THE GLOBAL
CLASS WAR

THE GLOBAL CLASS WAR

How America's Bipartisan
Elite Lost Our Future—
and What It Will Take
to Win It Back

Jeff Faux

WILEY

John Wiley & Sons, Inc.

Published by John Wiley & Sons, Inc., Hoboken, New Jersey
Published simultaneously in Canada

For general information about our other products and services, please contact our Customer Care Department within the United States at (800) 762-2974, outside the United States at (317) 572-3993 or fax (317) 572-4002.

Wiley also publishes its books in a variety of electronic formats. Some content that appears in print may not be available in electronic books. For more information about Wiley products, visit our web site at www.wiley.com.

Library of Congress Cataloging-in-Publication Data:

Faux, Geoffrey P.
    The global class war : how America's bipartisan elite lost our future—
and what it will take to win it back / Jeff Faux.
        p.   cm.
    Includes bibliographical references and index.
    ISBN-13: 978-0-471-69761-9 (cloth)
    ISBN-10: 0-471-69761-3 (cloth)
    1. Social classes. 2. Elite (Social sciences) 3. Elite (Social sciences)—United
States. 4. International economic relations. 5. Globalization. 6. Canada. Treaties,
etc. 1992 Oct. 7. 7. North America—Economic policy. 8. United States—
Economic conditions—21st century. I. Title.
    HT609.F28   2006
    305.5—dc22

                                                            2005010215

Printed in the United States of America
10 9 8 7 6 5 4 3 2

For Shelby, Malcolm, Celia, and Stella,
who will define the future

*Merchants have no country. The mere spot they stand
on does not constitute so strong an attachment
as that from which they draw their gains.*

—Thomas Jefferson

*In all life one should comfort the afflicted, but verily, also,
one should afflict the comfortable, and especially when they are
comfortably, contentedly, even happily wrong.*

—John Kenneth Galbraith

*Whether we like it or not, a new era has begun, and a new
economic and cultural topography has been designed for us.
We must now find our new place and role within this
bizarre Federation of U.S. Republics.*

—Guillermo Gomez-Peña

Contents

Acknowledgments

Many people helped me work through and distill the ideas in this book. My debts are large and diverse, and I apologize to any I may have inadvertently overlooked.

I am particularly indebted to the direct assistance of Adam Hersh, who gathered, analyzed, and culled an immense amount of research materials and data; Gabriela Prudencio, who located and organized the final references; Mary Rolle, who assisted with both administration and research; and Colleen Lawrie, who did the many editorial and organizing tasks needed to produce the manuscript.

Many thanks to my editor, Eric Nelson, for his belief in the book, his sharp pencil, and his good advice. Also to Gail Ross, my agent, who persevered.

Thanks to the Board of Directors of EPI and my successor as president, Larry Mishel, for their help and encouragement. Financial support from the Carnegie Corporation Scholars Program was also critical for the early stages of this work.

The staff of the EPI was, as always, supportive in many different ways. Particularly helpful were Rob Scott, David Rattner, and Christian Weller.

A number of others directly or indirectly contributed ideas, insights, advice, and/or special information: Mariclaire Acosta, Arturo Alcalde, Mark Anderson, Dean Baker, Tim Beatty, Jared Bernstein, Josh Bivens, Ron Blackwell, Robert Blecker, David Bonior, David Brooks, John Burstein, Duncan Cameron, Bruce Campbell, Jorge Castañeda, Stephen Clarkson, Ben Davis, Elizabeth Drake, Tom Faux, Leo Gerard, Tony Giles, Bill Greider, Susan Gzesh, Elizabeth Haight, Jeff Hermanson, Carlos Herredia, Andrew Jackson, Robert Kuttner, Thea Lee, Antonio Lettieri, Jerry Levinson, Mark Levinson, Ifigenia Martinez, Antonio Ortiz Mena, George Natzsikas, Vicente

Navarro, Ricardo Pascoe, Sandra Polaski, Ronald Rapoport, Robert Rubin, Carlos Salas, John Schmitt, David Smith, and Michael Zweig.

Most of all, I owe more than I can express to Marjorie Allen, without whose personal support, intellectual engagement, and help in many other ways, this book would not have been written.

Any errors, omissions, and uncomfortable ideas the reader may encounter herein are of course the full responsibility of the author.

Introduction

The seed of this book was planted in a conversation I had with a corporate lobbyist in the main corridor of the U.S. Capitol in 1993. She was exasperated that I couldn't see the virtues of the proposed North American Free Trade Agreement (NAFTA), which her company was promoting.

"Don't you understand?" she finally said. "We have to help Salinas. He's been to Harvard. He's one of us."

"Salinas" was Carlos Salinas de Gortari, then president of Mexico.

The reference to "us" seemed odd. She and I were not in the same political party, and a one-year fellowship at the Kennedy Institute of Politics hardly qualified me as a "Harvard man." She, as it turned out, hadn't gone there at all. It took me a little while to understand her point: we internationally mobile professionals had a shared self-interest in freeing transnational corporations from the constraints imposed by governments on behalf of people who were, well, "not really like us." Despite the considerable political and social distance between Carlos Salinas and me, she was appealing to class solidarity.

At that moment, I realized that globalization was producing not just a borderless market, but a borderless class system to go with it.

Once the point was made it seemed obvious. Markets within nations inevitably produce groups of people who have more money and power than others. So, it would be odd if global markets were *not* creating an international upper class of people whose economic interests have more in common with each other than with the majority of people who share their nationality.

In the years since that conversation, I have found that the morphing of national elites into a global governing class explained the politics of the new global economy better than the standard interpretations offered by the media punditry. Certainly, the bipartisan embrace of

1

2 GLOBAL CLASS WAR

NAFTA by American elites could be adequately understood in no other way: not in the familiar drama of Republicans versus Democrats, nor in the traditional trade politics of industry rivalry, nor by Yankee imperialism or the pursuit of some clear notion of the national interest—and certainly not in the simple-minded mantra of "free trade" that saturated the newsprint and airwaves. As Jorge Castañeda, who later became Mexico's foreign secretary, observed, NAFTA was "an accord among magnates and potentates: an agreement for the rich and powerful in the United States, Mexico, and Canada, an agreement effectively excluding ordinary people in all three societies."[1]

Despite the enormous amount of airwave and newsprint chatter about NAFTA, Castañeda's point was met with silence. In the public discussion of *domestic* politics, the simple and obvious truth that the rich and powerful collude for their own benefit is occasionally acknowledged. In the public discussion of *international* politics, almost never. The possibility that the mobile, cosmopolitan, and privileged of different nations would find common cause in designing the global marketplace never seems to have crossed the minds of the mobile, cosmopolitan, and privileged pundits who explain globalization to the American public.

It is therefore no surprise that the citizen is presented with a description of how it works that is—to be charitable—confusing. The front section of the morning paper and the three-minute segments on the evening news talk glibly of American interests and European interests and Chinese interests as if globalization were simply economic competition among separate nation-states representing the collective interest of their citizens.

At the same time, the pundits assure us that nation-states are irrelevant. The peripatetic Thomas Friedman regularly and breathlessly informs the readers of the *New York Times* that neither the United States nor the United Nations runs the world, but rather Wal-Mart, a herd of electronic day traders, and the entrepreneurs of Asia. Having broken out the chrysalis of their nation-state economies, transnational corporations and financial speculators are said to have no more regard for borders than do the monarch butterflies that drift with the winds from Canada to Mexico and back. It is on that basis that the central bankers and corporate CEOs tell governments that they must not do anything to disturb the butterflies or they will fly away.

The problem of poverty is almost always described as a conflict between rich countries and poor ones. But as the late Michael Harrington, whose book *The Other America* inspired the War on Poverty in the 1960s, observed to me, "Never forget, there are rich people in poor countries and poor people in rich countries."

The self-styled internationalists of the media have been uninterested in exploring this and similar contradictions in their explanation of how the global economy works. By and large, the punditry has confused the simple and age-old process of people in different countries trading to acquire goods they don't produce at home with the privileges taken by those who run giant transnational corporations to corrupt governments, undermine social mores, and defy protections of people and the environment at will. That having been done, the world is divided by those who are for or against "globalization." If you are against corporate abuses you must be against all international trade, which makes you an ignorant protectionist—and if you drink coffee imported from another country, a hypocrite as well. The argument reflects the art of the propagandist, and is aimed at stopping conversation and silencing opposition.

A political commentator named Amy Goodman said recently that the job of a journalist is "to go where the silence is."[2] In that spirit, this book starts by demonstrating how America's bipartisan governing class protects its privileged clients while abandoning the rest of us to an unregulated, and therefore brutal and merciless, global market. It is not the only place from which to examine globalization, but it is the place where the "silence" is.

That modern mass consumption societies divide along economic class lines should not be news. Nor should it be surprising that the rich and powerful of different parts of the world are drawn to one another's company in the upscale resorts, boardrooms, and social events where they congregate. But until recently, wealth and power—however diversified the portfolios—have been rooted in national market systems.

All markets have rules and, therefore, have a politics, which reflects conflict and bargaining over the rules for economic advantage. In stable modern societies, the bargaining takes place within a social contract—supported by laws, institutions, and customs—that assures that enough benefits of growth trickle down to keep a majority of citizens productive and loyal: what is good for General Motors becomes good for America.

The relentless integration of national economies raises the question: what then are the politics of the global market—a market without the common laws, institutions, and customs that would enable the economic classes generated by that market to negotiate a social contract?

The politics of the global economy are currently the equivalent of a one-party system, dominated by a virtual network this book calls the Party of Davos, after the now famous meeting place in Switzerland where the world's political and economic elite have their annual "convention." The platform of the Party of Davos is simple: enhance the bargaining position of corporate capital in the global economy. In the absence of global government, the transnational investor class represented by Davos depends on support from the elites running the major nation-states of the world, the U.S. superpower being the most important.

Although there are some substantial differences between the core leadership of the Democratic and Republican parties on domestic matters, and some tactical differences on foreign policy, the two have worked hand in hand to help so-called American corporations disconnect themselves from their obligations to the American people. Led by Robert Rubin, the Clinton administration used the economic instruments of free trade, financial deregulation, and the leverage of the International Monetary Fund and other financial institutions to further the world strategies of transnational banks and manufacturers. Led by Donald Rumsfeld and Dick Cheney, the Bush administration continued these policies and expanded the use of the U.S. military to extend investment opportunities at home and in the Middle East.

It is therefore not surprising that NAFTA, a joint project of the leaders of both parties, should serve as the template for, as the first head of the World Trade Organization, Renato Ruggiero, described it, the "constitution" of the global economy.

Like all constitutions, NAFTA reflects an underlying political philosophy—in this case, what is known throughout most of the world as neoliberalism. Despite the fact that the American governing class has been trying for more than two decades to impose this ideology on the rest of the world, the term is virtually never heard in the United States. Neoliberalism is a vision of society in which competition for wealth is the only recognized value and virtually all social decisions are left to unregulated markets. Its modern version treats huge transnational corporations as if they were small entrepreneurs. It reduces the role of a democratic government to the protection of private property. It is a world in which, in the words of a title to a 1996 book by Robert Kuttner, "everything for sale."[3]

Since the end of the cold war, America's unique superpower status has intoxicated its political elites with the idea that they have the right, indeed the moral obligation, to impose their own notions of how others should run their societies. Phrases like "American imperialism" and "American empire," which were once used only by marginal left-wing critics, are now proudly asserted by Washington policy intellectuals.

This is not the first time in American history that investment opportunity has marched under the banner of a messianic crusade to enlighten the world. But in the past, when what was good for General Motors was good for America, the economic benefits generally trickled down to the people back home. Today, the new post–cold war globalization has disconnected the fate of America's citizens from those who own and control the great transnational corporations with American names. Economic success these days is not, as many would have it, a matter of being connected to the global economy. Illegal immigrants, downsized factory workers, and laid-off telemarketers are all connected to the global economy—as are design engineers, accountants, and computer programmers stunned to learn that their jobs have been outsourced. The successful are not just connected, they are connected to the top—to the people who run the Party of Davos.

Globalization did not cause America's growing inequalities. Rather it allowed the rich and powerful to detach themselves from the bonds that had connected the economic fate of Americans of all classes since World War II. Ronald Reagan's breaking of the air traffic controllers' union in 1981 signaled big business that it could violate the domestic social contract. Clinton's passage of NAFTA in 1993 signaled that big business could abandon it completely.

The unraveling of financial security in America has been masked so far by the country's capacity to borrow and spend the savings of others. Simple arithmetic tells us that this is not sustainable. The United States cannot continue much longer buying more from the rest of the world than it is selling, allowing massive private pension liabilities to grow, and postponing the public investments in health, education, and technology necessary to work its way out of debt. Both political parties share responsibility for America's deteriorating financial position, but George W. Bush's reckless fiscal policy has clearly accelerated the day of reckoning and will make the inevitable drop in the average American's living standards that much more painful.

The erosion of support for the war in Iraq has already demonstrated the limits of the neoconservative military strategy. The political reaction to the coming economic crisis of neoliberalism is likely to force the American governing elite—whoever next lives in the White House—to spend less time, energy, and resources concentrating on what is going on in the rest of the world, and more time concentrating on looming economic problems at home. But "home" has changed. Thanks to NAFTA, we now have a domestic economy that spans the continent and includes Canada and Mexico, two other sovereign countries whose economies are permanently linked to ours.

Moreover, one of these nations is decidedly third world, where one hundred million people—with more than 40 percent living on less than two dollars a day—are overseen by a thin layer of oligarchs. Neoliberalism in Mexico has been a failure. Living standards for ordinary citizens are worse than they were ten years ago, while the rich, allied with American and Canadian capital, have gotten richer. Migration, which NAFTA was supposed to end, continues relentlessly. Indeed, the transfer of Mexican unemployment and poverty to the United States is the reason why Mexico has not yet descended into chaos. This also cannot go on forever. Mexico is a social and political bomb ticking away at our doorstep.

Like it or not, the people of North America now share an economic future. If we want to survive and prosper in the world of brutal competition that our ruling elites have set loose, we will have to create a new democratic continental politics—one that recognizes that the majority of ordinary citizens of Canada, Mexico, and the United States have more in common with each other than they do with the transnational elites who now govern their nations.

Finally, of course, this book is the story of how the global class war is conducted in the United States, and to some extent among the people of its northern and southern neighbors. No doubt the order of battle is different elsewhere. It is the author's immodest hope that this book will inspire others to explore these questions in their own societies.

1

NAFTA: Class Reunion

This fight is not a traditional fight between Democrats and Republicans, and liberals and conservatives. It is right at the center of the effort that we're making in America to define what the future is going to be about.

—President Bill Clinton, September 1993

Bill Clinton's Party

As the C-SPAN videotape of the White House event of the morning of September 14, 1993, begins to roll, the camera's eye picks up the trim pinstriped figure of Robert Rubin. He strolls through the crowd of several hundred men and women in business suits settling into their chairs in the stately East Room. Rubin, the ex-cochair of the investment firm Goldman Sachs, is chief of Bill Clinton's Economic Security Council— and soon to become his secretary of the treasury. He has the cool, unruffled look of an impresario, confident that all the details have been handled, patiently waiting to sit back and watch the show.

The camera angle widens onto a sea of some three hundred suits. We can pick out the most prominent faces of Washington's political class: the Democratic Speaker of the House and Senate majority leader; the Republican House and Senate leaders; the secretaries of state, treasury, and other cabinet officers; nine state governors. Others, not so well-known to the C-SPAN audience: lobbyists for the world's largest multinational

9

corporations; executives from the Business Roundtable, Chamber of Commerce, and other business associations; the Mexican ambassador; the Canadian ambassador. Colleagues all, they greet each other and chat while they wait for the ceremonies to start.

The *official* purpose of the event was to celebrate Bill Clinton's signing of three so-called side agreements to the proposed North American Free Trade Agreement.[1] NAFTA, as it was called, would create a single continental market in which goods, services, and money could freely cross the borders between the United States, Canada, and Mexico. The idea had been first proposed by Ronald Reagan in 1979. After his election, it took more than a decade to percolate through the think-tank seminars, the op-ed columns, and the policy speeches that the governing classes of all three countries use to communicate with themselves—and each other. Finally, in the summer of 1992, the administration of Reagan's Republican successor, George H. W. Bush, negotiated an agreement with the governments of the two neighboring countries. NAFTA had not yet been approved by the Democratically controlled Congress when Bush lost the 1992 election to Clinton.

The trade deal was fiercely opposed by labor unions, environmental groups, and other parts of the Democratic Party's political base, which feared that it would encourage American business to outsource production to Mexico in order to gain cheaper labor and escape environmental regulation. So the underlying *political* purpose of the White House event was for Clinton to convince skeptical corporate lobbyists and their Republican allies that he was committed to their fight against his own party's base in order to get NAFTA approved.

During the campaign, Clinton had hedged. He had said that he would not support NAFTA unless enforceable workers' rights and minimum environmental standards were added. "I'd be for expanded trade with Mexico and all these other countries," he said in San Diego, "but only, only, if they lifted their wage rates and their labor standards and cleaned up the environment so we could both go up together instead of being dragged down."[2] Later, in Raleigh, North Carolina, he repeated that he would not sign NAFTA unless it was amended to protect environmental standards and workers' rights.[3]

On November 4, 1992, he was elected president. One major cause of his victory was the turnout of the Democratic base, particularly low- and moderate-income working-class families reacting to the 1991–1992 recession. "It's the economy, stupid," his campaign manager famously said. Had the unemployment rate in the fall of 1992 been 5.5 percent rather than 7.5 percent, George H. W. Bush would have no doubt been reelected.

The other cause was the maverick businessman Ross Perot, who used his considerable fortune to buy his way into the presidential campaign. Perot pulled business, conservative, and right-wing populist votes away from Bush by hammering the Republican president on his budget deficits and his support of NAFTA.

Vice President Al Gore appears. Applause. He stands to the side. The camera's eye returns to the empty podium, behind which is a double door opening on a long red-carpeted corridor. The camera's eye waits expectantly. The band strikes up "Hail to the Chief." Bill Clinton and ex-presidents George H. W. Bush, Jimmy Carter, and Gerald Ford appear at the far end of the corridor, walk briskly toward us, and, four abreast, enter the East Room. Rubin and the crowd of dignitaries rise and give them a prolonged standing ovation.

The joint entrance of the president and the ex-presidents, two Democrats and two Republicans, symbolized the bipartisan support of the Washington establishment for NAFTA. Such joint appearances are rare, usually employed to show national unity at some time of extreme national danger. But NAFTA was not a response to a national crisis threatening the nation's citizens, it was an international opportunity for the nation's elites to make rules for the post–cold war global economy that would benefit them and their corporate clients. NAFTA foreshadowed the establishment of the World Trade Organization, the economic model imposed by the World Bank and the International Monetary Fund on developing countries, and the terms under which China's enormous labor market would later be poured into the world economy. NAFTA did not create globalization, but it showed the governing classes of both developed and developing countries how globalization could be used to disconnect themselves from the constraints and obligations, imposed democratically or otherwise, by their national communities. The story of how NAFTA was conceived, argued for, and finally delivered shows how they did it.

Among other things, NAFTA was the first demonstration of the way globalization was shifting the domestic U.S. politics of international trade. Until then, disputes over tariffs and other trade policies were generated by the competing interests of different sectors of the economy—various manufacturers, food producers, shipping companies would jockey for this or that advantage. The workers, the managers, and the investors of each sector were united against the others. But the politics of NAFTA were different: it was workers on one side and managers and investors on the other—*across* economic sectors. NAFTA thus reflected something new—that trade was now a dispute between those who could make money by investing somewhere else, and those whose job or business or concern for the environment was stuck in America.

After the election, NAFTA was the first priority of Clinton's new trade representative, Democratic attorney Mickey Kantor, a liberal California political activist. Kantor was initially cool toward NAFTA, but he was a tough lawyer and very loyal to his presidential client. He immediately opened up talks with his Mexican and Canadian counterparts to come up with a way to solve the contradictions in his boss's campaign rhetoric.

The Mexican and Canadian governments resisted. After all, they had already negotiated a deal with the United States. Opening it up again to satisfy domestic American politics was not only irksome, but embarrassing. It reminded their own electorates, once again, that they were second-class citizens on their continent. "We are," as one Canadian diplomat put it, "two very thin slices of bread at the top and bottom of a huge sandwich."

But they, especially the Mexicans, very much wanted the deal. So, several months later, Kantor brought back "side agreements" that he claimed protected labor and the environment. But the side agreements were just that; they were outside of NAFTA, and thus did not have the status of an international accord approved by the legislatures of each nation. NAFTA had established common protections and rights for multinational corporate investors that the governments of the three nations were not allowed to weaken. These included patent protection, banking regulations, and the right to challenge environmental laws. The side agreements on labor and the environment, however, were little more than admonitions to each nation to enforce its own laws. No common standards were set; any of the three nations could still eliminate its minimum wage, outlaw unions, dismantle health and safety standards, or loosen restrictions on the industrial pollution of air and water at will. Returning from the negotiations with Kantor, Mexico's finance minister, Jaime Serra Puche, happily assured Mexican businesspeople that the side agreements were meaningless.[4]

Leaders of the unions and most environmental organizations felt betrayed. Without their members, money, and energetic support, Clinton would not have been elected. Yet here he was, less than a year into his presidency, joining with their corporate adversaries and stabbing them in the back. And for an idea that was the brainchild of Ronald Reagan, no less!

Trade, But Not Free

Reagan had some very strong ideas about economics. One, growing out of his Hollywood experience as a millionaire actor, was that taxes were always too high. Another, growing out of his generation's experience after World War II, was a strong belief in free trade.

For most of its history, the United States had been a protectionist nation. The founding fathers—Washington, Adams, Hamilton, Jefferson, Madison—all supported high tariffs. The Tariff Act of 1789, which set high duties for a wide range of imports, was the second congressional bill signed by President George Washington. Over a century and a half, American industry developed behind the shelter of high tariffs, which were designed to limit competition from the more technologically advanced nations of Western Europe. In 1832, Henry Clay, reflecting the prevailing wisdom of the time, stated, "The call for free trade, is as unavailing as the cry of a spoiled child, in its nurse's arms, for the moon or the stars that glitter in the firmament of heaven. It never has existed; it never will exist."[5]

Protectionism was the underlying economic conflict of the Civil War. Southern plantation owners, who sold their cotton on the world market, wanted to buy cheaper European manufactured goods.

Northern industrialists wanted protective walls in order to build their textile, steel, and machinery companies. Led by Abraham Lincoln and the Republican Party, the protectionists won the war.[6] Over the next eighty years, tariffs remained high, as America went on to become the world's most productive economy. The United States was a trading nation, but it was not a free-trading nation.

World War II dramatically changed the attitude of America's governing elites toward trade protections. At war's end, American industries dominated world markets. With the factories of Europe and Japan devastated, they had virtually no foreign competitors. At the same time, Washington's leaders feared that when the federal government stopped its massive wartime spending, the country would fall back into the depressed conditions of the 1930s, where there was not enough demand to keep factories operating and workers employed. Increasing exports to a world digging out of the rubble of war made sense.

America's market was also an important weapon in the growing competition with the Soviet Union for the allegiance of the elites of the impoverished third world. Access to the U.S. consumer was a powerful counterweight to the ideological appeals of communism. Russia's economy was much less advanced and was busy protecting its own industries. Moreover, since it was a communist state, a larger proportion of its resources were devoted to public services that were supplied locally. American diplomats asked of the leaders of poor nations, "Would you rather earn dollars or rubles?" For all but the most committed Marxists, it was a no-brainer.

A policy of encouraging more imports into the United States was made possible by tapping the other major asset with which America emerged after World War II—the world's hard currency. Everyone wanted dollars. So the U.S. government could require that cash-strapped countries use foreign aid to buy American goods. American governments also lavished generous subsidies on domestic agriculture, aircraft, and other industries in order to further assure successful competition in world markets.

The arrangement was not, as Henry Clay would have pointed out, "free trade," in the classical sense of competition among unsubsidized laissez-faire economies. Nevertheless, it was crucial to support the package of international policies and new institutions—the Marshall Plan, the International Monetary Fund, and the World Bank—with which the American governing class shaped the noncommunist world after World War II. More importantly, it became part of the story of a confident, triumphant, outward-looking postwar America, whose prosperity was in sharp contrast to the decade of depression before the war.

So, to Reagan and others of the generation that had experienced both the depths of the Depression and the buoyant years that followed, expanding trade seemed both symbol and substance of that transformation.

The GOP Fast Track to Mexico

The Reagan/Bush administration had already, in fact, taken the first step toward NAFTA by completing a free trade agreement with Canada in 1989. CUFTA, the Canada-U.S. Free Trade Agreement, created what was close to a common market for goods and money, but left out the protection of labor, the environment, and other parts of the social contract that had evolved in both economies. Canadian and American living standards, however, are quite close, and Canada's worker and environmental protections are generally stronger than those in the United States. So the creation of a trade and investment agreement without social standards—while the precedent troubled some—was not sufficient to make the free trade agreement with Canada a major political issue in the United States, and Congress approved it by a comfortable margin.

With the Canada-U.S. Free Trade Agreement as a rough guide, the business-dominated governments of Bush in the United States, Carlos Salinas de Gortari in Mexico, and Brian Mulroney in Canada began negotiations over NAFTA in 1990. Each country's negotiating team was in constant, close touch with its nation's business groups. Often these business "advisory" committees rented rooms in government buildings or hotels right down the hall from the negotiators.

On the U.S. side, more than 90 percent of the members of the official Advisory Committee for Trade Policy and Negotiations (ACTPIN) represented multinational corporations. As Jeffrey Garten, Clinton's undersecretary of commerce, wrote in 1997, "The executive branch depends almost entirely on business for technical information regarding trade negotiations." He observed that American firms had become "de facto agents of foreign policy."[7]

None of the three governments permitted their country's trade unions, environmental groups, or other civil society organizations to become seriously involved in the negotiating process. All three had a common line: trade agreements were business matters, and each nation's interests would be taken care of by the business lawyers and consultants who were able to approve, reject, or amend the proposed language during the day—and in the evening bond with the negotiators over drinks and dinner.

Sending people who understood the complex language of trade agreements to meetings was expensive. Thus those who hovered around the negotiations were more Wall Street than Main Street. They tended to be from large companies, banks, and investment houses. American agribusiness corporations such as Cargill, Archer Daniels Midland, and Monsanto, who were looking to open up permanent new markets for their government-subsidized products, had lawyers whispering in the ears of U.S. negotiators. Representatives of Mexican processed-food corporations, such as Minsa and Maseca (the largest producers of flour) and Bimbo (a major producer of bread, cookies, and snacks), who wanted to buy cheaper raw materials subsidized by the U.S. taxpayer, were constant companions of their government's trade bureaucrats. Small citrus farmers in the United States had less clout. The even tinier corn farmers in Mexico might not even know a deal was being made that would put them out of business.

As the NAFTA negotiations proceeded, opposition began to form in all three countries, although it was much stronger and more organized in the United States and Canada. The Bush, Salinas, and Mulroney governments and their business and media allies dismissed opponents as "protectionists," ignorant of Economics 101. They assured legislators and the public that the benefits of free trade would be so vast as to overcome any economic costs or political inconvenience. The magic of free trade would make everyone a winner; as each country's exports rose, profits would flow and jobs would grow. It was, apparently, the only exception to Milton Friedman's proposition that there is no free lunch.

Polls showed that majorities in each of the three countries were opposed to NAFTA. Workers worried that jobs would be lost to imports. Small businesses were worried that they could not compete with transnational corporations. In Mexico, the opposition was muted because the country was ruled by one party, the Partido Revolucionario Institucional (PRI), which at that point had been in power for a half century. The PRI controlled the unions and Salinas controlled the PRI. In Canada, large numbers worried that the agreement would further endanger their social safety net by the erosion of the tax base. Since CUFTA, Canadian companies had been threatening to move south to the United States, where taxes were lower. Nationalists in both Canada and Mexico were worried that NAFTA would mean that their countries would be further tied to, and subordinated to, the giant United States.

It actually didn't matter what most Mexicans or Canadians, or even their legislators, thought. Carlos Salinas's party had an iron grip on the Mexican Congress. Mulroney, as prime minister, for the moment, controlled the majority of votes in the Canadian parliament.

But Democrats controlled the U.S. Congress, and in the House of Representatives the majority was opposed. So Bush's strategy was to get Congress to renew the president's "fast track" authority, under which the president can send trade agreements to Congress for an up-or-down vote, allowing for no amendments. Fast track passed narrowly on May 23, 1991. Then Democratic majority leader Richard Gephardt, who was skeptical of NAFTA, voted for it and brought a couple of dozen Democrats with him. He warned, however, that he would not support NAFTA unless it had sufficient safeguards for labor and the environment.

With fast track in hand, Carla Hills, Bush's U.S. trade representative, and her Mexican and Canadian counterparts concluded the NAFTA agreement in August 1992. Given the negative polls, Bush decided not to seek congressional approval until after the election in November.

Clinton Hops Aboard

The crowd in the East Room settles down and Vice President Al Gore steps to the podium, and begins. "There are some issues," he intones, "that transcend ideology. That is, the view is so uniform that it unites people in both parties. . . . NAFTA is such an issue . . . made possible by a long series of commitments by presidents in both parties."[8]

*   *   *

Since the war in Vietnam, no issue had divided Democrats like the question of NAFTA in particular, and trade policy more generally. Clinton aide Gene Sperling later said, "I found this to be the most wrenching and agonizing issue I dealt with in my eight years in the White House."[9] Uneasiness about trade had been growing among the Democrats' base—trade unions, environmentalists, cities and towns dependent on manufacturing—for more than a decade.

As the rest of the world recovered from World War II, America's unusual commercial advantages faded. In the late 1960s, jobs in the apparel and shoe industries began to move out of the country as producers found cheaper labor overseas. The assembly of television parts and consumer electronics followed, and in the mid-1970s the U.S. trade balance turned into a chronic deficit. Soon, heavy industries like steel and autos were losing jobs to overseas competition.

Books by economists such as Lester Thurow, Pat Choate, Robert Reich, Ira Magaziner, Barry Bluestone, and Benjamin Harrison put America's industrial decline into the national policy chatter. The AFL-CIO, with the support of some businesspeople, proposed a national development bank to help manufacturing industries modernize. But Jimmy Carter's economists were cool to the proposals, and their Republican counterparts, who moved into the White House in 1981, were ice-cold. In 1984, Democratic presidential candidate Walter Mondale, who had previously supported these ideas, abandoned them when he ran for president. Instead, Mondale, at the urging of Wall Street investors like Robert Rubin of Goldman Sachs, made balancing the budget the number one campaign issue. Presenting himself as a fiscal conservative, Mondale proposed to raise taxes to cut Reagan's deficit, a decision that destroyed any chance he had to win the election. In 1988, Michael Dukakis ran as an apostle of a new high-tech economy, with little concern over the outsourcing of industrial jobs that had grown from a trickle to a widening river.

Labor's frustration was shared by a growing middle-class environmental movement, worried that American industries were also outsourcing to escape antipollution regulations. In the past, industrial unions had generally resisted environmental regulations, but some trade union activists began to understand that they and the environmentalists had a common interest in restraining corporations from threatening to outsource production in order to cut wages or stop environmental laws.

On the other hand, unions and environmental groups were committed to the election of a Democrat. So Clinton's promise in the 1992 campaign that he would not support a NAFTA without social protections gave them an argument to get their rank-and-file voters to the polls. It was particularly important for the labor unions. The Republicans had succeeded in reformulating working-class issues away from the traditional "bread and butter" concerns to social issues like abortion, gun control, and affirmative action. Leaders of the manufacturing unions found their ranks swelling with "Reagan Democrats." Making the case that a Democrat in the White House would fight harder for their economic interests was crucial to getting out the labor vote for Clinton.

Clinton's first budget, which was narrowly passed in the spring of 1993, was a disappointment to his liberal constituency. After twelve years of Republican rule, they had expected their party—which now controlled the White House and the two houses of Congress—to expand domestic spending in order to make up for years of austerity. But Clinton, acting on the advice of Robert Rubin and Treasury Secretary Lloyd Bentsen, had made deficit reduction, not social spending, his first priority.

Once Clinton had tilted his budget to please Wall Street, presumably giving the administration some points with the business class, Democratic activists expected that the White House would turn to health care. But Rubin and Bentsen pressed Clinton to put NAFTA first, even though a prolonged fight over the issue would divert the White House's attention and energy away from the health care issue that was much more important to Bill Clinton's party and his place in history.

So it was not surprising that when the president they'd elected announced his support for Bush's NAFTA, many Democrats felt double-crossed, and mobilized against him.

The more voters heard about NAFTA, the less they liked it. By July, a Gallup poll showed 65 percent of Americans opposing the agreement, and only 28 percent in favor.[10] In the House of Representatives, several dozen old-style isolationist Republicans joined the liberal Democrats, making a majority of members opposed to the treaty. Meanwhile, Ross Perot was stomping around the country warning that if the treaty passed, Americans would hear a "giant sucking sound" of jobs leaving the United States for Mexico. More than eight and a half million people were still unemployed in August 1993, and the media was calling the modest increase in economic growth that had accompanied Clinton's first nine months in office the "jobless recovery." In April 1993, Clinton's budget director, Leon Panetta, told the press that the administration did not have the votes to pass NAFTA.[11]

Clinton aide George Stephanopoulos also thought at that point that NAFTA was a mistake: "I believed that we should go forward with the agreement only if it included our promised protections for labor and environment, which would be a spur, I believed, to higher wages and safer working conditions."[12] Mickey Kantor himself didn't see why they had to pursue NAFTA, and many Democrats in Congress scratched their heads in bewilderment, and some in anger, that the president would consider making it a priority.

Under these circumstances, and given Clinton's debt to his labor and environmental constituencies, the Republicans and the business establishment were skeptical that he would go all out for their priority. They were absolutely opposed to including any enforceable labor and environmental standards, even if it meant letting the agreement fall through. And they doubted that he would turn his back on the party's base so soon after that base had put him in the White House.

In early September, Robert Rubin and Mack McLarty, Clinton's chief of staff, organized a meeting with the president to decide whether NAFTA or health care would be the administration's next priority. The meeting also included Secretary of State Warren Christopher and Treasury Secretary Lloyd Bentsen. Rubin, while at Goldman Sachs, had had extensive dealings as an underwriter of several of Mexico's privatization schemes and had personally known Carlos Salinas since the 1980s. Bentsen had made a business fortune as head of a financial holding company with business interests in Mexico. McLarty had been the head of a large natural gas company and ran a family business with trucking and transportation interests. Christopher had worked for a corporate law firm whose clients did business with the Mexican government and he headed a State Department that was anxious to complete a major diplomatic project with Mexico

and Canada. Against this group were Hillary Clinton and Ira Magaziner, her health care consultant.

In her memoirs, Hillary Clinton writes, "By late August, [Trea-
sury Secretary Lloyd] Bentsen, Secretary of State Warren Christopher
and economic advisor Bob Rubin were adamant about postponing
health care reform and moving forward with NAFTA. They believed
the free trade agreement was also critical to the nation's economic
recovery and NAFTA warranted immediate action. Creating a free
trade zone in North America would expand U.S. exports, create jobs,
and ensure that our economy was reaping the benefits, not the burdens, of globalization."[13] Robert Rubin later said that he never
thought, and did not argue, that NAFTA would create many jobs.

In any event, the president decided to put NAFTA ahead of
health care. The White House would join Republicans in launching
a no-holds-barred campaign against the Democratic opposition.

On the advice of Henry Kissinger, Clinton invited former presidents George H. W. Bush, Jimmy Carter, and Gerald Ford to the
White House signing. (Ronald Reagan was ill, and inviting Richard
Nixon would have turned off the NAFTA supporters among the
Democrats.) Kissinger was the perfect tutor for a new Democratic
president trying to convince Republicans and their business allies
that they could count on him to champion Reagan's vision. At first,
Bush and Ford hesitated, so McLarty called on his friend Ken Lay of
the Enron Corporation to persuade them.[14]

After the White House rally, Bill Daley, brother of Chicago's
Democratic mayor, set up a war room in the White House, and the
administration started a full-court press on wavering members of
Congress. Business opened up its coffers and the Mexican government spent $50 million on Democratic and Republican lobbying
firms.

Meanwhile in Canada, a similar drama was playing out. Jean
Chrétien, head of the Liberal Party and the newly elected prime
minister, had made criticism of NAFTA a key part of his campaign.
He had denounced the earlier Canada-U.S. Free Trade Agreement
in harsh terms. "Free trade is a monster," he had said in 1990. "By
the time we get to power, it will have had too many babies to kill."[15]

The Clinton/Republican alliance was worried. Unemployment was
high in Canada, and Chrétien had run a strongly populist campaign.

He had said he would only sign the agreement if tight conditions were added, particularly protections for Canada's energy and water supplies and prohibitions against U.S. antidumping laws. If Canada pulled out there was a good chance that a U.S.-Mexico NAFTA would die in the U.S. Congress.

After Chrétien's October 25 election both Clinton and Salinas called to congratulate him, and ask nervously where he stood on NAFTA. They shouldn't have worried. It turned out that while Chrétien was raging against NAFTA as a sellout of Canada's sovereignty, his chief aides were quietly assuring Canadian corporate leaders that this was all for show, to keep working-class voters from voting for the more populist New Democratic Party. And so it was. One of Chrétien's first acts was to announce that he had changed his mind and would now support NAFTA. Like Clinton, he insisted that he would impose conditions. And as with Clinton, the conditions were a political fig leaf. Chrétien signed an agreement that did not differ significantly from the deal he had excoriated on the campaign trail.

Back in Washington, Democrats in the House were reluctant to fight against their president as strongly as he fought against them, so Ross Perot moved in to fill the vacuum. The swaggering, squeaky-voiced Perot was a perfect image for the administration to target opponents as ignorant "know-nothing" protectionists. Gore and Perot met in a televised debate on November 9, eight days before the House vote. Perot, supremely confident, did not prepare. He spouted generalities and got peevish when pressed. Gore waved a copy of the infamous Hawley-Smoot Tariff Act of 1930, conjuring visions of the Great Depression that could return if NAFTA was defeated. On most people's scorecard, Gore won.

The NAFTA campaign demonstrated Clinton's extraordinary political skills. Normally the burden of proof would have been on the administration, which was, after all, proposing something new. Instead, the White House succeeded in making Perot the issue, specifically his colorful claim that the agreement would produce the "giant sucking sound" of jobs moving to Mexico. The onus was shifted to the opponents, demanding that they defend their "protectionism," even though there was no protectionist proposal on the table.

By making NAFTA a referendum on protectionism, Clinton and the Republicans avoided a debate over the actual agreement. Once the issue had become the defense of the theory of free trade rather than the defense of this specific agreement, a vast majority of economists rallied to the cause. A week after the White House conference, the administration released a letter to the press, signed by 283 prominent economists, supporting the agreement. A follow-up survey by a radio network revealed that few, if any, had read the actual text.[16]

With the simple story of enlightened free traders versus protectionist ignoramuses, the press had little patience for finding a devil in any of the details. Thus, in the East Room gathering, Clinton assured the audience, "There have been 19 serious economic studies on NAFTA by liberals and conservatives alike; 18 of them have concluded that there will be no job loss."[17]

With one or two questions, any journalist could have discovered that the eighteen "studies" were simply abstract exercises with what economists call General Equilibrium Models. Among other things, these models are constructed to assume a state of permanent full employment. In other words, the studies could not have concluded that *any* policy would result in unemployment because unemployment did not exist in the computerized cyber-world they created.

Although the finalized "side agreements" clearly would not protect the environment, they were very useful as a wedge to divide the environmental movement. Some environmental groups—those with upper-class constituencies reluctant to be accused of protectionism—agreed to support NAFTA if the environmental side agreement was strengthened a bit. It was, and they did. Others, including the Sierra Club, Friends of the Earth, and Defenders of Wildlife, remained opposed.

With the question of jobs neutralized and at least some of the environmental movement peeled off, the political clout of big business and the ability of the White House to trade projects and favors for votes won the day.

"The national press was unabashedly pro-NAFTA," wrote the *Washington Post* media critic Howard Kurtz after the congressional votes. "From George Will and Rush Limbaugh on the Right to Anthony Lewis and Michael Kinsley on the Left, most of the nation's brand-name commentators led the cheerleading for NAFTA." The

New York Times, the *Washington Post*, the *Wall Street Journal*, and most of the major regional papers supported the agreement. National Public Radio featured a left-right "debate" over NAFTA between two former members of Congress, both of whom actively supported the agreement. On Veterans Day 1993, the *Washington Post* carried ten pro-NAFTA pieces in just one edition.[18] When Senator Byron Dorgan of North Dakota complained that the *Post* had devoted sixty-three feet of editorial space to pro-NAFTA arguments and only eleven to arguments against, Meg Greenfield, the editorial page editor, replied, "On this rare occasion when columnists of the Left, Right, and Middle are all in agreement I don't believe it is right to create an artificial balance where none exists."[19] At the same time, a July 1993 Gallup poll reported that ordinary Americans, as opposed to Washington columnists, opposed NAFTA 65 to 28 percent.[20]

Energized by Gore's performance, the White House went through the time-honored process of buying up the members who had been sitting on the fence. Tom Nides, who was Mickey Kantor's chief of staff, told John MacArthur, who wrote a history of NAFTA, "This was won member by member—figuring out what was in the district, figuring out who we could influence, how we could work it. A lot of things traded hands during this period of time."[21]

On November 17, 1993, after a long and bitter debate, the U.S. House of Representatives voted to approve NAFTA. Up to the very end, the outcome was in doubt, and only last-minute horse-trading by Bill Clinton's agents on Capitol Hill bought enough votes to save the agreement. One member of Congress told the press that he'd been offered so many bridges for his district that all he needed was a river.

Clinton won, but he paid a high price. The fight over NAFTA made a major contribution to the two great debacles of his administration: his failure to pass a national health care plan, and the loss of the House of Representatives in the 1994 election. As the journalist Eric Alterman put it, "The final days of the NAFTA debate offered the gruesome spectacle of Bill Clinton leaning all of his six-foot-three, two-hundred-something-pound frame on members of his own party to convince them to support a treaty pushed primarily by foreign-paid lobbyists, multinational corporate moguls, and Republican reactionaries. In doing so, the president rewarded the political

forces that have despised him and kicked the shins of his loyal supporters."[22]

Even in Mexico, Clinton's behavior seemed odd. Jorge Castañeda, who later became Mexico's foreign minister, noted, "Clinton's
voters were either indifferent or frankly hostile to NAFTA. Instead
of a universal and accessible health care system, Clinton gave them
the Mexican market, with the blessings of Henry Kissinger."[23]

When the NAFTA vote had been won, James Robinson, former
head of American Express, said, "NAFTA happened because of the
drive Bill Clinton gave it. He stood up against his two prime con-
stituents, labor and environment, to drive it home over their dead
bodies."[24]

The High Price

Health care was the historic mission of Clinton's presidency, and his
abandonment of the effort a year later guaranteed him a very modest place in history even before the Monica Lewinsky scandal. Theda
Skocpol of Harvard, who chronicled Clinton's aborted health care
proposal, wrote:

> During the fall of 1993, the Democratic Party's usual sure donor
> and grassroots supporter, the AFL-CIO, diverted resources and
> attention to the battle against NAFTA. Many activists were greatly
> embittered by the Clinton administration's support of NAFTA, and
> union leaders "turned off the spigot" for the NHCC [National
> Health Care Campaign] during the very period when opponents of
> the fledgling Clinton Health Security plan were channeling large
> resources into oppositional advertising and organizing. . . . Presi-
> dent Clinton may have given away his last chance to mobilize
> Democratic support for his crucial Health Security initiative by de-
> voting to NAFTA so much time, energy and arm-twisting of peo-
> ple in Congress.[25]

The loss of the House of Representatives was an even greater
disaster. Republican control of the House put Clinton on the defen-
sive for the last six years of his presidency and enabled the GOP to
build a case for impeachment. More importantly, for the previous
forty years the House, which had been the protected political citadel

to which Democrats could retreat during the years that the White House, and sometimes the Senate, wasn't under their control, was captured by Republicans. Control of the House had enabled Democrats to resist the most egregious conservative demands of the Reagan presidency. Because Democrats chaired the committees, corporate lobbyists were forced to give them a greater share of campaign contributions than they would have otherwise. Control of committees allowed Democrats to hire congressional staff that offset the greater ability of the richer corporate-sponsored Republicans to employ lobbyists and experts to support conservative positions in the public debate. Given the Republicans' naturally greater access to wealth in a political world increasingly dominated by money, Democratic control of the House was the vital element in a genuine two-party system.

Would the Democrats have held on to the House if there had not been the bitter fight over NAFTA? Obviously, no one knows. But the effect of NAFTA clearly was negative. Bill Clinton had been elected in 1992 because the Democratic base was enthusiastic and because Ross Perot, running against the budget deficit and NAFTA, had siphoned off Republican votes. In 1994, core Democratic voter turnout was low, and independents who had favored Perot broke heavily in favor of the GOP.[26] Despite Gingrich's fierce promotion of NAFTA inside the beltway, his widely advertised Contract with America, which the Republicans took to the people that year, never mentioned foreign trade. Clinton took the blame, and Gingrich took the House. The Democratic Party still has not recovered.

Frightened by Newt Gingrich and the radical right, the Democratic constituencies came back to Clinton in 1996. But by then the very effective and well-funded conservative Republican political infrastructure had put its own stranglehold on the House, where incumbency is the biggest asset in an election.

The political consequences of Clinton's NAFTA decision also came back to haunt the Democrats in the presidential election of 2000. The fight over NAFTA organized the North American antiglobalist movement that erupted in the streets of Seattle against the World Trade Organization in December 1999. Its energy fueled the 2000 Green Party candidacy of Ralph Nader, which denied Gore the electoral votes of New Hampshire and enough votes in Florida to allow the Republican Supreme Court majority to deny him the presidency.

Neither Clinton nor anyone else could have foreseen the conse-quences of his decision. But he was one of the smartest, most calcu-lating politicians that had ever occupied the White House, and the risks were obvious. NAFTA, Clinton acknowledged in his memoirs, "came at a high price, dividing our party in Congress and infuriating many of our strongest supporters in the labor movement."[27]

Follow the Money

In response to the criticism of the weak side agreements, Mickey Kantor said that the final agreement was the best deal he could get. The Mexicans and Canadians, he asserted, simply would not agree to include any labor or environmental standards in the agreement.

Kantor's claim is suspect, especially regarding the Mexicans. As we shall see, Salinas desperately needed NAFTA. Clinton and Kantor were in the perfect negotiating position. Salinas was a drowning politician and NAFTA was his only lifeline. Antonio Ortiz Mena, a Mexican economist who was a member of his country's NAFTA negotiating team, said later that if the United States had demanded enforceable social standards, Salinas would have reluctantly accepted it. "We didn't want labor or environmental standards in the agree-ment, but Salinas had bet everything on getting a trade agreement with Mexico. He couldn't have walked away from the agreement."[28]

Allen Sessoms, who was with the U.S. embassy in Mexico City at the time, also said he had no doubt that the Mexicans would have accepted an enforceable social clause on labor and the environment as part of NAFTA. "The Mexicans would have accepted anything," he agreed. "And the Canadians would have come along, reluctantly. Canadians were reluctant about the whole thing. They were in just because they wanted not to be out. Washington never pushed. I still don't understand why."[29]

Certainly, Clinton could not have been intimidated by Newt Gingrich. Whatever Gingrich's bluster, the Democrats at the time were in control of the House and Senate. Moreover, as he was to prove two years later when he trapped the overreaching Gingrich, who had just became Speaker of the House, into the politically disastrous shutdown of the federal government in 1995, Clinton could handle him. Clinton ought to have been able to use Gingrich's arrogance to political advantage, and to slide off the NAFTA hook. Given the preliminary vote count in the House, it would not have been hard to tell the business groups that if they wanted NAFTA they would have to pressure Gingrich to compromise on social protections. If the business groups did not, it would have exposed them as being more interested in escaping social regulation than "free trade."

The experience of Mark Anderson, an AFL-CIO official, is further evidence that the administration did not want worker protections in its trade agreements. After having secured NAFTA, the Clinton White House began talks on a bilateral trade agreement with Chile. In an effort to avoid repeating the split between organized labor and the administration, Anderson went to Chile in 1994 and returned with a commitment from the politically influential Chileans to agree to enforceable worker rights in exchange for a treaty giving more access to the American market. Under these conditions, the AFL-CIO was willing to endorse a trade deal. "I told Kantor and others that we would go along," says Anderson. "But they just brushed me off. They weren't interested."[30]

We can only conclude that the central obstacle to having worker and environmental protections in NAFTA was not the resistance of the Mexican and Canadian negotiators, but the resistance of American multinational business.

Thus, for many on the losing side of the NAFTA vote, the explanation for the president's behavior was simple. He had always been eager to ingratiate himself with big business. Clinton had been chairman of the Democratic Leadership Council, a business-funded Washington group that had championed the strategy of pro-business "centrism" for the party. Under the ideological cover of a "third way" between right and left, the brilliant and charming Arkansan became a prodigious fund-raiser on Wall Street, and delivered the Democrats to a business agenda.

Clinton's relationship with business was built on a foundation put in place by Democratic strategists ten years before, after Reagan won the White House and the Republicans took over the Senate. In 1981, Tony Coelho, who was at that time a congressman from California, expanded the Democrats' fund-raising operation by targeting corporate lobbyists who were willing to pay for access to the Democrats in control of the House committees. Given the widespread assumption that the Democrats were certain to remain the majority in the House of Representatives, which they had controlled for all but four years since 1933, it seemed like an obvious strategy. "Business has to deal with us whether they like it or not," boasted Coelho, "because we are in the majority."[31]

Coelho was a success. Business contributions to the Democrats steadily rose in the 1980s. Clinton's 1992 presidential campaign rhetoric portrayed him as the outsider who would clean up Washington and Put People First. But as Charles Lewis, director of the Center for Public Integrity, noted, "Clinton was no stranger to Washington or its money politics." By the time the New Hampshire primary came around, more than half of Clinton's staff came from inside the beltway, including several heavy-hitting consultants and lobbyists whose firms were collecting handsome fees from transnational corporations and foreign governments. These included Thomas Hoog, vice chair of Hill and Knowlton, Anne Wexler of the Wexler Group, and Samuel "Sandy" Berger, who would later become Clinton's national security adviser. In the campaign of 1992, Clinton received at least $853,295 from the financial industry alone.[32] Clinton took Coelho's fund-raising strategy to another level. He wanted business to contribute to Democrats not because they had to, but because they wanted to.

Once Clinton was in the White House, the coffers opened up for him and for his party. In the campaign of 2000, the Democrats raised $340.3 million from business. Labor's contribution to the party was $52.4 million.[33]

Republican Congressman Duncan Hunter observed that "Clinton in a perverse way, has acquired the twofer that the Republicans honestly acquired under Theodore Roosevelt: by appealing to labor they managed to win the exclusive backing of labor; at the same time, by appealing to multinational corporations, they managed to take a large share of businesses."[34]

David Bonior, the then Democratic whip in the House, who had led the House opposition to NAFTA, said Clinton was motivated by "the same thing that drives everything; it's power and money. And they go hand in hand. And money provides the opportunity for power. You get the money from being on the side of those who have it."[35]

2

"Good Jobs" and Other Global Deceptions

The Mexican government, along with the Bush Administration until 1992 and the Clinton Administration since then, drew up an accord among magnates and potentates: an agreement for the rich and powerful in the United States, Mexico and Canada, an agreement effectively excluding ordinary people in all three societies.

—Jorge Castañeda (1995)

We all know that money talks in American politics. But Clinton's decision to drive George Bush's NAFTA over the dead bodies of those who elected him was not a simple matter of trading votes for dollars. It reflected the complex interaction of money, ambition, power, and ideology that drives both Democrats and Republicans to try to shape the future of global society around a social model in which the corporate investor is king.

The effort has largely been driven by American leaders, but it is an international phenomenon. Indeed, Clinton represents a stock character in the national melodrama of modern democracy: the left-of-center leader, elected by popular reaction to conservative policies, who continues the same policies in a trendier or more populist style. Among the other leading men at the time were Britain's Tony Blair, Canada's Jean Chrétien, Germany's Gerhard Schröder, South Korea's Kim Dae Jung, and Argentina's Carlos Menem.

Much of the world's punditry—right, left, and center—tells the story of these populists-turned-realists as the inevitable consequence of the powerlessness of the nation-state in the face of global capital mobility. To the right, this process is a necessary constraint on democratic government's tendency to pursue egalitarian policies. To the left it reflects capitalism's outrageous suppression of democracy. Both agree that nation-states are no match for financial markets. According to the familiar plot, nations are guided or blackmailed by capital markets: "Either you follow policies that we approve of, or we will go elsewhere." Overwhelmed by the fear that capital will flee, interest rates will rise, businesses will collapse, people will be out of work, and political careers will be destroyed, the populists are kept in line.

This widespread perception is accurate, but incomplete—and therefore misleading. Globalization is not an invading army or a ship carrying a plague that lands on the shore from afar. Its origins are as much domestic as they are foreign. NAFTA, the prototype international agreement for the dismantling of public regulation over business, was not thrust upon the governing class of the United States, Mexico, or Canada. It was created by them.

The "winds of global competition," said the president, have put the American middle class under severe stress. Under these circumstances, he claimed, people were vulnerable to "fear tactics" and "adverseness to change." But they have to face reality. The question he said, is simple: "Are we going to compete and win, or are we going to withdraw? Are we going to face the future with the confidence that we can create tomorrow's jobs, or are we going to try against all the evidence of the last twenty years to hold on to yesterday's?"[1] The correct response was not to resist the winds of change but to "embrace" them.

Clinton was certainly correct that the world economy faced by Americans had changed. The revolutions in information technology, electronic communications, and passenger and freight transportation had dramatically accelerated the mobility of capital. By 1993, among the major, and many of the minor, economies, there was one seamless financial market. Major products—automobiles, computers, appliances—were being produced from components in a variety of worldwide locations. Even retailing was becoming less a local activity as consumers around the world shared an increasingly common advertising-driven culture.

But markets do not exist in the state of nature. They are human artifacts, defined by sets of rules. Simple markets have simple rules, such as common weights and measures, the meaning of a handshake, and the accepted value of currency. Complex markets have complex rules, like the New York Stock Exchange's prohibition of insider trading, restrictions on borrowing, and limits on how fast a price can fall.

Because markets are made up of socially determined laws or rules, all markets generate politics to settle conflicts over the content of those rules, how they are enforced, and who has the right to establish them. To a large extent, the jockeying for advantage in the setting of market rules is the subject of politics in the modern world. Politics, as a famous American political scientist noted, is essentially an inquiry into the same question that is addressed by the study of economics: "who gets what?"[2]

When markets expand, so must the rules, so there was logic to the three countries of North America agreeing on new rules to accommodate expanded trade among them. But any such change in market rules would clearly have an implication for "who gets what?" So the question was not why Clinton supported establishing new rules for a steadily integrating North American economy, but why he supported the NAFTA rules, designed by his political adversaries, to allow *their* constituencies to get more, and *his* to get less.

That NAFTA was supported by American's financial and political elite does not by itself mean it was not good for the rest of America as well. The United States is a capitalist trickle-down economy, so it is not unreasonable to claim that, as Charlie Wilson, who was Dwight D. Eisenhower's secretary of defense, once said, "What's good for General Motors is good for America." And General Motors, like most of our multinational corporations, stood foursquare for NAFTA.

The conscientious citizen trying to understand the debate over NAFTA would have heard from most of the media pundits that the agreement would help the United States succeed in the global economy in three ways. First, it would create new jobs and raise living standards in the United States. Second, it would stop most illegal immigration from Mexico by creating a sustained economic boom south of the border. Third, it would support Carlos Salinas, who represented the forces of democracy in Mexico.

"NAFTA means jobs," said the president to the C-SPAN audience. "American jobs, and good-paying American jobs. . . . NAFTA will generate these jobs by fostering an export boom to Mexico. . . . In 1987, Mexico exported $5.7 billion more of products to the United States than they purchased from us. We had a trade deficit. Because of the free market, tariff-lowering policies of the Salinas government in Mexico, and because our people are becoming more export-oriented, that $5.7-billion trade deficit has been turned into a $5.4-billion trade surplus for the United States. It has created hundreds of thousands of jobs."[3]

Clinton's central economic argument was the same as Bush's: labor and environmental standards were not necessary because NAFTA would generate an increased demand for workers in the United States much greater than any possible loss because of Mexico's cheaper labor. Indeed, the arguments were essentially the same as those that business lobbyists regularly make against minimum wages, health and safety rules, and other laws that protect workers within the domestic American economy.

Clinton claimed that NAFTA would stimulate a long-term economic boom in Mexico, which would suck in American exports faster than it shipped out exports—exactly the opposite of what Ross Perot had claimed. Inasmuch as Americans were on the average more skilled, the jobs created for them would pay more. In effect, NAFTA would move workers in both countries up the job ladder, with Mexicans replacing Americans at the bottom and Americans moving up.

Undersecretary of Commerce Jeffrey Garten predicted that NAFTA would ignite Mexican economic growth south of the border of "between a supercharged 6 percent a year, worthy of Asia's tigers, and a startling 12 percent per year comparable to China's recent economic growth."[4] Rudiger Dornbush of MIT, one of Salinas's former economics professors, also predicted that Mexico's growth rate would double to 6 percent for the next ten years. "Soon people will be talking about the Mexican miracle," he said.[5]

"The President and this administration would not be for NAFTA if we did not believe it would create jobs," said Clinton's commerce secretary, Ron Brown. "If we accept the proposition that U.S. exports equal U.S. jobs, and NAFTA helps exports to Mexico, we must believe that NAFTA increases U.S. jobs." Robert Rubin added that if NAFTA wasn't signed, an angry Mexican government might increase tariffs on American goods or make a deal with Japan, whose workers would get the jobs.[6]

Rubin's warning was echoed by Lawrence Bossidy, chairman and CEO of Allied-Signal. "It won't happen overnight," he said, "but the long-term consequences are dire. Clearly Mexico is an up-and-coming country. If we don't pass this legislation, we'll lose a chance to unite the Western Hemisphere. In that vacuum, the Europeans would like to align with Mexico; so would the Japanese."[7]

So far as anyone could tell, neither the citizens of Europe nor Japan spent much time dreaming of "alignment" with Mexico. As for the businessmen, Salinas had gone to the business/government meeting in Davos, Switzerland, in 1989 to plead with European corporations to invest in his country, and was rebuffed.

Throughout the debate, American corporate lobbyists assured Congress that their clients' interests lay in the Mexican *consumer*, not the Mexican *worker*. The representative for Eastman Kodak promised, "With these trade barriers out of the way, Kodak anticipates it will double its U.S. exports to Mexico to $250 million by 1995 and double them again to $500 million by the year 2000."[8] Scott Paper's lobbyists said, "With the reduction in tariffs and trade barriers, along with a growing consumer class for Scott's products, exports will increase and bring more jobs to the U.S."[9] Johnson & Johnson promised eight hundred new jobs.[10] General Electric promised ten thousand.[11]

The administration's claim that NAFTA would create a significant number of net new jobs for the United States was never plausible. To begin with, at the same time Clinton was telling Americans that their trade surplus with Mexico and Canada would rise as a result of NAFTA, Mulroney and Salinas were telling Canadians and Mexicans that *their* countries' surpluses with the United States would increase. You didn't need a PhD in economics to know that it was arithmetically impossible for all three nations to increase their net surpluses with each other.

For the United States especially, the then current trade surplus with Mexico was clearly temporary. Foreign speculators had been pouring money into Mexico, gambling that when NAFTA was signed, the value of their stocks and bonds would rise. The resulting demand for pesos (in order to invest in Mexico, foreigners have to buy pesos) inflated the value of the Mexican currency relative to the dollar. This made Mexican exports to the United States more expensive and U.S. exports to Mexico cheaper, producing the small U.S. trade surplus with Mexico.

It was well-known on Wall Street that the Mexican peso was overvalued relative to the country's international competitiveness. The question was not whether it would fall back, but when, and by how much. Neither did the president's own chief economists believe that NAFTA would produce jobs. Laura Tyson, chair of the Council of Economic Advisers, Joseph Stiglitz, who would later win a Nobel Prize, and Alan Blinder, who Clinton subsequently appointed vice chair of the Federal Reserve Board, were all top-notch economic minds. Protecting their professional reputations, they never offered their own forecast of the jobs that would be created by NAFTA. Instead, the White House quoted a prediction by economists at the Institute for International Economics, a business-backed Washington think tank, that NAFTA would create 200,000 net new jobs in two years on the assumption that the trade surplus with Mexico would widen. The study actually estimated a gain of 170,000 but was rounded up to 200,000 by Kantor.[12] Later, Julius Katz, who had been deputy U.S. trade representative under George H. W. Bush and a major player in Clinton's bipartisan campaign to pass NAFTA, told the *Wall Street Journal* that they had used "totally phony numbers."[13]

As the president's prominent advisers knew but did not say, the theory of free trade holds that its benefits do not come in the form of increased employment but rather in the form of lower prices. This is based on the assumption that the larger markets created from free trade will increase economies of scale for businesses and permit greater specialization, therefore making them more productive and able to sell goods at lower prices. Yet, if the members of Congress—certainly Bill Clinton himself—had been asked to list the most important economic difficulties that the country faced, the problem of U.S. consumers not having enough cheap toys, electronics, or apparel would not have made anyone's list. Then, as now, the United States enjoyed the largest, most varied, and cheapest-priced consumer goods market in the world. Even so, according to the details of the study cited by the White House, the annual benefit of NAFTA in lower prices to American consumers was close to zero.[14] As Harvard economist Dani Rodrik observes, "No widely accepted model attributes to postwar trade liberalization more than a tiny fraction of the increased prosperity of advanced industrial countries."[15]

While the potential job gains from NAFTA were vastly exaggerated, potential losses were dismissed. The Clinton/Republican alliance argued that lower wages in Mexico would not attract U.S. businesses because, in theory, low wages would be offset by lower productivity. But although rising productivity permits employers to pay more, it does not require them to. And in Mexico they generally did not. Thus, at the time of the NAFTA agreement, the productivity of Mexican export firms was about 80 percent of the productivity of U.S. firms in the same industry. Their wages, however, were only 10 to 15 percent of American levels. In the 1980s, manufacturing productivity in Mexico rose 28 percent, while real wages fell by 24 percent. Even before NAFTA, U.S. business managers openly admitted that they moved production to Mexico to take advantage of low wages, and the Mexican government was advertising itself to U.S. businesses as a haven for cheap labor.[16]

In May 1993, a small group of American congressmen, headed by then congressman Richard Gephardt, visited a four-year-old Sanyo Corporation maquiladora factory in Tijuana. Maquiladoras are factories that are allowed to ship products to the United States with little or no duty, if they use American raw materials and other inputs. This factory made television receivers and parts. The manager of the plant told the visitors, "It took us two years to catch up to the Koreans. And now," he said, "we are at the productivity level of our plant in Arkansas." And what was the ratio of the entry wage between his plant and the one in Arkansas? Without hesitation, he replied, "One to ten."[17]

Tomatoes or Tomato Pickers?

The political writer Elizabeth Drew later observed that in the campaign to pass NAFTA, "Anti-immigration was a sub-theme used, usually *sotto voce*, by the treaty's supporters."[18]

The voice was not always so sotto. Said President Clinton to the White House audience, "And there will be less illegal immigration because more Mexicans will be able to support their children by staying home." Added ex-president Jerry Ford, "We don't want a huge flow of illegal immigrants into the United States from Mexico. . . . If you defeat NAFTA, you have to share the responsibility for increased immigration into the United States, where they want jobs that are presently being held by Americans."[19] If Congress does not approve NAFTA, warned Jimmy Carter, "The illegal immigration will increase. American jobs will be lost."[20]

In fact, there was no widespread clamor in the early 1990s for Washington politicians to do something about illegal immigration. It was an issue exaggerated by NAFTA supporters. The idea that NAFTA would reduce the increasing flow of Mexican migrants to the United States showed that the high-minded "internationalist" elites—who had tarred NAFTA's labor and environmentalist opponents as anti-Mexican—were happy to use xenophobia in their own cause.

Nor was it just the Americans who used it. Addressing the U.S. Business Roundtable in 1990, Carlos Salinas said, "Where do you want Mexicans working, in Mexico or in the United States? Because if we cannot export more, then Mexicans will seek employment opportunities in the United States. We want to export goods, not people."[21] Thea Lee, the trade economist at the AFL-CIO, remembers Salinas asking Americans in another meeting, "Do you want our tomatoes, or our tomato pickers?"[22]

Globalization's Poster Boy

"Under Carlos Salinas," said George H. W. Bush at the White House rally, "a truly courageous young leader, Mexico has changed and they have moved on environmental matters and on labor matters and they're working closely with us in the narcotics fight. They're

good neighbors and they're good friends and they are good partners. And on a wide array of fronts, Mexico's courageous young
president has tangled with his own bureaucracy, taken on his own
special interests; moving to privatization, he's dramatically improved
Mexico."[23]

Bush's praise of Carlos Salinas was echoed throughout the American political and media establishment. Clinton called Salinas "one of
the world's leading economic reformers."[24] Former secretaries of
state, Democrat Cyrus Vance and Republican Henry Kissinger, told
readers of the *Washington Post*'s op-ed page of Salinas's "dynamic
leadership." *Fortune* magazine wrote of his commitment to "growing clean." *Time* gave him a special 1993 Latin American man-of-
the-year award. The *Wall Street Journal* called him "a man of extraordinary vision." *Newsweek* was awed by his "courage in tearing
Mexican policy from its traditional path." The columnist Georgie
Anne Geyer celebrated his economic transformation as "a drive
toward democracy."[25] One member of Congress, after listening to a
damning critique of the claim that NAFTA would create jobs,
responded, "Well you may be right about the economics, but we
have to help Salinas, don't we?"

Mexican president Carlos Salinas de Gortari, forty-five at the
time of the NAFTA debate, was the scion of a wealthy Mexican business and political family. His father had been minister of commerce
and industry and a prominent leader in the Partido Revolucionario
Institucional.

The PRI was quirky mixture of crony capitalism and socialism
designed to unify the major factions after the long civil war that
followed the overthrow of the dictator Porfirio Díaz in 1911. The
party managed a system in which each major constituency—such as
big and small business, workers, and small farmers—was represented
in the party's leadership by state-supported organizations that protected the interests of their members. The PRI's economic policies
were based on isolationist politics and protectionist economics.
Guiding the development of domestic industries to serve internal
markets was considered the priority "national project."

Mexico was not a democracy, and one-party rule eventually led to
corruption and heavy-handed intolerance of dissent. In the 1950s,
efforts to create independent unions by railroad workers, teachers,

and peasant organizations were brutally suppressed, with leaders jailed and killed. In 1968, the government answered a student protest in Mexico City with bullets and bayonets. Hundreds were killed or disappeared. Peruvian author Mario Vargas Llosa had dubbed Mexico under the PRI as the "perfect dictatorship," meaning that it had the appearance of democracy and the reality of authoritarianism. Still, the system brought political stability and widening prosperity and worked for most Mexicans. Until the early 1980s, the country enjoyed solid economic growth, a more equal distribution of income, and a reduction in poverty.

Moreover, Mexico was an oil producer, so its prospects looked even brighter after world oil prices shot up in the 1970s. Expecting—as did most of the world—that the price of oil would continue to rise, the Mexican government and businesses borrowed heavily from international banks more than willing to lend. When oil prices collapsed at the beginning of the 1980s, so did the peso. Mexico was faced with a rising foreign debt that had to be paid back in dollars while its dollar earnings from the oil business were shrinking. The country plunged into recession.

The crisis brought a new generation of Mexican leaders to power, supported by a network of businesspeople who were growing restive under the restrictions of the PRI's social contract. Breaking a tradition of going to Europe for their training, many studied economics at Harvard, Yale, and the University of Chicago and came back committed to what financier George Soros once called "market fundamentalism." During the 1980s, as minister of planning and budget under President Miguel de la Madrid, Carlos Salinas led this group of self-styled "technocrats" as they privatized state owned enterprises, deregulated business, and broke down the traditional collective landholdings in rural communities. In 1986, Mexico embraced the world trading system by joining the General Agreement on Tariffs and Trade.

Salinas, who knew the American political class as his predecessors did not, quickly became Washington's favorite third world leader. Until his later public disgrace he was the Clinton administration's choice to head the new World Trade Organization.

Certainly, the Mexican political system was in need of reform. But Salinas and the technocrats were not bent on breaking the PRI's power. Rather, they wanted to destroy the power of the labor and peasant constituencies within the PRI that were restraining the global ambitions of the business elite. Under the PRI, so long as they didn't threaten the system itself, union members had the right to job protection, peasants had the right to land, and poor consumers had the right to subsidized corn flour and milk. In order to give investors more leverage and flexibility, Salinas had to destroy those rights. Andres Oppenheimer, who chronicled the Salinas years in his book *Bordering on Chaos*, observed, "Wall Street investment firms had finally found a Mexican leader they could trust."[26]

For Salinas, the issue of democracy was beside the point. As Mexican historian Enrique Krauze notes, "The call for that *Reforma Política* was growing in volume and breadth. . . . But the truth was that Salinas de Gortari never took that call seriously. None of the arguments convinced him—least of all the obvious moral ones such as the capacity of democracy to form responsible citizens, who would have the maturity to discuss their disagreements without resorting to weapons or brute pressure. The pretext for putting off democracy was, as always, an assumed danger from the Left—even in 1989, when communism was collapsing, the cold war was ending, and (on the other side of dictatorship) gorilla governments like Pinochet in Chile and Stroessner in Paraguay were being replaced by the vote. Only three governments in Latin America would continue to shut their doors to democracy: two geographical islands (Haiti and Cuba) and the historical island of Mexico."[27]

For many Mexicans, democracy might have been worth the wait, if in fact their lives had improved. But Salinas's reforms of the 1980s had not delivered. Poverty rose, inequality got worse, and the GDP per capita fell from an annual rate of 3.3 percent in the 1970s to a miniscule 0.1 percent in the 1980s, which meant virtually no growth for the entire decade.

Salinas was picked in 1988 by de la Madrid to be the PRI candidate for president, which was presumed to be tantamount to election. But, reflecting the widespread unrest over the failure of the PRI's free-market reforms, a group of PRI-istas bolted from the party and ran an independent candidate, Cuauhtémoc Cárdenas. Cárdenas was the governor of Michoacán state, and the son of Lázaro Cárdenas, Mexico's most revered president, who had nationalized the oil industry in the late 1930s. On election night 1988, the Mexican government was shocked to find Cárdenas ahead. After a hurried meeting with his political advisers, President de la Madrid had his government announce that the computers had broken down. One week later Salinas was declared a narrow winner. The actual ballots were collected, hidden in the basement of a government building, and subsequently burned. De la Madrid, in his memoirs published in 2004, acknowledged that once the government saw that Cárdenas was winning, it simply stopped counting the votes.[28]

Cárdenas decided not to contest the election in the streets. "An order from him," wrote Enrique Krauze, "would have sent Mexico up in flames. But perhaps in memory of his father, the missionary general, a man of strong convictions but not a man of violence, he did the country a great service by sparing it a possible civil war."[29]

That a leftist almost became president of Mexico and therefore might have set back Salinas's plans to open up the country to foreign investment made Washington nervous. Preventing that in the future was on the minds of many NAFTA promoters. By locking Salinas's specific neoliberal agenda into an international treaty the U.S. and Mexican elites in effect were colluding to prevent the Mexican people from freely choosing different policies even if Salinas's reform failed. After one debate on Capitol Hill, Kantor took me aside privately and lectured me on how the agreement would keep the left from taking over in Mexico. In 2004, Robert Rubin recalled, "Salinas once told me that the best thing about NAFTA was that in the next crisis it would prevent Mexico from going back to the old statist protectionist days."[30] If, as they frequently claimed, the Clinton/Republican coalition was trying to encourage democracy in Mexico, it was an odd strategy to reward the man who stole that country's presidential election.

The people running trade policy in the Bush and Clinton administrations obviously knew of the circumstances of the 1988 election. Nor could they have been unaware that the man in whose cause they were asking American workers to risk their jobs and living standards was running a government with close ties to narcotraffickers, at the same time that the U.S. government was spending $12 billion a year to pursue a war on drugs.[31]

Mexico had long been a source of high-quality marijuana for U.S. consumers, but in the 1970s Washington persuaded the Mexican government to spray the fields with the toxic chemical paraquat.

The program dramatically reduced Mexican exports to the United States and shifted the business to Colombia. But in the 1980s, under the "reform" governments of de la Madrid and Salinas, the Mexican marijuana business rebounded. More importantly, Mexican narco-traffickers became big-time providers of cocaine to the U.S. market. By the end of Salinas's six-year term, drugs were contributing $30 billion in foreign exchange to the Mexican economy and had taken public corruption and violence to new levels.[32]

In 1985, a U.S. Drug Enforcement Agency agent, Enrique Cama-rena, was kidnapped in Guadalajara in broad daylight, tortured, and killed. His mutilated body was left as a calling card from one of the drug cartels. The head of the DEA at the time told the PBS documentary *Frontline*, "We determined that the individuals who took Camarena off the streets were law enforcement personnel." The problem was widespread: "Governors, ministers, corruption in the office of the attorney general of Mexico—very, very high up."[33]

In 1989, the commander of the National Police, Luis Esteban Villalon, was found with $2.4 million cash in the trunk of his car, and was eventually convicted of having given a bribe of more than $20 million to another Mexican official in order to protect the infamous drug boss Juan Garcia Abrego.[34] In 1993, Roman Catholic cardinal Juan Jesus Posadas Ocampo was gunned down at the Guadalajara airport by members of the Tijuana Cartel after his car was mistaken to be that of a rival drug lord.

By the time Salinas's term ended, it was widely known that the drug kingpins had permeated virtually every important sector of the Mexican government, including the office of the president. In 1995, the Swiss, not the U.S. or Mexican, government uncovered some $130 million in cash that Carlos Salinas's brother, Raul, secretly sent to Swiss banks with the help of Citibank in New York. Raul claimed the money was part of an investment fund financed by wealthy businesspeople. No evidence of the existence of such a fund was ever found.

In 1995, the writer Jorge Castañeda, who five years later would become foreign minister in the government of Vicente Fox, wrote, "While neither the Bush nor Clinton administrations ever acknowledged that the NAFTA accord would stimulate drug trafficking, they both knew perfectly well that it would. The DEA [Drug Enforcement Agency] and the U.S. Customs Service confided as much to anyone curious enough to ask."[35]

The dark side of the Salinas family could not have been unknown to the Bush family itself. Raul and George H. W. Bush's son Jeb, later governor of Florida, were close enough to vacation together, both at Bush's home in Miami and at Salinas's ranch in Puebla. According to the *Dallas Morning News*, Raul Salinas's former private secretary testified to U.S. authorities that Raul Salinas Lozano, the father of Raul and Carlos, "was a leading figure in narcotics dealings that also involved his son, Raul Salinas de Gortari, his son-in-law, Jose Francisco Ruiz Massieu, the No. 2 official in the governing Institutional Revolutionary Party, or PRI, and other leading politicians, according to the documents. Mr. Ruiz Massieu was assassinated in 1994."[36]

In 1995, Carlos fled the country in disgrace, and Raul was convicted and imprisoned for ordering Ruiz Massieu's murder. Ten years later, with Carlos returned and once more influential in politics, a Mexican court overturned Raul's conviction on the grounds that the evidence in his trial had been tainted.

On a flight to Mexico City in July 1994, my companion Marjorie Allen sat next to William Perry, who had handled the Mexico desk for Ronald Reagan's National Security Council. We were all official outside observers of the 1994 presidential elections. At one point, Marjorie asked him about rumors we had heard regarding the Salinas family's connection with drugs. He seemed to consider the question naïve. "Of course," he said. "Everyone knows that: it's the father and the brother."

"The intelligence on corruption, especially by drug traffickers, has always been there," said Phil Jordan, who headed the DEA's Dallas office from 1984 to 1994, to the *Dallas Morning News*. But "we were under instructions not to say anything negative about Mexico. It was a no-no since NAFTA was a hot political football." According to the *News*, "Other former officials say they were pressured to keep mum because Washington was obsessed with approving NAFTA."[37]

Both Robert Rubin and Lloyd Bentsen had known Carlos Salinas personally, and certainly the combined intelligence apparatus of the U.S. government, despite its many failings, was competent enough to know there were connections between the Salinas family and the drug lords. But the Clinton administration seemed uninterested in knowing much about the nature of the Salinas regime. As Jorge Castañeda concluded, the American policy class had a stake in its ignorance of Mexico. An "incestuous" relationship had developed "among brokerage firms and investment banks peddling Mexican paper, self-styled experts on Mexico advising those financial institutions and Bush and Clinton Administration officials who sought to avoid at all costs embarrassing or weakening their new found friends in the Salinas regime. . . . Even correspondents for the U.S. press in Mexico fell for Salinas' charm and urbanity, and for their editors' discreet but persistent suggestions that Mexico's modernization be reported on 'fairly.' Enhancing that temptation was the laissez-faire ideology sweeping both parties, with its thought-paralyzing mantra of 'free trade.' "[38]

After NAFTA had passed, the reality behind the Salinas hype became apparent. On the day the agreement went into effect, a rebellion broke out in the southern state of Chiapas. A few months later, Luis Donaldo Colosio, the PRI party candidate to succeed Salinas, was assassinated. Even today, many people believe that he was murdered by drug dealers afraid he might have tried to reduce their influence in the PRI-controlled government. Finally, as we shall see in detail in chapter 6, Carlos Salinas, whom the Washington establishment had proclaimed an honest, modernizing economic reformer, was found to have hidden the facts of a catastrophic drop in Mexico's foreign reserves from the world's financial markets. When Salinas left office, Mexico was bankrupt and he had to flee the country as an international fugitive from justice.

You're on Your Own

Bush, Clinton, Gingrich, Rubin, Kissinger, and the other prominent promoters of NAFTA told the American people that what was good for the Business Roundtable was good for America. We were all together in this brave new world of international competition. As Clinton put it, "Are we going to compete and win, or are we going to withdraw?"

There is no doubt that the world had become more competitive. In the early 1990s the op-ed pages and the business press fretted over the expansion of Japan's economy, which in a few decades had risen from the ashes of World War II to challenge American businesses in auto, consumer electronics, machinery, and high-technology industries. Japanese businessmen were buying up venerable American landmarks like Rockefeller Center, and Japanese tourists descended on the world's resorts and luxury stores buying goods that most Americans could not afford. Across the Atlantic, the European Union was consolidating and it was clear that at some point it would be the world's largest consumer market. Looking further into the future, one could see the challenges of the awakening giant of China. In the absence of NAFTA, Jimmy Carter warned, "The Japanese and others will move in and take over markets that are rightfully ours."[39]

But who was the "we"? Who would take the markets that were "rightfully ours"?

Certainly the people who filled the East Room that September morning knew that "we" meant them. Republicans and Democrats shared the sense of historic mission. The call to sail into the future on the winds of change was exciting and inspiring. Certainly *their* boats would rise with the tide of globalization. They were connected to the worldwide networks of money, old school ties, political institutions, and, most importantly, the great transnational enterprises that were being liberated to abandon any obligations to the nation that nurtured them as they searched the world for profit. For them, this new unregulated global market meant career opportunities, investment deals, foreign assignments, and the steady knitting together of a global safety net of professional contacts—people like themselves all over the world, who would never have to wait in line at the unemployment office or sign up for job retraining in a drab neighborhood center and be lectured on developing good work habits.

The governing classes of Mexico and Canada were also sure that the American "we" now included them. NAFTA meant privileged access to the U.S. market and partnership with the world's only superpower, which would make them even bigger players in the global economic game. What greater proof of this than the prospect of Carlos Salinas becoming head of the new World Trade Organization?

But it was not at all clear to what degree this particular proposal represented an economic opportunity for the other residents of Canada, or Mexico, or the United States. Many sincere people were persuaded that it was, yet a careful look at the fine print of the claims for NAFTA showed that its central assertions were so weak that not even most of the NAFTA champions in the U.S. government believed them.

Actually, there *was* a way that North American economic integration might have increased the competitiveness of the people who worked there. It was for the three countries to merge into a customs union, that is, to create one single internal market and a common tariff and trade policy with the rest of the world. This would have created a larger protected internal market, so that American—and Canadian and Mexican—businesses could produce more efficiently by (1) taking advantage of economies of scale, (2) getting privileged access to each other's raw materials and technology, and (3) providing integrated government on education and training, research and development, and business subsidies.

Senator Ernest Hollings of South Carolina, the chair of the Senate Commerce Committee, supported such a plan.[40] "A common market for the Americas," he wrote in *Foreign Policy* magazine, "with a common external tariff, could be an effective vehicle for competing with the emerging trade blocs in Europe and Asia." Along with it he also proposed requiring "the countries of North America to enter into a social contract to establish minimum standards for labor rights and environmental protection as well as to protect the individual liberties that are the foundation of a democracy."

But big business was opposed to a social contract. And the biggest of them were also not interested in a customs union. That is because the purpose of NAFTA was not to make either North America as a whole or its constituent nations more competitive. It was to make North America's corporate investors more competitive by giving them access to cheap labor and—as we shall see—government assets in Mexico. In fact, the corporations who convinced Clinton to run over the bodies of his allies were not committed to North America at all. It really did not matter where they got their cheap labor, so long as it was cheap. Any place was the same as another— Mexico, China, or Central America, or back in the United States and

Canada if the wage competition encouraged by trade agreements put enough downward pressure on wages and job security.

NAFTA was thus a giant step down the road toward liberating the transnational corporate investors to chase down profits anywhere in the world. But it was not the last step. As soon as NAFTA was signed, the Clinton/Republican coalition that had promoted the agreement immediately extended it to the entire world through the World Trade Organization, and brokered the entrance into the WTO of China's enormous labor market where wages were suppressed with bayonets. When George W. Bush, a charter member of the coalition, became president, he picked up Clinton's program without skipping a beat, making trade agreements with Jordan, Singapore, and Chile and proposing to extend NAFTA to Central America and all of the Western Hemisphere with a Free Trade Area of the Americas.

There were, of course, important differences between the Republicans and Democrats who filled the East Room. But the NAFTA debate revealed how closely the Washington political class still followed Ronald Reagan's script. It wasn't just his idea of a "free trade" zone for North America that they had embraced, it was the worldview he represented—happy-faced social Darwinism. The American voter who listened carefully to Clinton and Newt Gingrich—Reagan's intellectual heir—explain the future would hear a very similar ending. Their common story went something like this:

We are entering an information age that is obliterating economic national boundaries. It is a time of change equivalent to the shift from the agricultural to the industrial age. The resulting deregulated global economy is bringing freedom, democracy, and technological wonders to the rest of the world. In order for you to survive and prosper in this new global market you will have to compete against some six billion people out there, most of whom will work for a lot less than you will. The price of labor is set in South China, where people will work for one-twentieth or less of your wage. If you want to live better than the Chinese, you have to be more than twenty times more efficient. Therefore, you should get all the technical training you can get, be willing to work longer and harder, and make wise investments. You are on your own.

Bill Clinton, of course, understood that this was producing some anxiety. After all, he had been elected because, in his own words, most Americans were "working harder for less." So he continually assured his constituency that he felt their pain. Moreover, as a Democrat, he believed that government had a role in helping individuals make the "transition" to this new competitive global economy. So Democrats would like to help people adjust to the expanded world of dog-eat-dog. But anyone who paid attention to Clinton's speeches on the budget would have realized that they shouldn't expect too much.

As he later put it, the era of big government is over. You are on your own.

3

The Governing Class: America's Worst-Kept Secret

You have to understand, we're a country club crowd.

—Steel executive

The existence of a class of people who manage the government, who influence those who manage the government, and who interpret it all to the voting public, is hardly in doubt. The people in the audience at Clinton's White House rally were not a cross section of America. They fit the generally accepted definition of political elites: those "who are able, by virtue of their strategic positions in powerful organizations to affect outcomes regularly and substantially."[1]

The late Walter Lippman, one of twentieth-century America's most prominent political writers, argued that a governing class was essential to the workings of democracy. A modern society, he wrote, needs "a specialized class of men" with the training and talent to understand a complicated modern world whose workings are invisible to the ordinary person, who, even if he might have the capacity, does not have the inclination to master the issues.

49

The philosopher John Dewey disagreed. "A class of experts," he wrote, "is inevitably so removed from common interests as to become a class with private interests and private knowledge, which in social matters is not knowledge at all."[2] The result, he warned, is a democracy that risks both unaccountability and error.

Dewey's solution was to educate the citizen to take more responsibility. But the complexity of the modern world certainly has accelerated faster than our capacity to teach citizens to identify their own interests, let alone the national interest. Indeed, the pervasive phrase "the national interest" is one of the cloudiest concepts in our political environment. It hides more than it reveals, and has the effect of giving the ordinary citizen the false impression that a democratic consensus has been reached and therefore no longer has to be debated.

In the six months before the U.S. invasion of Iraq in April 2003, the *Washington Post* and the *New York Times* together carried a total of 363 references to "U.S.," "national," "America's," or "American" interests.[3] The articles reported that these "interests" were attacked, threatened, complied with, served, violated, undermined, pursued, spread, and defended. But nowhere were we told what these interests actually were, and why we should consider them to be the nation's.

By and large, governing-class intellectuals just assume away Dewey's concern. One of the most prominent, Harvard professor of international relations Joseph Nye, tells us, "In a democracy, the national interest is simply what citizens, *after proper deliberation* [italics added], say it is. . . . If the American people think that our long-term shared interests include certain values and their promotion abroad, then they become part of the national interest. Leaders and experts may point out the costs of indulging certain values, but if an informed public disagrees, experts cannot deny the legitimacy of their opinion."[4]

It is hard to take seriously Nye's explanation that American leaders simply pursue the country's national interest on the basis of what the "citizens, after proper deliberation, say it is." From NAFTA and the WTO to the war in Iraq, America's policy establishment—like that of most countries—did its best to discourage debate beyond the range set by the consensus at the top. NAFTA and the WTO were misrepresented as "free trade," the virtues of which were asserted as so obvious as to be beyond the scope of any "proper deliberation" by the citizenry. To this day Washington pundits speak admiringly of Clinton's ability to roll over public opinion to achieve his trade agenda. George W. Bush's stubborn insistence on promoting unpopular programs with misrepresentation and lies is generally considered in Washington to be his great virtue.

The case that the national interest is established by the "proper deliberation" of the citizenry is weakest when it comes to foreign affairs, where reality is so easily hidden from the public and repackaged to suit the agendas of those who govern. Claims about the facts on the ground in America, such as unemployment or prices or crime in the streets, are to some extent verifiable by the experience of the ordinary citizen. It is much harder to get the facts about what is happening on the ground in Iraq, Afghanistan, Colombia, or Korea. Precisely because of the general ignorance and lack of interest in foreign policy, presidents are drawn to the exercise of it.

The negative political reaction to the Bush administration's inept response to the destruction of New Orleans by Hurricane Katrina was swift. Journalists there were free to transmit the images and sounds of catastrophe—the bodies floating in the street, the cries of the abandoned and bereft, the outrage of overwhelmed local officials. In contrast, it took the public years to understand the administration's disastrous mishandling of the Iraq occupation. The news from Iraq was controlled and the citizens' perceptions were easily clouded by lies and misrepresentations (for example, that Saddam had weapons of mass destruction and was allied with al Qaeda) that they did not feel confident to judge. Iraq was a faraway abstraction and the Bush administration was able to use nationalist feelings to morph support for the troops into support for the war. New Orleans was a place people knew. When the administration tried to hide its mistakes behind the heroism of the rescue teams, the media was not so easily intimidated and thus the public was not so easily fooled.

Every president since FDR has found it easier to play politics in the international rather than the domestic arena.[5] Voters understand the domestic questions better. Therefore, they are more divided over them, making it more difficult for a president to define the national interest in domestic affairs.

The emergence of the United States as a global superpower, whose governing class has "interests" all over the world, has coincided with the expansion of the power of the executive branch and the weakening of Congress—most of whose members are kept in as much ignorance of foreign affairs as the people who elect them. The imperial presidency at home is an inevitable product of imperialism abroad.

Who Rules?

Newcomers to Washington are advised that if they want to know how power really works, they should read the society pages of the *Washington Post*. While not exactly offstage (like actors, politicians are hardly ever offstage), the continuous flow of Washington's social life nurtures a congeniality hidden behind the public veil of partisan politics. The newly arrived committed liberal Democrat or conservative Republican from beyond the beltway is often shocked at the chumminess of his heroes with their ideological enemies at embassy receptions, trade association dinners, and other haunts of the Washington social habitat.

The chumminess is understandable, given the similarity of background and experience of most Washington players. Most of those in the audience at the White House NAFTA rally were in the upper reaches of the distribution of income and wealth in America. The bulk of them came from families whose income and social status was substantially above average. They tended to have gone to the best schools, and to have classmates and social connections with others in the elite networks.

Membership in this governing class is not solely an inherited position. There is plenty of room for the extraordinarily ambitious, talented, and lucky individual of obscure origins. People with an aptitude for governing are constantly moving through the outer concentric circles of power—from city councils and state legislatures, from local businesses, universities and law firms in the hinterland, and from military assignments—toward power in Washington. As with most other occupations in America, a successful career requires some work, some talent, and some luck. To get to the power, money is essential. And the power and the money are almost always connected through the large business corporation.

In his classic study *Who Rules America?*, G. William Domhoff identifies three overlapping circles of people connected at the top of the American social pyramid: "the power elite." One circle is the network around government, which he calls the Policy Formation Organizations—political and technocratic Washington. The second comprises managers of the Corporate Community. The third is the Social Upper Class—the super-rich who live on their investments.

The corporation is the ultimate source of power for all of them. Ownership of financial assets supports the Social Upper Class, many of whom, as individuals, are uninterested in political power. The corporation supplies both ownership income and salaries for its managers. It provides salaries, retainer fees, and campaign contributions to technocratic and political Washington.

The Governing Class

Domhoff points out that "most appointees in both Republican and Democratic Administrations are corporate executives and corporate lawyers, and hence members of the power elite."[6] George W. Bush owned an oil company, as well as a being a former owner of the Texas Rangers. His vice president, Richard Cheney, is known worldwide as the former CEO of Halliburton. Lesser known is his service on the board of directors of Electronic Data Systems, Procter & Gamble, and Union Pacific. Bush's chief of staff, Andrew Card, had been General Motors' chief lobbyist in Washington for seven years. His secretary of state, Condoleezza Rice, formerly provost of Stanford University, was on the board of directors of Chevron and Transamerica. Former secretary of state Colin Powell had been director of Gulfstream Aerospace and America Online. Secretary of Defense Donald Rumsfeld was chief executive officer of pharmaceutical giant GD Searle for seven years, held the same job with General Instruments for three years, and was a director of Kellogg, Sears Roebuck, the *Chicago Tribune*, and Gulfstream Aerospace. His former secretary of the treasury, Paul O'Neill, was chair of Alcoa and a director of Lucent Technologies. His first secretary of commerce, Donald Evans, is the son of a Shell Oil manager and was the CEO of Tom Brown, Inc., a Texas Oil company. His second was CEO and chair of Kellogg. The secretary of labor, Elaine Chao, was a manager at Citicorp and the Bank of America and was a director of Clorox, Dole Foods, and Northwest Airlines.

Clinton's first secretary of state, Warren Christopher, was a corporate lawyer and director of Lockheed Martin, Southern California Edison, and First Interstate Bank. His first secretary of defense, Les Aspin, a member of Congress, was part of a family-owned business in Wisconsin. His first secretary of the treasury, Lloyd Bentsen, inherited millions and was head of his own insurance company. Robert Rubin, his second treasury secretary, came from Goldman Sachs. His first CIA head was a corporate lawyer and director of Martin Marietta. Even Clinton's minority appointments came from business. His secretary of agriculture came from a large landholding family in the South. His secretary of commerce was a corporate lawyer, whose firm paid him $580,000 a year while he was chair of the Democratic Party. His secretary of energy was the former executive vice president of North States Power. His secretary of housing and urban development was the head of an air charter company.

Clinton's first secretary of labor, Robert Reich, did not come from business. He was an old friend and a Harvard professor. But he made his reputation by studying corporate strategies and was virtually unknown to the trade unions. In fact, a Democratic president had not appointed someone from a labor union as secretary of labor since John F. Kennedy in 1961, when he appointed the steelworkers' lawyer, Arthur Goldberg.

But membership and rank are not fixed. Elections at any given time determine which individuals sit in the limited number of musical chairs available. Some members of Congress who lose elections go back home, or weaken their ties to the governing class. Others stay on in Washington, becoming lobbyists with the K Street law firms that in recent decades have usurped the role of the career bureaucracy in policymaking. The university president or major law firm partner moves up when he or she becomes a cabinet officer, and down when the party loses power. Being today's deputy secretary of commerce is more important than being yesterday's secretary of commerce. Just below those whose faces appear in the society pages are armies of aides, contractors, journalists, and others whose livelihood is a function of their proximity to the rich and powerful.

The business corporation is by far the most privileged institution in American society, and the people who manage the largest of them are naturally the country's most powerful people. Thus neither the lopsided distribution of income nor the even more lopsided distribution of wealth fully reflects the way economic power is concentrated in America, because it leaves out the leverage that accompanies control of a corporation. When Jack Welch of General Electric, Sandy Weil of Citigroup, or Ken Lay of Enron walked into the Bush or Clinton White House they walked in not just as rich men, but as men who could deploy vast accumulations of capital far beyond their own substantial wealth.

Corporate money flows into the political mainstream in many forms—in direct payments to lobbyists and influential insiders, campaign cash contributions bundled by executives, plush jobs for defeated politicians and retired high-level civil servants, grants for think tanks, fellowships for journalists, and in the promise of bringing jobs in the congressman's district or the threat to lay off workers in the senator's state. It is the glue that connects the leadership of the two-party system. Thus, a chorus of political pundits told the country during the election campaign of 2004 that the loyalties of the electorate were fiercely divided. But at the top, much of business, despite the obvious preference for Republicans, remained surprisingly bipartisan. The same four financial firms—Citigroup, Goldman Sachs, UBS AG, and Morgan Stanley—were among the top ten donors to both George Bush and John Kerry.

The influence of those who control large corporations reaches far beyond the number of cabinet officers with corporate experience. It pervades the other major institutions that in theory should be a check on their power—federal and state government, the courts, the military, government bureaucracies, universities, political parties, churches, foundations, and the variety of organizations that make up civil society, including labor unions. The civil service is full of accountants, tax lawyers, contract specialists, and others steadily acquiring the knowledge, experience, and contacts that they expect will land them a job in private business at three times their government salary. Corporate influence is so pervasive in Washington and state governments that it is almost invisible—the way air is to mammals and water is to fish. Every day, virtually every waking hour, Congress, the executive branch, and the courts are flooded with business lobbyists and lawyers promoting the tax breaks, subsidies, regulatory changes, and other objectives of their business clientele. As NAFTA illustrated, and as all but the most hopelessly naïve observer of life in the capital understands, the process of government is now overwhelmed by the influence of money. Patrick Griffin, who became top lobbyist after working in the Clinton White House put it succinctly: "Washington has become a profit center."[7]

Business is not the only institution that lobbies. Labor unions, environmental organizations, universities, and others also hire people to influence the government. And there are about 250 lobbyists in Washington registered to represent foreign governments. But the corporate money overwhelms. The one hundred top spenders on Washington lobbying laid out almost $4.5 billion between 1998 and mid-2004. The U.S. Chamber of Commerce headed the list with $194 million. The AFL-CIO and the Trial Lawyers Association—widely identified by the media as "powerful" interests—ranked seventy-fourth and seventy-seventh respectively.[8]

Moreover, on any important issue in which the interests of business corporations as a class are at stake, they rarely lose. The last instance of a major law that passed over the significant opposition of the business community occurred more than three decades ago in the first year of Jimmy Carter's presidency—the Occupational Health and Safety Act of 1975. The last instance of a Democratic president publicly challenging the prerogatives of big business was when John Kennedy forced the major steel companies to rescind their simultaneous price increase in October 1962.

The punditry must of course acknowledge—and sometimes deplore—the crass dependence of America's governing class on corporate money. But this, the citizen is told, is not decisive. People who give large amounts of money to political candidates do not get favors, goes the story they only get "access." But as Congressman Romano Mazzoli (D-KY) put it, "People who contribute get the ear of the member and the ear of the staff. They have the access—and access is it. Access is power. Access is clout. That's how this thing works."[9]

The corporate lobbyists' explanation of what they do drips with hypocrisy. Democrat Anne Wexler told author Joel Bakan that she lobbies to "educate" the overworked members of Congress so they have an "understanding of what the issues are." Hank McKinnell, CEO of the transnational drug company Pfizer, says that their contributions are a way to "participate in the national policy debate," and that they do not "give us anything special in return."[10]

The notion that $5.4 billion would have been paid to Washington lobbyists in 2003 and 2004 (double the amount spent on federal elections) for nothing but the privilege of helping out the democratic process does not pass the laugh test—and we all know it.

The relationship between Congress and lobbying business has become even more incestuous over the last few decades. In the 1970s only about 3 percent of retiring members of Congress went to the K Street lobbying and law firms. Today, it is more than 30 percent. Chairmen of committees and subcommittees become lobbyists getting paid up to $2 million a year to influence legislation in their former committees. Representative Billy Tauzin was the chair of the House Energy and Commerce Committee that, among other things, oversees the drug industry. When he retired from the House he became the head of the chief lobbying association for the pharmaceutical industry, with hardly a raised eyebrow among the political establishment.

Politicians and the punditry commonly complain of the breakdown of "civility" across party lines in Washington, and hands were thrown up in horror when Republican House leader Tom DeLay tried to banish Democrats from the top jobs among the K Street lobbyists. But in reality, the Democrats and Republicans among those in Washington who represent the big money have never been more integrated.

It also used to be that there were very separate lobbying firms for Republicans and Democrats. But despite DeLay's effort, the corporate money increasingly intends to cover all bases, and the important lobbying firms and industry associations are today more bipartisan, not less. So it was no real surprise that after Senate Democratic majority leader Tom Daschle was defeated in 2004, he was recruited to the firm of Alston and Bird by ex–Republican majority leader Robert Dole. "He's got a lot of friends in the Senate, and I've got a lot of friends in the Senate," Dole joked. "And combined, who knows—we might have fifty-one."[11] Daschle's wife was already in the business, as a major airline industry lobbyist.

At the same time, Jack Oliver III, who was vice chairman of finance for Bush-Cheney '04, and Steve Elmendorf, former chief aide to Democratic leader Richard Gephardt and deputy manager of Kerry-Edwards '04, formed their own lobbying partnership after the

2004 campaign. Elmendorf told the *Washington Post* that after the election he went to yet another lobbyist, Bobby Koch, brother-in-law of George W. Bush, who put him together with Oliver.[12]

Another example of how this works was Bill Clinton's end-of-presidency pardon for the notorious Marc Rich, an oil magnate who was long a fugitive from U.S. justice. The Belgian-born Rich (who was naturalized and later renounced his U.S. citizenship) had faced criminal charges for massive tax fraud and selling oil to Iran during the hostage crisis. Rich's wife made major contributions to the Clintons and then hired a bipartisan team of insiders to lobby the White House: Republicans Lewis Libby, who became chief of staff to Richard Cheney; William Bradford Reynolds, a top official in Reagan's Justice Department; and Leonard Garment, Richard Nixon's White House counsel. The Democratic side was represented by Clinton's ex-White House counsel Jack Quinn, whose partner was former Republican Party chairman Ed Gillespie. Clinton pardoned Rich while turning down petitions for people who already served jail time for lesser crimes.

Corporate interests are not monolithic. Corporations compete among themselves for tax breaks, subsidies, and regulatory decisions. As in the courts of Louis XIV or Catherine the Great, individuals continually jockey for power within the corporate class. The international business press regularly delivers stories of Shakespearean intrigue, deception, and betrayal in the boardroom. In the summer of 2004, for example, the media was inundated with the scandal of Conrad Black, for decades one of the most powerful business moguls in the world, being charged with having stolen roughly 90 percent of the profits of the Hollinger Corporation, itself a publisher of such papers as the *Chicago Sun-Times*, the London *Telegraph*, and the *Jerusalem Post*. Black had put on his board prominent political figures such as Henry Kissinger; Democratic powerhouse and former ambassador to Russia Robert Strauss; Richard Burt, former ambassador to Germany; and Richard Perle, top Reagan Defense Department official and superhawk adviser to George W. Bush.

Moreover, the traffic of power is a two-way street. It moves from corporations to government and back. At a "not for attribution" dinner of congressional Democrats in 2003, a prominent Wall Street financier told the members of Congress that his colleagues in New York were deeply concerned with George W. Bush's fiscal and trade deficits. They were worried that the dollar would fall so far that foreign investors would unload their U.S. bonds causing a financial panic. "So, why don't we read about these concerns in the *Wall Street Journal* or the *New York Times*?" asked one congressman. "Well," said the financier sheepishly, "we all have business to do with the administration."

Republicans are more aggressive in leaning on individual businesses to serve their political agenda, particularly with the media. Richard Nixon during the Watergate scandal threatened to "sic" the Federal Communications Commission on the *Washington Post*'s ownership of TV and radio stations. George W. Bush's White House is notorious for pressuring the media. When the Bush FCC used an incident in which singer Janet Jackson's breast was momentarily exposed during a halftime football game to sanction Viacom, the corporation's chairman, who had portrayed himself as a "liberal Democrat," announced his support for Bush's reelection. "I vote what's good for Viacom," he said.[13]

Democrats like to think that they do not abuse their power this way because they are nicer people. Perhaps. It may also be that they are more timid and cannot match the Republican passion for their cause. But most likely it is that Democrats, with their connections to workers and environmentalists, do not feel fully accepted by the corporate class and must therefore be more careful about stepping on those CEO toes.

Class Unconsciousness

The influence of money on American politics is a fact of life. It would follow that the rich have more influence on public decisions than the rest of us. It would also seem to follow that the rich, as a class, act together in their common interest.

Yet the idea of the rich as a political class is quickly dismissed by the punditry as obsolete Marxist "conspiracy theory." The accusation that someone is waging "class warfare" is one of the most effective conversation stoppers in American political life.

The promotion of shared class interest is natural human behavior; people who are alike tend to socialize with each other, reinforce each other's views of the world, and act together when their common interests are at stake. It would be odd if the richest and most influential individuals did not act in their common interest. Indeed, Adam Smith himself was a conspiracy theorist. As he famously observed, "People of the same trade seldom meet together, even for merriment and diversion, but the conversation ends in a conspiracy against the public."[14]

The constraints on the public discussion of economic class seem to apply primarily to those at the top. The poor are studied to death by government agencies and liberal foundations as a substitute for a serious national effort to combat poverty. We know who the poor are, what they eat, how they behave. The ostensible purpose of the research is to guide policies aimed at changing the behavior of those at the bottom.

Another, more commercially motivated research industry studies the middle class, breaking it into small niches (for example, upwardly mobile urban white women between twenty-five and thirty, retired seniors in the Southwest, non-college-graduate males in medium-sized cities, and so on). Most of this research—conducted at universities as well as private survey research firms—is driven by the desire of corporate managers, politicians, and others who sell to mass markets to better identify the most profitable "niches." As with studies of the poor, research on the middle class is also aimed at attitude and behavioral change—in this case, to get consumers to buy certain products or vote for certain candidates.

In contrast, there is comparatively little serious research on the composition and behavior of the American elite. In the academic world, departments of sociology, political science, and economics are parts of the university system run by people of or near the governing class. Scrutinizing and publishing reports on their behavior as a class might suggest some practical-change agenda as well, a prospect that they would clearly rather not encourage.

Of course, political, sports, and entertainment figures, including business celebrities like Donald Trump and Ted Turner, fill the pages of newspapers and magazines and soak up TV airtime and tabloids. They are icons to be worshipped or envied as individuals, but not a class to be examined for its collective impact on our lives.

Class as Style

Indeed, one of the most successful political strategies of our time is the reinterpretation of class as an issue of cultural and lifestyle division rather than group differences in wealth and power. The culturally elite atheist intellectual, who from time to time morphs into an out-of-touch-with-American-values bureaucrat, is a familiar caricature in the screaming echo chambers of the conservative media. Liberal Democrats are relentlessly painted as members of the pointy-headed "chattering class" who use Big Government to pander to minorities, gays, feminists, and other segmented constituencies.

Accompanying this sleight of hand is the identification of Big Government only with unpopular causes of the left. Never mind that the largest subsidized industries are agriculture and defense, economic sectors that consistently support the conservative political agenda. Never mind that Republican administrations have used Big Government to dictate social conformity and undercut constitutional rights. Never mind that Republican administrations have used Big Government to override states' rights to regulate corporations in banking, insurance, telecommunications, and other sectors. Big Government is associated in the electorate's mind with social liberalism, to the great benefit of social conservatism.

Thus, the shift in the political discussion to cultural class "values" further widens the country's economic disparities. As the author Thomas Frank noted, "When two female rock stars exchange a lascivious kiss on TV, Kansas goes haywire. Kansas screams for the heads of the liberal elite. Kansas comes running to the polling place. And Kansas cuts those rock stars' taxes."[15]

The conservative interpretation of class as a social and cultural phenomenon is not totally inaccurate. The civil rights and Vietnam conflicts of the 1960s splintered the Democratic Party's broad-based New Deal coalition that had been united around issues of economic class. Since then, liberal identity has been defined by issues of gender, race, sexual preference, disability, and other subclass categories that emphasize differences among their own core constituencies. The institutions that unite the traditional Democratic constituencies but make business uncomfortable, such as the labor unions and the local political clubs, were gradually marginalized by the party, a process that accelerated in the 1980s with the expanded influence of corporate money. The result was that liberalism's accomplishments have been aimed at niche political constituencies. Thus, notes Elaine Bernard, executive director of the Trade Union Program at Harvard University, "The boss cannot fire you because of your race. He cannot fire you because of your gender. He cannot fire you because of your sexual preference or your disability. He can just fire you for no reason at all."[16]

Social liberalism has much to be proud of. Discrimination remains, but the official and unofficial lowering of barriers just on the basis of race or gender or disability or sexual preference has been significant, including forcing more diversity at the top. Twenty-five years ago a black Republican secretary of state, a black female national security adviser, and a black conservative Supreme Court justice would have been impossible to imagine. The same is true of a woman running Honeywell, Hewlett-Packard, or Time Inc.

But *class* divisions have worsened. Not only is the distribution of income and wealth getting more top-heavy, but the institutions— primarily organized labor—that championed the cause of the working class (as the slogan says, "The people who brought you the weekend") have been steadily losing influence in the party that claims it speaks for working families. The disdain of the Clinton White House staff for the labor unions to which they owed their election was well-known. The tone was set from the top, as an anecdote told by Clinton's labor secretary Robert Reich suggests. A year after having run over his labor union supporters with NAFTA, Clinton refused to put sufficient pressure on the two Democratic Arkansas senators who were needed to pass the one piece of legislation that the AFL-CIO wanted from him, legislation ensuring the right to strike. The union presidents came into the White House hurt and angry. Clinton was "red-faced and upset" at having to meet them. "Who the hell set this up?" he yelled at his staff. But after a few minutes of his professing to understand their problems and passionately expressing his commitment to workers, in the abstract, the union presidents gave him a standing ovation—and left empty-handed.[17]

The Top Fifty Thousand

Conventional wisdom asserts that America is a middle-class country, because that's what most Americans say they are.

When pollsters ask Americans if they are lower, middle, or upper class, 80 to 90 percent typically select "middle." In fact, the middle 80 percent of the distribution of income in America covers a huge range. In 2002, it spanned $10,620 to $114,112.

The media often stretches the range further. Steve Case, the former chair and CEO of America Online, was frequently referred to in the press as coming from the "middle class." Yet as G. William Domhoff notes, "His father was a corporate lawyer and his mother a descendant of a sugar plantation owner. He grew up in an exclusive Honolulu neighborhood, attended a high-status private school in his teens and graduated from Williams College, his father's alma mater. He received his start at the company that later became AOL through his older brother, already established as an investment banker and a member of the company's board of directors."[18] In another common confusion of "class," Bill Gates is celebrated as a college "dropout" who made good. But Gates's story is not what most of us think about when we hear the word "dropout." He is the son a well-to-do corporate lawyer and went to a private prep school, before entering Harvard. He dropped out to form Microsoft.[19] Bill Clinton's origins were more modest, but they hardly deserve the label "poor" or "humble" the media often gives them. His mother was a registered nurse and his father a partner in an auto dealership, which in most of 1950s America were above-average circumstances. Writer Garry Wills notes, "This was no Dogpatch, as one can tell from the number of Clinton's childhood friends who went on to distinguished careers."[20]

The initial response to pollsters is clearly limited by the choices presented. When respondents are offered a fourth choice, "working class," the results shift. According to the National Opinion Research Center of the University of Chicago, in 1998, in the middle of an economic boom, 45 percent of the public considered themselves "working class" whereas 46 percent said they were "middle class." Five percent said they were lower and 4 percent upper class.[21]

The term "working class" carries a huge ideological burden in American culture. It is commonly associated with images of downsized blue-collar industrial workers, who in 2003 represented only 12 percent of the labor force. So the survey results undoubtedly understate the extent to which people think of themselves as working, rather than middle, class.

Another way to define "working class" is to separate those whose income depends on work from those whose income is derived from investment. In the early 1990s, Robert Reich estimated that 80 percent of the workforce was labor-dependent and 20 percent composed of wealthy people who lived off their investments or "symbolic analysts," that is, highly paid professionals who sold their specialized services in the global market. Sociologists Robert Perucci and Earl Wysong come up with similar numbers, identifying 20 percent of the population as "privileged." These are people with high incomes, extensive power on the job, and income security. The vast majority of these are a "credentialed" class of managers and highly paid professionals. At the top is a super-rich class of 1 to 2 percent of Americans who live on investment income and are protected by their vast wealth.[22]

Professor Michael Zweig of the State University of New York at Stony Brook divides the labor force into three broad classes, based largely on the power people have in and around their job. He estimates that in 1996 the working class—those with no power—represented the bottom 62 percent of the country's workers. Its members are now overwhelmingly in the service sector, almost half female, and roughly 10 percent unionized. He breaks the middle class into three groups: small businesspeople, supervisors and middle managers, and professionals. Together they make up 36 percent. Zweig estimates the "capitalist" class—the top managers and directors of corporations employing more than five hundred workers—at roughly two hundred thousand people. From this group he winnows out those who serve on the boards of directors of only one major corporation and adds some major political and cultural leaders affiliated with the major corporations. He concludes with an estimate of an American "ruling class" of roughly fifty thousand people[23]—1.7 percent of Americans.

Fifty thousand is clearly too many to comprise some secret conspiracy. But the class system in America is not born of a secret conspiracy. Domhoff observes, "Not everyone in this nationwide upper class knows everyone else, but everybody knows somebody who knows someone in other areas of the country, thanks to a common school experience, a summer at the same resort, membership in the same social club, or membership on the same board of directors. The upper class at any given historical moment consists of a complex network of overlapping social circles knit together by the members they have in common and by the numerous signs of equal social status that emerge from a similar lifestyle."[24]

Breaking into the Ruling Class Is Getting Harder, Not Easier

But does it matter? The United States appears to be a mobile society, where people easily move up and down the socioeconomic ladder. So what if there are classes? If your position depends on your abilities and not the class that you were born into, what's the problem?

Compared to many other places in the world, and other times in history, America today certainly provides more opportunities for talented people to better themselves. Our history has many examples of people who climbed from humble origins to places of power and wealth. The Horatio Alger story of the poor boy who rises to riches represents an icon of the American experience.[25]

But the United States is not as mobile as the official catechism would have it, and the evidence is that it is getting less so. In the roughly three decades following World War II, the distribution of income and wealth became more equal and mobility among classes improved. Labor unions gave greater bargaining power to workers, educational opportunities were expanded, and government-subsidized housing gave working-class Americans access to a wealth-building asset. Then, after the 1970s, both trends reversed. For example, 74 percent of families that were in poverty at the beginning of the decade of the 1970s remained there at the end. During the decade of the 1990s, despite the fast overall economic growth and the increase in two-earner families, 77 percent remained poor. During the 1970s, 73 percent who started the decade in the top 20 percent remained there. In the 1990s, 77 percent stayed at the top. Sons of fathers in the bottom three-quarters of the socioeconomic scale were substantially less likely to rise out of their class in the 1990s than they were in the 1960s.[26]

James Heckman, a Nobel Prize–winning economist at the University of Chicago, concluded, "The big finding in recent years is that the notion of America being a highly mobile society isn't as true as it used to be."[27]

The persistence of inherited status is often rationalized as the natural result of genetically transmitted characteristics. Race and gender, for example, are significant determinants of economic status. We know that good-looking, intelligent people are more successful, and although we can argue over the degree to which good looks and intelligence are inherited, that genes play some role is not in doubt. Still, the overwhelming evidence in the last twenty years is that inherited *status* is more important than inherited genes. In an exhaustive analysis of the research, professors Samuel Bowles and Herbert Gintis concluded in 2002 that "wealth, race, and schooling are important to the inheritance of economic status, but IQ is not a major contributor, and . . . the genetic transmission of IQ is even less important."[28]

Conventional wisdom among the globalist elite is that inequality is the price a society must pay for increasing social mobility, reflecting greater opportunity. Thus, for example, the governing class never seems to tire of telling Americans how lucky they are compared with the citizens of Western Europe who are so protected from competition that they have no incentive to succeed. Yet, although the United States has the highest level of income inequality among all advanced societies,[29] a child born to poverty actually has a greater chance of moving up the class ladder in Western Europe and Canada than in the United States. Economist Miles Corak, who analyzed dozens of studies on this point, told the *Wall Street Journal* in May 2005, "The U.S. and Britain appear to stand out as the least mobile societies among the rich countries studied."[30] France and Germany, regularly ridiculed by the American elite for economic policies that supposedly discourage ambition, actually provide more room for mobility than does the United States. Canada and the Scandinavian countries, home of high taxes and generous welfare, are, according to the numbers, even greater lands of individual opportunity.[31]

Yet over the last thirty years the gap between the EU's and U.S.'s GDP per hour narrowed from 35 to 7 percent. Productivity per hour of work in Austria, Denmark, and Italy is at U.S. levels. In France, Belgium, Germany, Norway, and Ireland it is higher.[32] Returns on investment in Europe have been the match of America's for the previous decade. Moreover, this has been accomplished without the huge amount of overseas borrowing that has sustained the American

economy. As a special report by the *Economist* in June 2004 concluded, "The widely held belief that the euro area economies have
persistently lagged America's is simply not supported by the facts."[33]

It is precisely this economic dynamism that has allowed Europe
to maintain its social safety net and economic democracy in spite of a
more competitive world. You can become a billionaire quicker in
America, but your chances of living a longer, more secure life, with
time for your family and friends, free from the anxiety of economic
ruin if you get sick, and a higher-quality education for your children,
are much greater in Western Europe. European workers have taken
more of their productivity gains in leisure—primarily in longer holi-
days and shorter workweeks. Over their lifetimes, Americans work
an estimated 40 percent more hours than do workers in France,
Germany, and Italy.

The immediate cause of reduced economic mobility in the United
States has been the closing off of avenues of escape from low-wage
jobs. The traditional job paths into the middle class—unionized industrial jobs and unskilled government service—have shrunk. While
opportunities for further upward mobility have declined, rising costs
have priced people in the lower end of the income distribution out
of the market for a college education, the springboard for the next
generation.

In the decade of the 1990s, after adjusting for inflation, the annual cost of undergraduate tuition plus room and board rose 21 percent at public colleges and 26 percent at private ones.[34] The annual
cost of sending a child to Harvard is now $41,500. Of course, subsi-
dies and loans are available for the extraordinary child of poverty. But
for the only moderately gifted person from poor or ordinary families, opportunities are slipping away. For example, they must compete with children from families who can afford to pay $400 an hour
to a tutor who knows how to raise SAT scores. Then they must
compete against children who simply go to the best schools because
their parents went there. The *Economist* reported in late 2004 that
"legacies"—children admitted because their parents are alumni—
made up a significant share of the student body. "In most Ivy League
institutions, the eight supposedly most select universities of the north-
east, 'legacies' make up between 10% and 15% of every class. At Harvard they are over three times more likely to be admitted than others.

The students in America's places of higher education are increasingly becoming an oligarchy tempered by racial preferences."[35]

Children of wealthier families are further fast-tracked by the growing importance of internships—the new apprentice system for careers in the most competitive and attractive fields, such as communications, entertainment, and politics. Each year, several thousand young people come to Washington to work for no money, or very little, in order to make career connections and add to their résumés for prestigious graduate schools. They work for congressional offices, at the White House, at newspapers and TV stations, think tanks, NGOs, lobbying firms, and for political consultants. Mark Oldman, co-founder of a career counseling center, told the *New York Times*, "It used to be that internships used to be a useful enhancement to one's resumes. Now it's universally perceived as an essential stepping stone to career success."[36]

But fewer college students can afford to take unpaid internships. At the very least, they have to pay for housing, food, and transportation away from home in an expensive city. For the large numbers who have to make as much money as possible in the summer to help pay for the rising costs of college, taking an unpaid internship is close to impossible.

Not, of course, *entirely* impossible. As in many areas of life in the United States, the extraordinarily committed person from modest means has a shot at success. In the summer of 2004, the *Washington Post* interviewed one student who worked two paying jobs as well as a full-time unpaid internship—eighty-nine hours a week. But by and large, the apprenticeship for careers in public policy is being reserved for children of families with the means. Those who must wait tables, deliver packages, or do other work to earn a living on their "vacation" fall behind in the race to find a place at the top of power structure.

Gaps between Classes

As the class structure of American society hardens, the gap between those at the top and the rest of the economy is widening. In 2002, the average income of the very top one-tenth of 1 percent of income earners—about 145,000 taxpayers—was over $3 million. It had more than doubled since 1980. This group's share of all income also more than doubled. The share of income going to the rest of those in the top 10 percent also rose, but much less. The share of income going to the bottom 90 percent fell.[37] Wealth is even more concentrated. In 2001, the top 1 percent of households held 33 percent of all Americans' assets and 40 percent of all financial assets.[38]

Those who insist that America is a classless society point to the spread of corporate stock ownership as evidence that we are becoming a nation of capitalists—an "ownership society," as George W. Bush terms it. But in 2001 the wealthiest 1 percent of households held 33 percent of all corporate shares. Since they own most of the stock—and presumably have more access to information—the benefits of the great stock market boom went primarily to those at the top. Obviously owning just a few of the ten billion outstanding shares of General Electric does not give you any real clout with the company or get you an invitation to the White House.

Still, it is true that corporate stock ownership has widened over the past decade. By 2001, 52 percent of all households owned stock. Of these holdings 70 percent was *indirect*, that is, in mutual funds or 401(k) plans. The broadening of stock ownership has been primarily driven by the shift away from defined-benefit *pension* plans—where the company invests and guarantees the pension payment—to the 401(k), which is not a pension at all but a personal savings plan to which the employer makes a defined *contribution*. The risks that there might not be enough in the pension plan to retire on have shifted to the employee from the employer.

But the risks do not get shifted to those who rule at the top. Instead, in addition to allowing the corporate managers and owners to escape their traditional obligations to their longtime employees, the 401(k) has provided opportunities for the corporate manager class to loot the life savings of their workers. As with so many companies that proclaimed themselves leaders of the "New Economy," Enron's executives created a corporate culture that celebrated the enterprise as one big, classless family. But the underlying economic relationship was class warfare; the corporation's managers were selling virtually worthless stock at high prices into their own workers' 401(k) plans. Inevitably the bubble had to burst, and top executives who understood the company's finances bailed out—leaving the workers' 401(k)s chock-full of virtually worthless stock. To add insult to injury, the people at the very top of the Enron pyramid got guaranteed-benefit pensions. Ex-CEO Ken Lay, for example, gets $457,000 a year for life.

CEO mismanagement of pension systems is endemic. In early 2005 the Pension Benefits Guarantee Corporation, the government agency that is supposed to insure private pensions, estimated that American corporations were underfunding their pensions to the tune of $450 billion. Meanwhile the agency was $60 billion in the red and facing a huge collapse of pensions in the airline industry. But, as in the Enron case, the CEOs who had been paid to take the risk offloaded it onto the employees. While United Airlines was reneging on almost $7 billion in pensions owed to more than 100,000 employees, the board gave its president an ironclad pension guarantee of $4.5 million. The board of Delta was equally generous to its CEO. US Airways went one better; six months before the corporation went bankrupt the board voted its CEO, Stephen Wolf, a $15 million golden parachute.[39]

"Certain things in life never seem to change," commented *New York Times* business writer Gretchen Morgenson, "and one of the most unfortunate constants is that when corporations behave badly, their rank-and-file workers are hit hardest. Executives always seem to vanish from the accident scene, toting their munificent pay packages; ordinary workers are left with little or nothing."[40]

Meanwhile, the upward redistribution of income continues because the system treats the class of corporate CEOs differently than it treats the rest of the workers. Roughly 60 percent of corporate directors are themselves CEOs of large corporations and are anxious to protect the prerogatives of their peer group. Conservatively measured, the pay of the average CEO rose from 26 times the pay of the typical worker in 1965 to over 310 times in 2000.[41]

Clearly, the owners and top managers of the nation's largest corporations have increased their bargaining power over those who work for them. In the last thirty years, union membership has dropped from 24 percent to 13 percent of the labor force—less than 10 percent in the private sector. As the collective bargaining position of labor has weakened, so has its political clout. The minimum wage, unemployment compensation, and the right to strike are among the legal rights that have been eroded.

The business media routinely rationalizes such disparities on the grounds that the individuals getting these salaries are "worth it." The "market" makes the decision. Thus, CEO salaries are said to reflect not a class society but a meritocracy. Since talent and aptitude for hard work are unequally distributed, so are the rewards.

In the early 1990s, many corporate boards announced that they had "reformed" the determination of CEO salaries by tying them to the corporation share price, considered the market's best measure of the company's value. In the dizzying Wall Street boom, CEO salaries and bonuses soared. Still, company-by-company analyses show little specific relationship between CEO pay and share prices. By 1999, *Business Week* magazine concluded that the connection between CEO salaries and company performance "has been all but severed in today's system."[42] The observation was prescient; when the market crashed in 2000 and stagnated for the next four years, CEO salaries kept going up.

If we don't pay the CEO a high salary, say the CEOs who make up a majority of boards of directors, they will be lured away by a competitor. Thus, in 1999, the board of Motorola gave its CEO, Christopher Galvin, $59.8 million in cash and stock. The chair of the compensation committee said they were worried about losing Galvin in this highly competitive market. Yet Galvin did not appear to be much of a "flight risk." His grandfather founded the company and his father had been CEO before him.[43]

The notion that the growing inequality between the majority of working Americans and those at the top of the income scale is purely a result of a failure of workers to keep up with technology also has been a fundamental governing-class doctrine for several decades. And for several decades the doctrine has been undermined by the facts. As economists Lawrence Mishel, Jared Bernstein, and Sylvia Allegretto have shown, the technology claim fails by virtually every economic measure applied over the last two decades. Just as the change in the ratio of wages in Mexico and the United States cannot be explained because of differences in productivity, so the change in income between workers and managers, and the change among workers themselves, cannot be explained by variations in productivity.[44]

Despite the evidence, the subject of "who gets what in America" is today dominated by the claim that income is distributed according to one's contribution to productivity—if the rich make so much, it has to be because they are more productive. The result gives the governing class a way to minimize public discussion of what every-one knows is true—that those with the most income and wealth have the most political power, and that they use that power to per-petuate themselves.

Things Change, the Corporation Remains

The moral justification for the Clinton/Gingrich promotion of a global economy without a social contract implicitly rests on an assumption about the nature of international markets, that is, that they operate like the idealized competitive market assumed by Adam Smith, David Ricardo, and other early theorists of capitalism. In this abstract world, unknown buyers and unknown sellers with perfect knowledge of the market compete on the basis of price alone, and individuals are rewarded according to their personal, individual efficiency.

Common sense and over a century of evidence had shown that this did not describe the way that the American economy works. Thorstein Veblen, Adolphe Berle and Gardiner Means, and John Kenneth Galbraith and untold thousands of antitrust lawyers, econ-omists, and muckraking journalists had explained to Americans that it was absurd to equate the behavior of these collective institutions of gargantuan market power with the small anonymous businesses. Yet the very power of big business to organize and deploy vast resources was a major contributor to economic progress. Since cor-porations could not be abolished, Big Government was essential to protect the citizenry from the abuse of private market power.

Common sense also suggested that a global market would be even more accommodating to the large corporation with its ability to organize resources, raise capital, and influence governments. But starting in the 1980s, some began to argue that the global market would actually reduce the power of large corporations. Global com-petition would be dominated by skilled individuals—to use Robert Reich's phrase, "symbolic analysts"—working for themselves or in small groups. Democratic theorists of this New Economy thought government would still be necessary to succor the poor, invest in roads, and police the streets. For Republicans, the closer government's role in the market was reduced to zero, the better. But both predicted that globalization would better reward individual efficiency as quick, flexible Lilliputian entrepreneurs tied down sluggish corporate Gullivers.

Computer technology, the Internet in particular, was said to have "changed everything" by flattening the hierarchies of the old "Fordist" production system. Business would now be managed horizontally with information shared widely and decisions made quickly. The old forms of "command and control" were giving way to dispersed networks with superior abilities to spot trends, anticipate problems, and cash in on opportunities. Above all, individuals were empowered to start their own companies and compete with the sluggish corporate behemoths, breaking up the markets into small niches that could be better served by small businesses. This was a central assumption behind the massive stock bubble of the 1990s.

That the bubble burst does not make this story completely wrong. Computer technology and the Internet had of course changed many things—as did the telephone, the automobile, and the television set. In the market crash's aftershock it became clear that the new economy hype had confused the ongoing process of change with a permanent social revolution. As the economist Joseph Schumpeter famously expressed it, capitalism is a process of "creative destruction." New industries are always growing, old ones always withering away. Assets are merged, bought, and sold. New names appear, old ones disappear. The large corporation—the foundation of class power in America—remains.

Thus, many of the high-tech start-ups were decimated and the patents and other assets were bought up by large, established corporations. It turned out in the end that the new technology could be best exploited by the managers within large corporations who had the global reach to deploy it.

The new technology and the lean business organization gave the corporations new bargaining power over Reich's symbolic analysts—turning them from employees with job security and pensions for their old age into private contractors with the market power of sharecroppers. The independent entrepreneur suddenly found himself at the mercy of the dinosaur institution that he was supposed to replace.

By the early twenty-first century, writes business analyst Barry Lynn, the management of large corporations, armed with the new technologies, was reasserting its "power over the would-be geekocracy by turning these 'knowledge workers' once again into 'plug-and-play' pieces. . . . In relatively short order, the militia of self-sufficient yeoman programmers, the New Model Army of educated contractors, had been reduced to a harried, frazzled, self-focused rout of the semi-employed."[45]

Loyalty to Whom?

The corporation is an instrument to power and wealth of the class that manages it. When a particular corporate instrument dulls and wears out, it is discarded. In the end, loyalty to one's class trumps loyalty to any specific corporation. For example, for decades, large U.S. manufacturing companies have complained loudly that they are at a competitive disadvantage in the global economy because of the expensive and dysfunctional U.S. health care system. U.S. firms must pay for health insurance for their workers, which in other countries is covered by public insurance programs. A car can be made in Canada, for example, for roughly $1,000 less than in America because the Canadians have a publicly funded national health care system.

Publicly funded national health care would clearly be a major benefit to large American manufacturers, who have been steadily losing markets both here and abroad. Accordingly, Bill Clinton expected that these corporations would support his health care agenda and designed his specific proposals with them in mind. Robert Rubin and Lloyd Bentsen told him that giving priority to the passage of NAFTA would bring them further along. But the CEOs of the large insurance companies were adamantly opposed. They demanded that their peers in other industries take a stand against the Democratic effort to "socialize" health care. The manufacturers withdrew their support from Clinton, despite their desperate need to find a way to reduce their health care costs. This was truly class solidarity.

One afternoon in the late 1980s, I gave a lecture to several steel company executives on trends in the U.S. economy. With charts on the wall, I described how the Reagan economic policies had priced American steel out of the market and led to the collapse of several firms and the downsizing of half the industry. The vice president of a major company interrupted me. "You don't have to explain the damage Reagan did to the steel industry," he said. "We know all about it. We lived through it."

"Then why do you guys support him?" I asked.

He leaned back in his chair and smiled. "You have to understand," he said. "He cut our taxes. And we're a country club crowd."

4

How Reagan and Thatcher Stole Globalization

I have long dreamed of buying an island owned by no nation and of establishing the World Headquarters of the Dow Chemical Company on the truly neutral ground of such an island, beholden to no nation or society. If we were located on such truly neutral ground we could then really operate in the United States as U.S. citizens, in Japan as Japanese citizens and in Brazil as Brazilians rather than being governed in prime by the laws of the United States. . . . We could even pay any natives handsomely to move elsewhere.

—Carl A. Gerstacker of Dow Chemical

That the "rich and powerful" have the most influence on American politics is hardly news. Even in the most socially advanced nations—in Scandinavia, for example—money makes some people, as George Orwell put it, "more equal than others." By and large, the majority of those who are less equal accept some corruption of the democratic idea of "one person, one vote" as inevitable in this less-than-perfect world.

Still, the stability of any society requires mutual dependence among its various parts. People need to trust that there is overlap between the interests of the small governing class and the rest of the population. Wide disparities of income, wealth, and power are tolerated if there is some understanding that those in charge will act in a way that creates opportunity for a satisfactory life for the majority of people who lack the connections, ambition, talent, or luck to be part of the ruling elite. History shows that people will stand for a great deal of inequality—and misery—if they believe that what is good for the master is good for the servant.

In any society, determining just how much inequality and misery people will stand for and when concessions must be made is the job of the politicians supported by the rich and powerful. With wise statecraft, ruling classes survive and prosper, even when regimes and economic conditions change. Warriors become landowners, aristocrats become businesspeople, and commissars become CEOs. Those who manage less well, who push the people too far, risk the guillotine.

When Both High Wages and High Profits Were in the National Interest

America's one-hundred-year leap from an agricultural society to the most powerful industrial economy in the world was accompanied by fierce conflict between capitalists and their workers. Before industrialization, capitalist business cycles had a limited impact on the majority of people who lived on farms. In hard times, families hunkered down, survived off what they produced, and waited for demand for their surplus production to return. When farmers aged, they could still contribute to the family enterprise when the next generation took over.

Industrialization changed farmers into urban workers who lived paycheck to paycheck with no cushion against hard times and no place to go when sickness or old age took away their ability to work for wages. Still, however much they might have hated the boss, workers generally believed that they needed him to keep the factory going in order to keep the paycheck coming. So the industrialists pushed workers to toil as hard as they could for as little as possible, assured by their clergymen and their economists that poverty for the majority was the inevitable result of both God's will and the scientific laws of supply and demand. Give workers a raise beyond what they need to sustain themselves, lectured the British economist Malthus, and they will just breed faster, increasing the supply of labor and bringing wages back down to their natural level—what it costs to keep them reproducing.

But as the American working class learned to read and as their ranks in the nineteenth century swelled with immigrants with socialist ideas, discontent and radical ideas spread with each economic downturn. The governing class responded to the growing anger with "progressivism," a set of policies aimed at relaxing tensions between labor and capital by using government to blunt some of the sharp edges of the unregulated market. Born into the Social Upper Class of G. William Domhoff's formulation, Teddy Roosevelt railed against the giant corporations. "I believe in shaping the ends of government to protect property as well as human welfare," he said in 1910. "Normally, and in the long run, the ends are the same: but whenever the alternative must be faced, I am for men and not for property."[1] The Democrats under Woodrow Wilson passed legislation restricting child labor and regulating consumer fraud. But there were limits. In 1916 Wilson had promised the electorate that he would not enter World War I. He broke the promise the next year. The socialist Eugene Debs, who had received almost a million votes in the election of 1912, publicly denounced Wilson for sending the working class to fight a rich man's war. He was promptly sent to the penitentiary.

The appeal of utopian socialism receded in the boom of the 1920s, but when the Great Depression struck, capitalism's governing class faced a graver challenge: the real-world alternative of communism. From the Russian Revolution in 1917 to the fall of the Berlin Wall in 1989, the distribution of income and wealth—and therefore political power—in the capitalist countries was constrained by the competition for the hearts and minds of the working class. Given the Soviet Union, communism was no longer just talk.

The governing class found an answer in the British economist John Maynard Keynes, who demonstrated that rising living standards and opportunities for the investor class depended on consumer spending. Since most consumers were workers, this required that they have money in their pockets to buy the products that they made. Henry Ford had made the point earlier; unless workers earned enough to buy the cars he produced, he couldn't get richer. The people who supplied the capital could only prosper if the people who supplied the labor prospered as well. Keynes's insistence that uninterrupted full employment was possible under capitalism, and that rising wages were the fuel that maintained and increased profits, provided a way to resolve the labor-capital antagonisms that seemed built into the market system, and in the 1930s threatened to tear it apart.

To the pre-Keynesian "classical" economist, a drop in wages, which reduced labor costs, motivated capitalists to invest. But Keynes showed that as wages dropped, so did consumer demand, creating a vicious downward cycle that threatened all of society. His answer was for government to act as an economic "stabilizer" to maintain full employment over the business cycle. When business and consumer spending declined, the government would run deficits to maintain purchasing power. When private borrowing and spending rose too fast, threatening inflation, the government would run surpluses to siphon off excessive purchasing power. Full employment was the answer to communism; without a surplus army of unemployed workers, the logic of Karl Marx's inevitable proletarian revolution broke down.

Keynes's ideas created a synergy between democracy and capitalism. From his perspective, growth was a function not just of the extraordinary captain of industry, but of *all* of the actors in the economic drama—the majority of whom were, by definition, ordinary. Prosperity depended on providing opportunities for people of average talent, luck, and connections. Trade unions, unemployment insurance, and other elements of the welfare state were helpful precisely because they maintained income and therefore supported the consumer spending that was necessary to support a job for everyone willing and able to work. Economic security—pooling risks through social insurance, subsidized higher education, and collective bargaining—was as important as the freedom to buy low and sell high.

Conflicts between workers and bosses over the distribution of benefits from economic growth were contained within a political climate that recognized the economic importance of both. But bosses had a natural bargaining advantage over workers. So labor unions and liberal government provided social balance—what economist John Kenneth Galbraith called "countervailing power"—to big business.

The social contract based on this "mixed" economy was a great success. For a quarter century following World War II, Americans got richer together. Companies owned by shareholders who voted Republican paid union wages to workers who bought the products and voted for Democrats.

In the United States, given the overwhelming importance of the conflict with the Soviet Union, Keynesian spending included what Dwight D. Eisenhower called the "military-industrial" complex—the incestuous back-scratching partnership between Pentagon officials, military contractors, and members of Congress eager for jobs. But it also included building highways, financing homes, and providing Medicare for the elderly and welfare for the poor.

Moreover, the promise of widely shared economic growth enabled the country to finally address its racial divisions. The boom of the 1960s created economic space for African Americans to move into jobs and even neighborhoods that had excluded them in the past. Martin Luther King Jr. and other civil rights leaders argued that poverty was a burden on the whole economy: if black workers earned more, they would spend more, enlarging the virtuous circle. The civil rights movement would not have been as successful as it was without the expanding demand for workers and rising opportunities for everyone in the decade of the 1960s.

Republicans and Democrats, liberals and conservatives, still warred with each other over budget priorities, but by 1971, Republican president Richard Nixon acknowledged, "We are all Keynesians."

The Ruling Class Rebels

But even the mild social democracy of the post–World War II era made America's economic elites uncomfortable. American unions are quite conservative compared with those in the rest of the industrial world, but still their expansion was a threat to the prerogatives of the corporate owners and managers. Even though it broadened their customer base, many managers resented the government telling them to serve minorities at their restaurants, motels, and lunch counters.

The 1970s saw minorities and women using government to limit the boss's prerogative to hire and fire and banks' freedom to discriminate against borrowers. Environmentalists and trial lawyers were beginning to interfere with corporate managers' power to mine and manufacture in the most profitable way.

In the late 1950s, a new generation of conservatives led by William F. Buckley Jr., a brilliant scion of a rich Connecticut family, began the takeover of the Republican Party. They detested the New Deal for its egalitarian instincts, but unlike their right-wing predecessors, they were neither anti-Semitic, nor snobbish toward Catholics, nor isolationists. They were hard-line anticommunists and supported a large and widely deployed military. Buckley's *National Review* was their initial organizing vehicle, transmitting conservative ideas and generating mailing lists that conservative activists used to recruit at elite colleges, country clubs, and business conferences.

The network overlapped with embryonic movements of the postwar intellectual right. These included the "objectivism" movement of the libertarian novelist Ayn Rand, a group of New York ex-socialists led by Irving Kristol and Norman Podhoretz, and a militant band of anti-Keynesian economists at the University of Chicago organized by Milton Friedman. Friedman was, in turn, a member of a group of European and American fervid believers in laissez-faire called the Mont Pelerin society. The society's founder, an Austrian economist named Frederich von Hayek, wrote the widely distributed book *The Road to Serfdom*, which proclaimed that any effort to interfere with the workings of supply and demand—including the most modest efforts to smooth out the business cycle—led straight to totalitarian communism. Start with Keynes, argued Hayek, and you will inevitably end up with Stalin. Among Hayek's followers was a young British conservative politician named Margaret Thatcher.

By itself, a call to return to the pre-Keynesian era of dog-eat-dog capitalism had limited appeal for ordinary voters. It was only when the neoconservative economic ideas were connected by the Republican Party with powerful reactionary social movements—such as the white backlash against civil rights, and the Christian fundamentalist crusade against abortion and homosexuals—that the ideas of Hayek, Friedman, and William Buckley's conservatives gained political and intellectual respectability. By 1964, they were strong enough to make their candidate, Barry Goldwater, the Republican nominee for president. Although Goldwater was trounced, the campaign finally established that the base of the party was now on the far right.

The Republican Party provided an umbrella that hid the fundamental contradiction between the interests of social conservatives and corporate investors. The former wanted to use government to limit the freedom of individuals to pursue their hedonist instincts. The latter wanted the government to facilitate the stimulation and commercialization of those same instincts. The organizing genius of conservative Republicans was to compartmentalize the two opposing value systems so they reinforced each other against what was perceived as a common liberal enemy. The social conservatives would bring grassroots energy. The corporations would bring the money.

In 1971, the U.S. Chamber of Commerce circulated a confidential strategic memo entitled "Attack on the Free Enterprise System," by Lewis Powell, a corporate lawyer who would later become a Supreme Court justice. The memo declared that the survival of the free enterprise system depended on the creation of a long-term, well-financed political campaign to change the way Americans thought about economics.[2]

Ideologically conservative foundations founded by super-rich families—Scaife, Bradley, Olin, Smith, Richardson, Coors—responded. They provided grants for books and conferences, endowments for think tanks like the Heritage Foundation, the Cato Institute, and the American Enterprise Institute, and university chairs for professors who shared their views. A prime target was the media. Journalists were wined and dined, invited to lectures and seminars, and even given scholarships to take sabbatical of a few weeks or a year at university programs designed to explain the world of economics from the conservative perspective. Nineteenth-century ideas that had been considered obsolete gradually filtered back into the mainstream dialogue.

At the same time, the fear that communism would appeal to Western working people, which had motivated the postwar capitalists to accept a more egalitarian social contract, was fading. Nikita Khrushchev's exposure of Stalin's crimes and the accomplishments of Soviet science and improvements in living standards had given the USSR the appearance of a dynamic society in the 1960s. But under the reactionary Leonid Brezhnev, Soviet society stagnated. The gaps in living standards between communist Eastern Europe and social democratic Western Europe widened. Russia remained a nuclear threat, but its attraction as a model of development became virtually nil in the first world and weakened considerably in the third.

The watershed U.S. election of 1980 represented the large pay-off of two decades of business investment in conservative ideas. A combination of inflation and unemployment had dogged the U.S. economy in the 1970s, reaching its crescendo in two back-to-back recessions at the end of the decade. Ronald Reagan had a clear expla-nation for what was wrong—Democrats' big government spending. Jimmy Carter, who had campaigned in 1976 against big govern-ment as a "bloated confused bureaucratic mess," was tongue-tied.

Reagan's attack on Carter for failing to curb inflation was taken from Hayek and Friedman, who argued that once government was allowed to engage in deficit spending it would not resist popular pressure to continue when the economy reached full capacity. At that point, the money supply from government deficits would expand faster than the production of goods and services. Wages would rise and prices would follow. Better for everyone in the long run to allow unemployment to continue until wages were low enough to reduce business and hire more workers. (It was on this point that Keynes had famously quipped that "in the long run, we are all dead.")

The Friedman-Hayek explanation of the inflation of the 1970s was not consistent with the facts. High prices were not driven by an economy overheated by either wage demands or government spend-ing on liberal programs. Rather, they were caused by two external shocks. The first was the unwillingness of Lyndon Johnson to raise taxes in order to pay for the Vietnam War. The second came from the formation of the OPEC oil cartel, which raised world petroleum prices in three separate stages in the 1970s, triggering a dramatic rise in the cost of living.

But by that time, the conservative campaign to change the way Americans thought about economics had permeated the media and the Democratic Party. Right after he was elected, Jimmy Carter the-atrically refused a routine congressional offer to renew presidential authority for the standby wage-price controls that Nixon had used effectively in the early 1970s. The free market, Carter asserted, would correct any inflation problem. With that fateful decision, Carter and his Democratic advisers denied themselves the instruments Richard Nixon had used to take the wind out of inflation's sails just before his reelection in 1972. Instead, they combated inflation by slowing down growth in the entire economy, even though the source of the problem was the oil industry, not a generally overheated market. Carter cut government spending and installed Paul Volcker as head of the Federal Reserve to raise interest rates. As a result, he faced re-election with the worst possible economy, rising unemployment, and rising prices.

On election day, Carter won only 41 percent of the vote and had 49 electoral votes to Reagan's 489.

Reagan's Intellectual Legacy

Stagflation continued, and by the 1982 congressional election Reagan's popularity rating was the lowest of any president two years into his term in modern history. But with no apologies to Keynes, Reagan ran a huge budget deficit that stimulated growth, and in 1984 he was reelected over Walter Mondale, who had promised the electorate that he would balance the budget. The Republicans built a political machine that retained the presidency in 1988 and went on to smash what had seemed like a Democratic iron grip on the House of Representatives six years later. American politics is still under the shadow of Ronald Reagan.

The idea that Keynesian economics failed (and the ideas of the New Deal with it) because of the stagflation of the 1970s has become a staple of media groupthink—and not just for the Fox News Channel or conservative talk radio. For example, it is the main theme of a six-hour 2002 PBS documentary, *Commanding Heights*, used in schools and colleges all over the country. According to the *Washington Post*, "No more important program for making sense of our life and times has been seen on the air in at least a decade and probably a good deal longer."[3]

The high-budget documentary, filmed in locations around the world and delivered in eye-catching dramatic images, was financed by Federal Express, British Petroleum, Electronic Data Systems, and two business-oriented foundations. The program associates Keynes and liberalism with the central planning of communism and interprets the history of the globe over the last twenty-nine years as a triumph of Hayek's laissez-faire ideas over Keynes's. Among other things, Reagan's deficits are overlooked, as is his mid-1980s big-government rescue and reorganization of the savings and loan industry.[4]

The purpose of the Reagan revolution was clearly not to eliminate government influence on the economy. It was to use government in order to shift the distribution of income and wealth upward and roll back the power of popular democracy to constrain the prerogatives of the corporate elite. As for social conservatism, it had never been high on the agenda of Ronald Reagan, a product of Hollywood—the heart of the hedonist beast.

Reagan's primary target was the unions. By breaking the air traffic controllers' union in his first year in office, he signaled to corporate America that the post–World War II accommodation of labor and capital was over. It was now open season on organized labor. The other target was postwar social safety nets. Murray Weidenbaum, who was his first chair of the Council of Economic Advisers, later said, "On the question of fiscal deficits, I recall [Reagan's] views going through three stages: one, they won't occur; two, they'll be temporary; three, when they stick, they'll serve a good purpose—they keep the liberals from new spending programs."[5]

Alan Greenspan, an acolyte of the radical libertarian Ayn Rand, and whom Reagan appointed to succeed Volcker as head of the Federal Reserve Board, was an eager and effective general in Reagan's class war. After Bill Clinton was elected, Greenspan and Robert Rubin teamed up to convince the president that cutting the budget deficit should be the highest priority. They argued that deficits were inflationary, that they threatened the long-term solvency of the Social Security trust fund, and, most of all, that the financial markets were demanding it. So Clinton obliged, starving his own liberal Democratic constituency in order to pay off the debts run up by the "fiscally responsible" Republican disciples of Hayek and Friedman. By the end of Clinton's term, his administration had become a champion of eliminating the entire national debt.

When George W. Bush took over the presidency and proposed a huge tax cut to give away the surplus that Clinton had painstakingly saved, Greenspan changed his position 180 degrees and supported it. As it turned out, Greenspan, like Reagan, was not as concerned about the deficit as he was in promoting the shift of income to the rich and powerful. Those Democrats who understood what had happened could only ponder how they had allowed themselves to be fleeced.[6]

Reagan's decision to renew class conflict in America paralleled a similar effort in Great Britain. Like Reagan's, the so-called conservative revolution of Margaret Thatcher was steeped in contradiction. Thatcher, who actually knew and read Hayek, was perhaps the most ideologically astute of the free-market fundamentalists who had begun to exercise power in Western Europe as the Soviet threat faded. Thatcher's class war also involved a minor front against the upper-class gentry that had dominated the Conservative Party. The daughter of a grocer, she projected a populist resentment against the old aristocracy. But her main conflict was with labor, and she set about destroying its claims to social solidarity. She understood that the logical conclusion of laissez-faire economics was to undercut social cohesion. "There is no such thing as Society," she said.

But laissez-faire economics was not enough to sustain Thatcher's individualist revolution. In 1982, the British economy was a shambles and her popularity had plummeted. She saved herself, not with an appeal to individualism, but by rallying British nationalism in a war to preserve the British government's ownership of a few islands off the coast of Argentina in which the Britons had no individual— only a collective—interest. Thatcher's political agenda—smashing the labor unions and undercutting the British welfare state—floated on the top of a celebration of big government's most socialized program, the military. The conservative revolutions of the 1980s in the United States and Britain had never been about fiscal responsibility or individual freedom. As Spanish political commentator Vicente Navarro commented, "Margaret Thatcher believes in the class struggle. And she wants to win it."[7]

"There Is No Mindset That Puts This Country First"

Ronald Reagan did not create a successful conservative economy. His America, like that of his Republican successors, was pumped up with public debt. This was not what Hayek, Friedman, and Greenspan preached.

Reagan did succeed, however, in redistributing income upward and undercutting the bargaining power of labor, both on the shop floor and in the ballot box. This, it turned out, was what Hayek, Friedman, and Greenspan really wanted. The result was to open up the political space for the corporate investor class to use the integrating world economy in order to slip the leash of social regulation. Friedman and Hayek failed to overturn Keynes on the question of how to run a *national* economy. Their profligate U.S. acolytes burst the bounds of what even Keynes taught was permissible borrowing. But their ideas triumphed in the way that the *global* economy was established on Social Darwinist, rather than social democratic, principles.

Certainly, a good case can be made that unions can often make a firm more efficient, and that social spending improves the quality of the labor force and the spread of innovation. But perceptions rule, and with the terms of the public debate still set by Reagan and Thatcher, business demand for lower wages and lower taxes became appealing. The world economy is globalizing rapidly, but it is far from completely globalized. Large chunks of the populations of Africa, the Middle East, Latin America, and Asia remain beyond the reach of transnational companies. But these companies are the channels through which the increased cross-border trade in investment flows. In 2000, thirty-four of the largest fifty economies in the world, measured by revenue, were corporations, fifteen were countries, and one was a government enterprise (the U.S. Postal Service).

Globalization per se is not a product of political ideology. The gradual expansion of world markets is a natural consequence of evolving technology, communications, and business organization in search of efficiencies of scale. Certainly it was not invented by Ronald Reagan or Milton Friedman. American corporations had been steadily investing overseas for decades. As early as the 1950s, a Ford Motor executive corrected a U.S. senator who referred to the company as "an American firm." We're an American company when we are in America, he said, and a British company when we are in Britain, and a Brazilian company when we are in Brazil.

But until the mid-1970s, investment in foreign countries was generally for the purpose of producing for their markets. Indeed, many countries required foreign manufacturers of any size to build in their markets if they wanted to sell to them. Gradually, spurred by increased competition from abroad and facilitated by changes in technology, the restless American corporate class began to see the potential of outsourcing production to places where labor costs were cheaper and weak governments could be bribed to keep them cheap. The ability to produce elsewhere and still sell in America would allow them to abandon the irksome twentieth-century American social contract. Just to threaten to move would give more bargaining power over workers and government.

But first they had to open up the U.S. economy to imports from the foreign countries where they would produce. This meant not just knocking down a few tariffs. They had to get the American governing class to commit to permanently eliminating import restrictions so that they could be sure that building factories overseas to produce for the U.S. market would pay off. Discrediting Keynes was essential to this strategy.

Keynes's economics required that the government's influence extend to, and be limited by, roughly the same space as the national economy. Just as locks in a canal need walls in order for the boats to be lifted and lowered by changing the level of the water, economies must have walls if the government is to be able to pump up or drop the level of economic activity. Borders to the economy are necessary to keep government-induced spending from drawing in imports, instead of expanding domestic employment.

Keynes was no protectionist. He well understood comparative advantage and the common sense of nations trading with each other in order to get products they could not easily produce themselves. He was the principal architect of the original Bretton Woods institutions—the International Monetary Fund, the World Bank, and the General Agreement on Tariffs and Trade—and had proposed an early version of the World Trade Organization in order to facilitate trade among nations. But he knew that the capacity of the government to maintain high employment was strongest when the economy was reasonably self-contained. He therefore cautioned countries to keep their foreign trade and investment at moderate levels.

The followers of Hayek and Friedman understood that the expansion of trade and financial flows beyond borders would be a dagger in the heart of the economic argument for national social democracy. The post–World War II social contract was built on the recognition that capital's profits depended on labor, not just as producers, but as consumers. Thus high wages were necessary for shared prosperity in an economy that depended on a growing domestic market.

But to the extent that the economy is globalized, high wages, and the taxes needed to pay for social protections, put domestic firms at a cost disadvantage with firms in other countries. If you can manufacture your goods anywhere, you'll choose the country with the lowest taxes and most desperate workers. The larger the international sector of the economy, the less power the government has to smooth out business cycles, sustain domestic prosperity, and maintain the social contract. Therefore, the less relevant government is to the economic management of the economy. Unions, which help create prosperity in a domestic mass consumption economy precisely because they maintain wages, become problematic when the economy depends on exports. Social welfare programs, which must be paid for in taxes, add to the costs of production and appear increasingly "unaffordable."

Liberating the transnational corporation in the global marketplace required other nations to open up as well. Many third world countries had their own systems of social protections and were suspicious of foreign investment, which was needed to build the factories for low-wage production. So the conservative campaign was duplicated abroad. With some guidance from the American conservative movement, business in other nations created similar ideological campaigns. In both Mexico and Canada, as in the United States, support for NAFTA was the result.

The Counterrevolution in Mexico and Canada

Since the 1930s, Mexico's economy had been managed by economists who adapted Keynes's ideas to the problems of underdevelopment. The state intervened in the economy not just to stabilize the business cycles but to organize investments in public and private infrastructure that would raise the long-term growth rate.

This was not a new concept. To the north, the government of the United States had been instrumental in shaping investments in transportation, communications, and agriculture that quickly populated the territories it had wrested from Mexico in the 1840s. In the late nineteenth and early twentieth centuries the Mexican government under the dictator Díaz had led a rapid modernization of the economy. But the economic policies pursued by the Partido Revolucionario Institucional after its founding in 1929 reflected the idea that development involved all of the country, not just the investors. It rested therefore on a social contract that gave a claim on the benefits of development to the urban workers and small farmers as well.

Despite the policy's success in producing steady growth, the Mexican oligarchs, the small group of families who still controlled most of the country's wealth, became increasingly discontent with the restraints on their privileges. The student unrest of the 1960s, which radicalized parts of the Universidad Nacional Autónoma de México, made them even more uncomfortable. So they began to finance private schools for the teaching of conservative economics, and as the career of Carlos Salinas symbolized, they sent their sons to graduate school at Harvard, Yale, and the University of Chicago where the influence of Hayek and Friedman was growing. When the students returned, the network of bankers and businessmen made sure they were placed in key jobs in the government.

With help from their U.S. counterparts, the Mexican governing class honed a critique of Keynes and his followers as too "statist," which was echoed by selected journalists. The debt crisis of 1982—like the energy crisis earlier in the United States—was their opportunity. When it struck, they provided the businessmen and their political allies with a simple explanation, and put Carlos Salinas on the road to the presidency.[8]

In Canada, the ideological campaign was spearheaded by the Business Council on National Issues (BCNI), created in 1975 and modeled on the U.S. Business Roundtable. At the core of its support were the large corporations in the banking and natural resource sectors and U.S.-owned firms, who provided the chief political force behind the Canadian free trade agreement with the United States as well as NAFTA.

The same pool of large corporations financed conservative think tanks and university economics departments that in the last twenty-five years have built a relentless case in the media for shrinking the welfare state. Chief among them is the C.D. Howe Institute in Toronto, supported by Canada's largest corporations and influential in both the Liberal and Conservative parties. Another is the Fraser Institute in Vancouver, which, like the Heritage Foundation and Cato Institute in Washington, is explicit in its radical conservative ideology. Its goal, says its president, is to "change the ideological fabric of the world."[9]

In Canada, the episode that marked the turning away from the Keynesian-inspired mixed economy occurred in 1980, when the Liberal Party presented its first budget after being elected. It had been returned to office on a pledge to expand social programs. But the BCNI objected and brought a group of American CEOs to warn Prime Minister Pierre Trudeau against alienating American investors. After an internal struggle, the Liberals reneged on their promise. Shortly afterward, the Liberal Party set up a Royal Commission on the Economic Union and Development Prospects for Canada, whose report was published under the next Conservative government of Brian Mulroney. As one history observes, it was "the perfect symbol of the now-shared ideology of the Liberals and Conservatives," laying the groundwork for "continental free trade, planning high unemployment, and the coming assault on universal social programs."[10]

As NAFTA demonstrated, the campaign to change the way the political classes thought about economics worked in all three nations. In the United States, corporate leaders were openly acknowledging the disconnect between their corporation and their country. "The United States does not have an automatic call on our resources," said a Colgate-Palmolive executive. "There is no mindset that puts this country first."[11] Jack Welch, the CEO of General Electric, who had once employed Ronald Reagan to give patriotic speeches, insisted that GE was a "borderless" corporation.[12]

And what about Henry Ford's point about the need to maintain consumer demand through high wages? As Reagan showed, U.S. purchasing power could be supported by America's unique capacity to borrow from other countries in order to pay for its trade deficit. At some point, this system would collapse, but inasmuch as the average CEO's tenure is less than ten years, there was a good chance that he or she would be out the door by then.

5

A Bipartisan Empire

Jake Gittes: *Why are you doing it? How much better can you eat?*
What can you buy that you can't already afford?
Noah Cross: *The future, Mr. Gittes, the future.*

—*Chinatown*, directed by Roman Polanski (1974)

When the cold war ended in the rubble of the Berlin Wall, most Americans thought that they—as a nation—had won. Their reward for shouldering the burden of periodic wars of containment and continuous military spending was to be a "peace dividend." Visions of lower taxes, investments in education and health care, revived cities, and even shorter workdays filled the popular press. The question of the future had suddenly shifted from "Who will win the cold war?" to "What kind of an America do we want to create?"

During the campaign of 1992, Clinton energized his Democratic base with promises to spend more money on education, training, and health care. Military industry would be converted to high-tech civilian needs—microsurgery, fast trains, and futuristic products to export. "The American People have earned this peace dividend," he said, "through forty years of unrelenting vigilance and sacrifice and an investment of trillions of dollars."[1]

But from the perspective of the American governing class, the average citizens had little to do with it; *they*, the people who ran the State Department and the Pentagon, Boeing and Lockheed, had won. Without detonating a World War III, they had defeated their Soviet counterparts who were armed with enough nuclear weapons to destroy the world. *They* were the heroes. Yet they understood that the American people would not be sufficiently grateful. Ordinary citizens were tired of the burden, they were ready to demobilize. In the hinterland, conservatives would want tax cuts, and liberals would want national health care.

The governing class had no intention of demobilizing. After a half century of wars, hot and cold, its members had acquired a taste for the "great games" of military and financial geopolitics. Now, in control of the world's undisputed superpower, they had a shot at truly dominating the world. The prospect of having to turn their swords into ploughshares—redirecting their energies to unheroic domestic tasks of eradicating urban poverty or cleaning up the environment, under the tiresome scrutiny of congressional committees, governors, mayors, and the undisciplined media that dogged domestic programs—was singularly unexciting.

So they did not do it. From the fall of the Berlin Wall to the invasion of Iraq, the American governing class redefined the overriding "national interest" from the project to contain and defeat the empire of the commissars to the project to expand the empire of the transnationals. They assumed, correctly, that, diverted by the media's presentation of politics as the clash of Democratic and Republican personalities, ordinary Americans would not seem to notice that the peace dividend had disappeared.

Wall Street Relieves the Sixth Fleet

As the Soviet Union collapsed, America's foreign policy intellectuals began to rearrange the world geopolitical map to explain the next great challenges that the people of the United States should support them to confront. Fresh out of the Bush State Department, Francis Fukuyama declared that Western culture was the final stage of history and that America's role was to impose it on the rest of the world. At Harvard, Samuel Huntington projected war against Islam abroad and Latin American immigrants at home. The *New York Times* pundit Thomas Friedman told Americans that they now had a duty to bring capitalism to the world's primitive peoples.

The military budget might have to take a momentary hit, and some of the technicians who made their living targeting Soviet missile sites might have to find other work. But with their victory over communism, America's governing elite now had the historic opportunity to shape, not just the future of the nation, but the future of the entire world. They would impose, in George H. W. Bush's phrase, a "New World Order."

A generation of such Americans had done it before. After World War II, those who had walked Washington's corridors of power led the world in the creation of the United Nations. They established the International Monetary Fund, the General Agreement on Tariffs and Trade, and other institutions to manage the noncommunist part of the global economy. On defeated Germany and Japan, the victorious Americans imposed electoral democracy, social welfare, a pluralist civil society, and defused the class warfare between labor and management.

New Dealers, who could not have succeeded in pushing their ideas on a postwar America, created models of social democracy in West Germany and Japan. For example, they required that large German corporations put workers on the boards of directors. Such an idea was a nonstarter in post–World War II America, where a Republican Congress was passing the Taft-Hartley Act, which curbed labor unions, and McCarthyism was blacklisting people who had written lyrics for 1930s musicals about the working class.

Four decades later, with the Soviet Union dismantled, and no power even close to matching America's, the chance to make history was arguably even greater. Like their liberal counterparts a half century before, American elites set out to rebuild defeated societies in Eastern Europe with ideas—in this case, from the right—that they could not quite sell in the America of the early 1990s, where people still resisted privatizing Social Security, selling off the national parks, and leaving their health care to the free market.

Thanks to the Coelho-Clinton fund-raising strategies, the Democrats had become almost as dependent on corporate money as the Republicans. Therefore it was no surprise that under both George H. W. Bush and Bill Clinton, the chief post–cold war priority was the opening up of foreign profit-making opportunities for transnational corporations with American names.

Not that commercial interests had not always been important. The American governing class had in the past deployed the military to support private profits, as episodes of gunboat diplomacy in Central and South America have testified. The U.S. involvement in World War I was a product both of Woodrow Wilson's vision of "making the world safe for democracy" and of his desire to make the world safe for Wall Street loans to Britain and France. Earlier, Wilson had laid out his vision of the military's role in securing corporate profits. "Concessions obtained by financiers must be safeguarded by ministers of state, even if the sovereignty of unwilling nations must be battered down."[2]

The cold war had been marked by the same mix of motivations. The American military saved Europe from Stalin's dictatorship, and its massive budget generated windfall profits for American firms. With its worldwide network of hundreds of bases, the U.S. military was a visible presence in every part of the noncommunist world where American companies wanted to do business. Not since the 1930s has any significant part of the American business community not supported a large military budget, and many high-ranking American officers are very close to corporate defense firms that shower them with perks and offer lucrative potential second careers after retirement. When an American ambassador promoted American commercial interests with a client country's finance minister, the latter was well aware he was talking with someone who was protecting his country from the menace of communism. "Never forget," a German businessman once said to me, "when General Electric walks into the boardrooms here, the Sixth Fleet walks in behind it."

In the "great game" that had been played with the Soviet Union, the markers were missiles, nuclear warheads, and geopolitical strategy. Now the game was opened up to investment bankers and manufacturing company CEOs, business and political advisers, transportation and housing experts, pollsters and educators, hospital administrators and retailers. People with American passports and a claim to expertise on almost anything spread out to the ex-communist countries. American government contracts for teaching the Bulgarians, Romanians, Latvians, Mongolians, and Russians how to set up stock markets, privatize state enterprises, and raise money for political parties were for the taking.

When the Soviets collapsed, the new leaders of Russia and Eastern Europe, and the old leaders of China and all but the few outposts of Marxism-Leninism in places like North Korea and Cuba were plugging themselves into the capitalist world as quickly as they could. America was the only game in town. But the model being sold was not the America that actually was, rather it was the oversimplified image of American cowboy capitalism—the left's nightmare and the right's dream.

After the Democrats came back to the White House in January 1993, the weight of influence in Washington shifted from the Pentagon and the State Department to Treasury and Commerce and the U.S. trade representative. Guns and tanks made way for trade and investment as the principal instruments of power and career paths into the governing class. The job of the commercial attaché in embassies abroad went from low to high status, and ambitious young diplomats, CIA analysts, and military officers signed up for classes in corporate finance and business administration. "In the first days of the Clinton Administration," says David Rothkopf, who was deputy undersecretary of commerce, "we were in a period of growth and boom in the world, and there was a real sense that the opportunities for the United States to take advantage and to lead in this period were enormous."[3]

The economists at the International Monetary Fund and World Bank who had been teaching the Thatcherite doctrine that all societies were just a collection of individuals driven only by the desire to get rich, triumphed. Those agencies abandoned what was left of the Keynes-inspired "statist" development programs handcrafted to the conditions of each specific country. Now they demanded that all client states adopt cookie-cutter programs of "structural adjustment" designed to eliminate restraints on capital investment from overseas. Since all economies were assumed to be the same, appearing to know the economy of any one country was less important than appearing to know what made America—the world's most important economy—succeed.

So there was plenty of work for those who wanted to be in the nation-building business—Democrats as well as Republicans, neoliberals and neoconservatives. University professors and NGO activists, many of whom had spent their careers trying to reduce poverty, unemployment, urban decay, and other by-products of capitalism, flew off to Moscow and Bucharest to lecture former commissars on how to create markets. The free market was a simple formula that one could apply without actually knowing anything about the country. Prominent economists like Jeffrey Sachs of Harvard wrote economic programs overnight for countries that he had just visited.

As one U.S. Agency for International Development contractor put it, paraphrasing Wordsworth's comment on the French Revolution, "Bliss was it in that dawn to be alive, but to be a business consultant from America was very heaven."

Emerging Markets, Sinking Societies

During the cold war, America's managers saw the world's poor and developing countries as regions of threat and danger—places where poverty and inequality bred communists. The strategy had been to protect those who were most opposed to communism—the very rich, the business class, the churches—with military aid to keep the army loyal and economic aid to dilute radicalism among the poor. The end of the communist threat transformed the most promising parts of the third world and the second world of former Soviet satellites in Eastern Europe into "emerging markets," places where American capital could profitably invest for higher returns.

Like the neoconservatives, these neoliberals saw themselves as noble, bringing democracy, freedom, and prosperity to the entire world. As Jeffrey Garten, a major champion of the strategy, said, "For 50 years the U.S. fought the cold war on certain principles, and one of them was we wanted to see capitalism and democracy spread, and we—most Americans make a link between the two. You have economic freedom that leads to political freedom and vice versa."[4]

Brushed aside by this simple dogma was the obvious fact that markets, per se, created neither freedom nor democracy. Most of the nations in the third world were brimming with markets. A visitor to Latin America or Africa or poor parts of Asia will find individuals selling everywhere—candy in the street, vegetables in the stalls, teenage girls in the alleys. The entrepreneurial spirit does not seem to be absent. The garbage-filled streets, the open sewers, the official corruption, the huge inequality of wealth, reflect not an absence of private ambition, but the absence of honest, competent government—to keep order, to educate the children, to improve the public health, and otherwise create the space for commerce to develop.

But honest accountable government was not what Washington's neoliberal reformers had in mind for the developing world. Like the catchphrase "national interest," the word "reform" is a code word—misleading to outsiders, precise to those who understand the code. To the public, the word seems one thing, implying the elimination of third world corruption, cronyism, and authoritarian rule. But for America's governing class, it has a different meaning—lifting restrictions on foreign ownership, privatizing state-owned utilities and other industries, lowering business taxes, and weakening labor unions and the social safety net to keep wages and costs low.

In his 1990 essay on the economic prospects for Latin America, economist John Williamson had already noted that these were the objectives for which there was a "Washington Consensus." In total agreement were the two parts of the Washington-based governing class, which Williamson identified as *political* Washington—congressional leaders and the senior members of the administration—and *technocratic* Washington—"the international financial institutions, the economic agencies of the U.S. government, the Federal Reserve Board, and the think-tanks." Williamson acknowledged that the demands Washington elites placed on other nations were not always followed by the U.S. government. So what? he concluded. It is still good advice.[5]

Was it? It is reasonable to assume a positive connection between economic freedom and democracy. But in the world of the Washington Consensus, economic freedom refers to the freedom of only one type of economic actor—the investor. Certainly, the freedom to buy and sell, invest and grow in competitive markets, can help prevent the concentration of economic wealth and political power that supports authoritarian government. But most people are not investors. Freedom in their lives begins with freedom from destitution, sickness, and exploitation. Moreover, free trade, which was at the core of the Washington Consensus, was definitely not the way the world's most advanced economies had themselves succeeded. The economies of the United States, Western Europe, and Japan grew under various regimes of *managed* trade, in which certain industries were protected in order to build them up to the point where they had a competitive edge in international commerce.

The assumption of the Washington Consensus, following Hayek and Friedman, assumes that the fundamental conflict over who gets what is between public and private sectors, bureaucrat versus entrepreneur. But in most societies the same class is in charge of both sectors. Corrupt and incompetent government reflects the top-heavy distribution of private wealth and power.

Making it more complicated, conditions that were barriers to foreign investment in poor countries were often also part of a fragile social contract of protections and the distribution of large and small privileges that the vast impoverished majority had managed to wring from elites with threats of mutiny and disorder. Ethnic customs, cultural traditions, and religious structures had created habits and values that worked against the neoliberal vision of each individual for himself. Property ownership was informal and often collective. Religious scruples discouraged lending. Social mores resisted the commoditization of sex that drives so much of Western marketing. Those in poverty put more value on security than on opportunity.

These cultural obstacles had to be smashed to make way for transnational corporate investment. It was now not enough to reinforce Woodrow Wilson's dictum that other societies had to honor "concessions obtained by financiers." The neoliberal program aimed to transform those societies—the values and culture of the people—in order to accommodate the demands for cheap labor and, eventually, expanding markets.

The task was breathtaking. It implied an effort at social engineering on the scale that in its global reach dwarfed the effort to create "socialist man" in the Soviet Union or Mao Tse-tung's Cultural Revolution. This market utopianism, like the withering away of the state in the communist future, would take time. The "false consciousness" of the people abounded. Left to themselves, they backslid; lured by populist demagogues, they demanded more collective goods like health care, education, retirement, public parks, and free concerts—and protections against the inequality of wealth and power that the market relentlessly generates. It was the special responsibility of the U.S. governing class to overcome the weaknesses of these human beings—for their own good.

The colossal arrogance that drives this enterprise is rationalized by a makeshift philosophy asserting that values of individualism, consumerism, and markets were universal and basic. It followed that underneath all cultures beat the heart of an "American," the stereotypical pure economic man defined by Friedman and Hayek. As the British writer John Gray observed:

> The contemporary American faith that it is a universal nation implies that all humans are born American, and become anything else by accident—or error. According to this faith American values are, or will soon be, shared by all humankind. Of course such messianic fancies are commonplace. In the nineteenth century the claim to be a universal nation was made by France, Russia, and England. Now, even more than in the past, it is a perilous conceit.[6]

This "perilous conceit" was an economic parallel to the CIA's assumption that a limited small-scale invasion of Cuba's Bay of Pigs would be enough to motivate the Cubans to welcome their "liberators" with open arms, that the South Vietnamese, inspired by American values would roll back the communists from the North, and the confident prediction that Iraqis would embrace the U.S. occupation of their country.

As in many other efforts to make over human beings, the cause of bringing out the hidden American inside the soul of people in other cultures justified uncompromising methods—the "shock therapy" or the "big bang theory of social change." Lawrence Summers, the Clinton administration's point man for the global makeover, along with his Harvard colleague Jeffrey Sachs, demanded that the countries in debt to the U.S. Treasury, the IMF, and the World Bank transform their economies overnight, that they immediately decontrol their prices, privatize their state enterprises, create stock markets, and rip up their subsidies to food, medicine, housing, and other basic necessities of life. Like the "shock and awe" tactics pursued by the U.S. military in the bombing of Baghdad, "shock therapy" was designed to obliterate hope and any tendency to compromise.

The Washington governing class claimed the moral authority to reorder other societies from the success of post–World War II Marshall Plan managers who had revived the economies of Europe. Indeed, Sachs later excused the failure of his program in Russia on the grounds that his team didn't have the money that was available to the Marshall planners. But as Walter Isaacson and Evan Thomas wrote in *The Wise Men*, the Americans who managed the Marshall Plan "wanted to restore Europe, not change it."[7] Thus, they were content to build on the pre-fascist values of democratic community and social cohesion, by widening and opening up the institutions by such means as putting workers on corporate boards of directors and building up the welfare state.

Some of the neoliberals were opposed. The United States and the Western European countries did not become sophisticated capitalist nations overnight, argued economist Joe Stiglitz and a few others inside the administration. Development requires education, honest courts, competent bureaucracies, and a social contract that reduces individual risk as tribal and extended family supports weaken. But Summers and Sachs had the full support of Washington.

Rubin and Bentsen could deliver the president on virtually any important economic matter. As the NAFTA vote showed, the Democratic and Republican members of the Senate Finance and House Ways and Means committees were also on board. Now that the menace of communism was gone, the contributions and lobbyists representing the transnationals had no interest in waiting for Mexico or Russia or Thailand to fashion efficient capital markets, create an honest and competent bureaucracy, and nurture indigenous institutions. There were profits to be made now! What, after all, was the point of winning the cold war?

Iraq: Sixth Fleet Politics, Wall Street Economics

The change of administrations after the 2000 elections did not alter this agenda. Not that there were no divisions between Republican and Democrat leaders. Differences on Social Security, tax policy, environmental regulation, budget priorities, and other aspects of domestic policy were profound and would have serious consequences for many Americans.

On issues of foreign policy, however, the distinctions between the two parts of the two-party system seemed more symbolic than substantive. Much has been written about the network of neoconservative conspirators that George W. Bush brought into the White

House when he became president: how Cheney and Rumsfeld and Wolfowitz and their extended ideological family chafed under what they considered Bill Clinton's indifference to military power and his softness on Iraq, and how, as soon as September 11, 2001, occurred, they seized the moment and launched their program—Afghanistan, Iraq, and the defining of a "war on terror" that extended to anyone in the world deemed insufficiently respectful to the American governing class and its partners.

It seems reasonable to assume that had Al Gore been president of the United States on September 11, 2001, he would have ordered the attack on Afghanistan. It is also reasonable to assume that he would not have invaded Iraq. We will of course never know.

But we do know that the bulk of the Democratic Party leadership—including the majority of Democratic senators—supported the war. With the exception of Congressman Dennis Kucinich, every Democratic presidential contender who was a member of Congress voted for the resolution authorizing the preemptive strike, leaping to the side of the president against the inclination of their own liberal constituency. Even after it was made clear that there were no weapons of mass destruction, John Kerry declared that he would have voted for the resolution anyway. Indeed, Kerry ran for president pledging that he would send another forty thousand soldiers to Iraq.

The ease with which the Democrats were stampeded into supporting the invasion has been chalked up to their lack of enough courage to buck the jingoistic tide unleashed by the more aggressive Bush. That was a factor. But the difference between the Clinton neoliberals and the Bush neoconservatives over America's fundamental role in the world is quite small. The leadership of the two parties is in accord with the notion that the American governing class has the authority and obligation to police the world. They only differ on the question of tactics.

The Democratic neoliberals were certainly more balanced, flexible, and largely more effective than the swaggering Republican neoconservatives who followed. As Chalmers Johnson, longtime student of the intersection between America's international economic and military policies, observes, "Bill Clinton was actually a much more effective imperialist than George W. Bush. During the Clinton administration, the United States employed an indirect approach in imposing its will on other nations. The government of George W. Bush, by contrast, dropped all legitimating principles and adopted the view that might makes right. History tells us that an expansive nation must at least attempt to disguise what it is doing if it wants to consolidate its gains. It must pretend that its exploitation of the weak is in their own best interest, or their own fault, or the result of ineluctable processes beyond human control, or a consequence of the spread of civilization, or in accordance with scientific laws—anything but deliberate aggression by a hyperpower."[8]

Contrary to the complaints of the Republican neoconservatives, the neoliberals did not abandon their military assets during the Clinton years. The "Sixth Fleet" remained important in impressing the world that those in charge of the U.S. government were able to intervene in any serious matter in any part of the globe. The military was essential to assure that the United States would continue to be the "indispensable nation" in the jockeying for power among the global elite.

As Madeleine Albright taunted Colin Powell in the early years of the Clinton administration, "What's the point of having this superb military that you're always talking about if we can't use it?"[9]

From a peak of $304 billion in 1989, spending on national defense had dropped 4 percent by 1993 under George H. W. Bush. In Clinton's first term defense spending dropped another 8 percent, but by his last budget (fiscal 2001, before the effect of the attack on the World Trade Center) national defense spending was back at the level of 1989 and by 2004 was almost 50 percent higher. In real terms, defense spending during the Clinton years averaged $278 billion, just under the $281 billion annual average for the non-Vietnam cold war years.[10]

In the 1990s, the U.S. commitment to NATO increased, the network of naval bases in the Pacific grew, and the American military was drawn into civil wars in Colombia, Kosovo, and other places around the globe. According to Chalmers Johnson, on September 11, 2001, there were 725 openly acknowledged American foreign military bases around the world, and many more that were not acknowledged. Moreover, U.S. industry continued to provide nearly half of all the arms sales in the world.[11]

Harvard historian Stanley Hoffman pointed out during the presidential campaign of 2000 that foreign policy "unilateralism" was an assumption of *both* the Democrat Al Gore and the Republican George W. Bush. Behind the bland public debate, wrote Hoffman, there was an elite consensus that "complacently envisages that America will remain preeminent in all the different realms of world power and that it will remain a model for other countries. It relies on the traditional way of analyzing world affairs; as a competition among states in which the United States had to keep watching potential rivals and 'rogue states' lest they sneak up on it and do it harm. At the same time it is optimistic about the benefits of globalization, which is supposed to spread prosperity around the globe and push countries toward democracy."[12]

Writer David Rieff notes, "While the atmospherics and aesthetics accompanying the use of American power indeed distinguish the current administration from its predecessor, in substance the Clinton and Bush teams have been remarkably of one mind on issues surrounding the unilateral application of U.S. military might."[13] Indeed, one reason British prime minister Tony Blair could get along so well with both Clinton and Bush might well have been because they were so close on the international issues that mattered most to Blair. "Be his best friend," Clinton told Blair right after the Supreme Court gave Bush the 2000 election. "Be the guy he turns to."[14]

They were also of one mind on promotion of transnational corporate interests. In a sense, Rubin and economist Lawrence Summers, his deputy who succeeded him as treasury secretary and went on to become president of Harvard, were to Clinton what Cheney, Rumsfeld, and Wolfowitz later were to George W. Bush. Rubin/Summers and Cheney/Rumsfeld/Wolfowitz represented the two Wall Street and Sixth Fleet pillars of the American governing class. The two pillars are firmly attached and integrated at their base.

Certainly the Bush team was as close to the transnational corporate crowd as were their predecessors. Cheney of Halliburton, Condoleezza Rice, who was on the board of Chevron Oil and had a tanker named after her, and Rumsfeld, who was CEO of the global pharmaceutical giant Searle, are people who understand the importance of being able to walk into any boardroom in the world with the equivalent to the Sixth Fleet behind them. Shortly after the attacks of September 11, 2001, Robert Zoellick, Bush's U.S. trade representative, was touting more NAFTA-type agreements to promote U.S. values in the war on terror. "Sometimes," he said of the attacks, "tragedy also presents opportunities for those who are alert."[15]

Whatever might have been the exact proportions of the various motivations for the *invasion* of Iraq—inaccurate intelligence, an alternative to Saudi oil, the Bush family's grudge against Saddam, the delusions that it would protect Israel, the flexing of U.S. military muscle—one major reason for the *occupation* was clearly oil. As the *Guardian* of London pointed out, it could cost as little as ninety-seven cents to produce a barrel of Iraqi oil—compared with three to four dollars for oil from the North Sea. At $30 a barrel that would generate $87.5 billion a year. "Any share," commented the *Guardian*, "would be worth fighting for."[16]

But here again, the distinction between what is good for American corporations and what is good for the American public gets lost. If Iraqi oil is pumped and marketed by U.S. oil companies, it will be sold at a world price on world markets, not allocated to the U.S. consumer.

The Iraq invasion took Summers's and Sachs's shock therapy to new heights—or depths. Where the neoliberals had been obliged to operate through the international financial agencies to impose conditions on local politicians reluctant to make their own constituencies suffer, the American occupiers of Iraq would not have to negotiate with anyone. The first proconsul in Iraq, General Jay Garner, thought of Iraq as a Middle Eastern version of the Philippines, that the U.S. military could use as a "coaling station." It was straightforward old-fashioned gunboat imperialism; no transformation of Iraqi society was required, simply enough internal order to accommodate American strategic pressure. Garner was quickly replaced by Paul Bremer, a former State Department official who had spent eleven years as managing director of Kissinger Associates and had a résumé of corporate directorships, club memberships, and connections with the Council on Foreign Relations and the Heritage Foundation.

Bremer took the opportunity to impose on the Iraqis an unadulterated NAFTA template that even Carlos Salinas could not have swallowed. He fired half a million government workers, slashed business taxes, gave investors extraordinary new rights, eliminated all import restrictions, and allowed 100 percent foreign ownership of all businesses except the oil industry—the future of which had not yet been decided. He even privatized the process of privatizing Iraq two hundred state enterprises to a private contractor, Bearing Point, a subsidiary of the transnational consulting giant KPMG.

As with NAFTA, the country's labor laws were left to the mercies of the local elite. Saddam Hussein's restrictions against forming unions and collective bargaining were just about the only economic policies that were not changed. Moreover, the Coalition Provisional Authority took away workers' bonuses, profit sharing, and food and housing subsidies, leaving them with Saddam Hussein's average basic salary of eighty dollars per month, which meant a drop in real wages— as well as in labor costs for foreign investors.[17]

The international industry of consultants, brokers, and advisers to transnational corporations that had flowered since the end of the cold war poured into Iraq. "Getting the rights to distribute Procter & Gamble products can be a gold mine," said one. "One well stocked 7-11 could knock out thirty Iraq stores; a Wal-Mart could take over the country."[18]

Well-connected people grabbed Pentagon and USAID contracts funded in part by Iraqi oil revenues that were supposed to go for the rebuilding of the war-devastated society. Kellogg Brown & Root, the subsidiary of Richard Cheney's Halliburton, alone was paid $1.6 billion on a sole-source contract to import fuel from Kuwait to Iraq, which it was later charged with doing at vastly inflated prices.[19]

The bungled attempt at the instant transformation of the Iraqi economy and society was a major contribution to the disastrous occupation. Many of the unemployed joined the guerrilla opposition, the surge of imports swept away local businesses struggling to get back on their feet, and the indifference of the Bush ideologues to the basic need for public infrastructure—water, electricity, transportation—spread public resentment. In the end, foreign investors naturally refused to put their money into such an incendiary world, and, despite the extraordinary wages and profits provided by the U.S. government contracts, the violence caused an exodus of foreign contractors.

The business opportunities generated by the Iraq war were well spread throughout the governing class, with Republicans and Democrats colluding on business deals that were often at cross-purposes with the Bush administration on policies. One example was a bizarre effort organized by the Carlyle Group, an extremely well-connected investment fund founded by a former Carter administration official. In 2003, the Carlyle Group proposed that the government of Kuwait give them a contract for helping the Kuwaitis secure $27 billion in reparations for damages in the first Persian Gulf War from future Iraqi oil revenues. As evidence that they had enough political clout to overcome the Bush administration's announced intention to minimize Iraq's debt payments, they offered to put the following Americans in Kuwait's service: George H. W. Bush; James Baker, his secretary of state; former British prime minister John Major; Madeleine Albright, Clinton's secretary of state; Carole Browner, Clinton's director of the Environmental Protection Agency; Democratic ex-senator Gary Hart; and Jeane Kirkpatrick, Ronald Reagan's ambassador to the UN.[20] The deal fell through when the proposal was leaked to the press.

The *Economist* called the occupation of Iraq a "capitalist's dream."[21] And so it was.

But in order to sell their agenda to the people—and to themselves—the people who want to rule the globe had to see themselves as motivated by more than money and personal power. Thus the neoliberal pursuit of NAFTA had to be attached to a grander concept than just cheap labor and financial speculation, so as Clinton expressed, NAFTA was about defining "what the future is going to be about."

Similarly, for the neoconservatives the invasion of Iraq had to be attached to something grander than simply oil and juicy military contracts. When the claim that it was a response to a threat of weapons of mass destruction and a regime in collusion with Al-Qaeda proved to be false, the neoconservatives also reached for the future. "The mission begins in Baghdad, but it does not end there," wrote William Kristol, editor of the *Weekly Standard* and Washington's most influential conservative strategist. "We stand in the cusp of a new era. . . . It is so clearly about more than Iraq. It is about more even than the future of the Middle East and the war on terror. It is about what sort of role the United States intends to play in the twenty-first century."[22]

The Democratic and Republican leadership of post–cold war America was indeed creating our future—of cheap labor, financial speculation, oil profits, and fat military contracts.

6

Alan, Larry, and Bob Save the Privileged

But the truth is they love it, they love every self-important minute of it. Suddenly they are at the forefront of what could be another greatest generation, not some blurry interregnum. . . . We see it when they emerge from counsels of state in the wee hours, caressing their shirt fronts, smoothing down those yellow dotted ties.

But it's after that, in the limo, gliding through the night, the crucial meeting over, the hard choices made—it's the glimpse through the tinted windows of us little people in the street that yields the truly meaningful moment for our leaders. Because it's all about service, really, all about giving back, isn't it? All about us regular folks out there in the vague night. Especially the children.

—Thomas Zengotita (2003)

Robert Rubin was the chief architect of the Clinton administration's global economic agenda. Son of a successful businessman, he had degrees from Harvard and Yale Law School and enjoyed a lucrative twenty-five-year career at Goldman Sachs where he rose to cochair of the board. He is a social liberal and a very productive fund-raiser for the Democratic Party since 1982, when he organized a million-dollar event under the tutelage of Robert Strauss, the legendary Democratic corporate lawyer.

In 1991, Rubin hosted a series of dinners with a select group of New York financiers for the purpose of interviewing Democratic presidential candidates. Investment banker Roger Altman, who attended, said the Wall Streeters believed the Democratic Party needed "a new and more forward looking economic policy." Organizers referred to it as an elegant "cattle show" and Bill Clinton got the blue ribbon. Rubin said he was "enormously impressed" with Clinton's grasp of "the issues important to us." Clinton aides told the *New York Times* reporters Nicholas Kristof and David Sanger that the dinner "was an important step in the business education of Mr. Clinton, who came to repeat and amplify the themes—especially the need to move away from protectionism and push for more open markets."[1] Banks, securities firms, and insurance companies contributed $1.7 million to Clinton's 1992 campaign.[2]

Smart, unpretentious, and practical, Rubin is a natural insider politician. Given his Wall Street credentials and his personal charm, he quickly became Clinton's most influential economic adviser. After the election, he moved to Washington, where he created and ran the new National Economic Council—the economic equivalent of the National Security Council. In a few months, Rubin had enough clout to override Hillary on the issue of whether NAFTA or health care should become the president's priority in the summer of 1993. With the retirement of Lloyd Bentsen, Rubin became U.S. treasury secretary in January 1995.

Rubin opens the memoir of his Clinton years with the Mexican peso crisis. In December 1994, almost a year after NAFTA became law, he is on a fishing vacation in Florida, waiting to be confirmed by the Senate to succeed Bentsen. Larry Summers, then Treasury's chief economist, calls Rubin from Washington. He tells him that investors around the world are dumping Mexican bonds and other securities in a near panic on strong rumors that the government is about to default on its debt. "I didn't know much about Mexico's economic problems," Rubin writes, "and I didn't understand why a peso devaluation was urgent enough to interfere with fishing."[3]

He was a fast study. The peso crisis was the first of a series of international financial emergencies that established Rubin's reputation as the world's premier crisis manager—the genius who kept the financial dikes from bursting in Mexico City, Bangkok, Seoul, and New York.

Mexico's crisis was representative. For several years prior to NAFTA, financiers had poured short-term money into Mexico, anticipating that the deal would raise the price of Mexican securities and other assets. In the self-fulfilling process of speculative booms, expectations of higher prices brought in new buyers, inflating prices further. The boom also pushed interest rates higher, so that in the year or so running up to NAFTA, investors could "arbitrage," that is, borrow money in New York for, say, 5 percent, and buy Mexican government bonds that paid 12 percent. The flood of money trickled down into the rest of Mexico—at least in the urban areas—and seemed to support predictions that Mexico would be a buoyant consumer market for American goods.

When NAFTA was finally consummated, speculators began to cash in, looking around the world for the next new financial play. The January 1994 rebellion in Chiapas and the political assassinations that followed further soured financial markets on Mexico. In addition, higher U.S. interest rates that year narrowed arbitrage profit, leading investors to further disengage.

But Carlos Salinas was determined to keep Mexico's currency from falling. He was campaigning to become head of the World Trade Organization and needed to maintain his reputation as a brilliant economic manager. He also wanted to ensure the political loyalty of the urban middle classes for his handpicked successor, Ernesto Zedillo, in the July 1994 election. With the disputed election of 1988 still a painful memory, the PRI had to deliver something to the more independent voters in the cities. A high-priced peso meant that consumers could buy imports cheaper, giving them a temporary sense of prosperity just before the vote. It was an old strategy, and it worked; Zedillo won the election.

But Zedillo would not be inaugurated until December. Moreover, the WTO was not yet established, and its director had not yet been selected. So Salinas kept borrowing money to buy pesos, maintaining their value and the illusion of Mexican prosperity.

Investors became even more jittery. In order to keep the money flowing in, Salinas issued special bonds—*tesobonos*—that would pay the holder in dollars. In effect, Salinas was now buying up pesos with loans that Mexico would have to pay back in dollars.

Still, he could not raise enough money to cover Mexico's growing trade deficit with the rest of the world. In the last two months of 1994, Mexican dollar reserves dropped from $17 billion to $6 billion—with $30 billion in debt coming due the following year.

Salinas left his successor holding the bag. Shortly after his inauguration in December, Zedillo met with a group of PRI insiders and told them that he had no choice but to stop supporting the peso. After the meeting, some of them called their brokers to sell their peso-denominated stocks and bonds. The word quickly spread; panicky investors dumped pesos, and within a few weeks the Mexican currency had fallen some 50 percent against the dollar. Among other consequences, the value of Mexican commercial bank reserves shrunk, so banks stopped making new loans and stopped rolling over old ones. With the money supply contracting, interest rates rose from 15 to 130 percent in two months. Business failure, unemployment, and personal bankruptcy quickly followed.

As Summers explained it to Rubin, the Mexican treasury would need an infusion of at least $25 billion, and probably more, in order to pay the foreign holders of *tesobonos* that were coming due and to keep the creditors at bay until the country could ride out the storm, that is, until the lower peso stimulated exports and a government austerity program cut consumer incomes so imports would fall and Mexico could start running a surplus to pay its bills.

To get the U.S. Congress to pony up the money, Rubin, Summers, and Fed chair Alan Greenspan told members that the entire world was now at risk. If Mexico defaulted, investors would likely pull their money out of other "emerging markets" (that the United States had been also promoting), causing a global economic meltdown. Rubin's memoir is a financial thriller complete with tense meetings with the president, clandestine trips to Mexico, and white-knuckle monitoring of minute-by-minute currency fluctuations. The Republican leadership in Congress was sympathetic. Newt Gingrich called it "the first crisis of the twenty-first century." According to Rubin, George W. Bush, the newly elected governor of Texas, "instinctively grasped what was at stake and became a strong public supporter of our aims and efforts." At one point, Rubin called Gingrich, who called Greenspan who called Rush Limbaugh to promote the bailout to the right-wing listeners of his radio show.

But Congress balked at putting out a sum of money that was equivalent to the cost of a fleet of B-2 stealth bombers. Partly it was politics. Republicans on the right did not want to help out Bill Clinton; Democrats on the left, having just lost their forty-year-old control of the House under Clinton's leadership, were in no mood to spend money to rescue a NAFTA that they had thought was a bad idea in the first place.

Finally Rubin and Summers found $20 billion in a half-forgotten Treasury Department fund that had been set aside to defend the U.S. dollar. They ordered the IMF to put up the rest, which it did.[4]

Class before Country

The money was not used to rejuvenate the Mexican economy. It did not underwrite job creation for the unemployed or debt relief for the bankrupted small businesspeople or aid to hospitals and schools that were suddenly broke. It was used to make whole the Wall Street holders of *tesobonos*, who had originally bought the risky Mexican bonds because Salinas was giving them a higher yield.

Mexican taxpayers would of course have to pay back the money their government borrowed to pay off Wall Street bondholders. And their financial burden did not stop there. The bailout was the opportunity to further tighten down the neoliberal screws on Mexico.

Rubin sent Summers on a secret trip to Mexico to make sure Zedillo understood what Rubin wanted: high interest rates for foreign investors, an austere Mexican government budget, and assurances of further "reforms" of the Mexican financial system.[5] Among the reforms was an accelerated timetable for the opening up of Mexican banks to foreign ownership that Mexico had agreed to in NAFTA.

Summers came back with a glowing report: Zedillo, who had a PhD in economics from Yale, was "firmly committed" to Rubin's demands.

As a business deal between the rich and powerful, the Mexican financial rescue was a success. By mid-May 1995, Rubin reports, "the Mexican economy was in a severe recession, but the country's trade deficit had turned into a surplus, the stock of outstanding *tesobonos* had been reduced substantially, and the peso had recovered somewhat." By November, the stock market had stabilized, and in 1997 the Zedillo government was able to borrow money from the private sector to pay back the U.S. loan.

But "severe recession" is a modest phrase for what happened to ordinary Mexicans. It was the steepest economic crash since the Great Depression. In 1995, GDP per capita fell 9 percent, wages fell 16 percent, domestic consumption fell 10 percent, and business investment dropped by almost a third. The formal unemployment rate, which vastly understates joblessness, doubled. At the same time, because of Zedillo's commitments to his U.S. partners, government budgets for social services, education, and health care were slashed. Poor Mexicans (half the population) fell further into poverty.

The middle class, upon whose prosperity Mexico's future depended, was decimated. Inspired by the NAFTA-driven boom of the early 1990s, middle-class Mexicans had joined the credit economy, taking out loans at variable interest rates to buy cars and houses and to start new businesses. When the crash came, incomes dropped, but prices and monthly interest payments rose. People who had borrowed $50,000 found that they now owed $100,000. Debtor organizations sprung up, refusing to pay bank loans and protecting their members when the police came to repossess their homes or farms. Some banks stopped repossessing cars because they had run out of space to keep them. A decade later, the Mexican economy had still not recovered from its "shock therapy."

Rubin said that had there been no rescue, it would have been worse—a global meltdown that would have had a devastating effect on the United States. He may, of course, have been right, but it is unclear why an investor who had made a confident long-term investment in a Polish or Brazilian business would pull out because of a crash in the Mexican peso. Moreover, to the extent that money was being pulled out of the world's hot markets, most would end up in the safe harbor of the United States, lowering interest rates and boosting the domestic economy. The Federal Reserve Board calculated that even under a "worst case" scenario U.S. economic growth would have been reduced by only one-half to one percent.

We will never know if Mexico or the United States or the world was really saved. We do know that the holders of Mexican bonds were saved. So it is hard not to conclude that at least a major objective of the bailout was to assure Wall Street that it could continue to move "hot" short-term funds around the world in search of fractionally better yield and that the risks against some catastrophic mistake would be covered by the U.S. Treasury and the IMF.

As Jorge Castañeda noted, "The fund managers and stock brokers of New York knew what they were doing when they invested in Mexican stocks and received colossal returns; they were taking a risk. Now, thanks to the package, the cost of that risk (which produced lavish returns for two or three years) has been transferred completely to the Mexican taxpayer. The American investors make the mistake. Mexicans are left to pay, becoming more indebted and dooming our economy and that of our children to indefinite stagnation."[6]

To Rubin, Summers, and Greenspan, the pain to Mexico was unfortunate but justified, because, after all, the problem was caused by the Mexicans. "Alan, Larry and I agreed about what had caused the crisis," Rubin later writes. "Mexico, despite reforms in many areas, had made a serious policy mistake by borrowing too much in good times, leaving it vulnerable when sentiment shifted."

But it wasn't "Mexico" that had made the serious policy mistake; it was the government of Carlos Salinas and Ernesto Zedillo, both of whom "Alan, Larry and I" had promoted to the American Congress as honest, competent reformers who had to be supported with NAFTA, even if it meant thousands of Americans losing their jobs. And it wasn't just "good times" that had caused the speculative bubble that popped when sentiment shifted; it was the hype of NAFTA by the U.S. government led by "Alan, Larry and I," coupled with the opening up of Mexico to foreign "hot" money. And it was Salinas's excessive borrowing that had pumped up the Mexican economy of the early 1990s, sucking in U.S. imports and temporarily creating the U.S. trade surplus, which the president, assured by "Alan, Larry and I," told Americans would continue indefinitely.

Greenspan, Summers, and Rubin also shared an ideological concern: the danger to the NAFTA model. Rubin writes, "With the implementation of the North American Free Trade Agreement

(NAFTA), Mexico was hailed as a role model for developing countries pursuing economic reform. The public failure of that model could deal an enormous setback to the spread of market-based economic reforms and globalization."[7]

The bailout was an essential part of the NAFTA model—a "free market" economy that provides a safety net for corporate investors and leaves the rest of society at the mercy of the brutal laws of supply and demand. Ninety percent of the Mexican *tesobonos* were held in New York—something that Alan, Larry, and Bob were surely aware of. Rubin's old firm Goldman Sachs was a privately held company at the time and we do not know the company's exposure in *tesobonos*, but according to the *Wall Street Journal*, Goldman Sachs was the single largest underwriter of Mexican equities and bonds from 1992 to 1994, in total worth $5.17 billion.[8]

There were other options. For example, rather than require Mexico to put its economy through the wringer in order to save the peso, the U.S. Treasury might have simply intervened in the peso market, buying enough to stop its free fall and then allowing it to decline slowly. This would have taken time, but the U.S. Treasury knew that Salinas had been propping up the peso since early 1994, and even had lent him some short-term money earlier to help. Another option for Salinas and Zedillo, knowing that they would have to devaluate, was to place controls on capital flight, such as Chile had successfully done under similar circumstances, and—with the leverage of some control over the foreign assets—to have sat down and negotiated loan term extensions with the *tesobonos* holders.

Such ideas would have been denounced as irresponsible "statism" by the U.S. Treasury, the World Bank, and the Dow Jones Corporation (publishers of the *Wall Street Journal*) where Salinas was now a board member. The conventional wisdom was that any such response would so turn off the global financial markets that Mexico would never get any more credit and its economy would be doomed. But Mexico would not have been the only country to stand up to its creditors, nor the last. A decade later, Argentina, which was in a weaker bargaining position than Mexico had been in, defaulted on its international loan payments and forced its creditors to settle for thirty-two cents on the dollar. The Mexican leaders, however, when faced with a choice between the *tesobonos* holders in New York and the vast majority of the Mexican people for whom missing a paycheck was a catastrophe, chose class over country.

The Committee to Save the World's Rich and Powerful

With the peso bailout, Alan, Larry, and Bob became the toast of Wall Street. The *New York Times* called them the "Committee to Save the World."

The NAFTA financial model—liberalization of trade and finance leading to a speculative bubble, a subsequent crash, and the protection of investors from the consequences of their own actions—was repeated in various forms in the 1990s throughout the global markets in Thailand, Brazil, Bolivia, South Korea, Indonesia, Russia, and Argentina.

The scenario would begin with the U.S. Treasury, the IMF, and World Bank and other financial agencies, in partnership with local elites, conditioning their loans on privatization, deregulation, and the opening up of their financial systems to foreign ownership. Anointed by the international lenders, the nations then become hot markets, identified by the global business media, the newsletters, and the e-mail chatter as ready to "emerge" from the pack.

Typically the initial effect, as in Mexico, is an economic boom in the large cities. The gusher of new money creates jobs and drives up the prices of land, producing instant millionaires and a few billionaires. Incomes rise faster than production, so imports rise faster than exports. To finance the gap, the country borrows at high interest rates from foreign lenders competing for higher yields. At some point investors become aware that the country's central bank is running out of the reserves needed to redeem the local currency that its consumers have been spending on imports. Devaluation looms. Investors dump their assets, whose prices suddenly collapse along with the value of the currency. With collateral now worth less, banks have to call in their loans to local businesses and consumers, and the financial crisis follows.

Alarm bells ring in the offices of the transnational bureaucrats in Washington. The assistants to Rubin at the U.S. Treasury, Michel

Camdessus at the IMF, and James Wolfensohn at the World Bank come up with a number for how much the country needs to "restore confidence" in the financial markets, that is, pay off the bondholders. In return for the money, they demand more "reforms," including drastic cuts in social services and subsidies for the poor, total elimination of the remaining restrictions on foreign ownership of banks, and a pledge to keep interest rates high to attract enough foreign money so that the currency will stabilize.

Negotiations follow. Bob Rubin makes the final round of calls and the deal is done. Unemployment, bankruptcies, and poverty increase, as do the crime and suicide rates and the number of children living in the streets. But the currency is stabilized and the holders of the country's bonds are assured that they will get their money back. The *Wall Street Journal* announces that the country has been "saved," and the debtor nations' leaders are congratulated for understanding that their first obligation was to pay their foreign debts. Borrowing resumes.

Socialism for the Rich

The world, of course, included the United States. Alan, Larry, and Bob were relentless champions of domestic financial deregulation as well. In 1999, they helped banking industry lobbyists get the 1933 Glass-Steagall Act repealed. Glass-Steagall had been designed to prevent the kind of crony capitalism that had caused the 1929 stock market crash. That crash had shown that when the same financial institution both sells company stock and provides a firm with commercial loans, the independent banking judgment as to the firm's creditworthiness becomes corrupted. So Glass-Steagall forbade it.

The big banks chafed under the restrictions. But Glass-Steagall had been a sacred text for Democratic populists like congressmen Wright Patman and Henry Gonzales who had for years chaired the banking committee in the House of Representatives. So after the GOP took over Congress in 1994, the banks mobilized to eliminate it, promising that they would keep "Chinese walls" between the different functions to separate them. With Rubin and Summers in charge of White House economic policy and the Republicans in charge of Congress, they killed Glass-Steagall, actually undercutting a milder proposal by a moderate Republican, Jim Leach of Iowa, who chaired the committee. The repeal of Glass-Steagall sent a strong signal to the banks that crony capitalism, widely condemned in the third world, was once again to be nurtured in America.

The practice of socialism for the financial markets and capitalism for the labor markets continued. In September 1998, the Committee to Save the World learned that a sophisticated New York hedge fund named Long Term Capital Management was about to fail. LTCM—open only to those who could afford to put up a million dollars—was run by a Wall Street veteran, John Meriwether, assisted by two Nobel Prize–winning economists. They used mathematical models to manage their portfolio. But the models did not work so well in the real world, and LTCM began to lose large amounts of money. The fund—like the treasuries of so many third world countries in crisis—was suddenly faced with more debts coming due than money to pay them. Its creditors were the crème de la crème of Wall Street: Citigroup, Goldman Sachs, Merrill Lynch, Bear Stearns, Chase, and Morgan Stanley.

Once again, the alarms went off. And once again the Committee to Save the World concluded that the collapse of financial civilization was inevitable if they did not rescue the Wall Street high rollers. So with the support of Rubin and Greenspan, the president of the Federal Reserve Bank of New York called a meeting of LTCM's creditors and leaned on them to lend LTCM another roughly $4 billion to float its way out of trouble.

A few years later, the impact of the repeal of Glass-Steagall was reflected in the collapse of Enron. The banks now had a stake in keeping the company's stock up and could continue to get fees for issuing new securities and other deals. So Enron's banks kept lending it money even after it was clear that the company was in serious trouble. The more unjustified their previous loans had been, the more incentive banks had to lend still more to try to avoid the company going bankrupt, which would reveal the banks' irresponsibility.

When Enron was on the brink of collapse, Robert Rubin, who by then had become chair of the executive committee at Citigroup—one of Enron's creditors—placed a call to Richard Fisher, a Treasury Department official, to suggest that the U.S. government ask the bank-rating agencies to hold off downgrading Enron stock while the creditor banks were deciding whether to lend Enron even more.

NAFTA's "High Yield" Club

Rubin is an intelligent and reflective man. He is not a Thatcherite hater of social safety nets. He thinks government should be responsible for retraining people who lose their jobs and that it should give more aid to the education of poor children, as well as do something to help people in the inner cities.

Nor does he idealize the corporate investors. "I remember, at the time of the South Korea crisis," he says, "being struck in discussion with a prominent New York banker by how little he and his company knew about a country to which they had extended a considerable amount of credit. . . . Though the basic hazard of investing in countries with major economic and political problems should have been obvious, the prevailing mentality was to downplay or ignore those risks in the 'reach for yield.' "[9]

But he is a member of the governing class first. He therefore sees the world through the lens of people like himself, people who he works with, plays tennis with. So despite the hazards of greedy ignorant bankers "reaching for yield," Rubin used his talent and influence to make it easier for the greedy and ignorant to gamble with other people's money. When they gambled and lost, if they were important enough, they had to be rescued—not to help his friends, of course, but to save the system and all the little people who would be hurt.

Rubin assures us in his memoir that he believes that "governments shouldn't worry about the tribulations of any particular firm or corporation, but if a situation threatens the financial system, some kind of government action might be the best among bad choices." In a speech given in 1998 during the Korean financial crisis, he declared, "We would not give one nickel to help any creditor or investor . . . [but] any action that would force investors and creditors involuntarily to take losses, however appropriate that might seem, would risk serious adverse consequences. It would cause banks to pull money out of the countries involved. It could reduce the ability of these countries to access new sources of private capital. And perhaps most tellingly, it would cause banks to pull back from other emerging markets."[10]

When the report of his call to Treasury on Enron leaked out, Rubin insisted that he was motivated by public service. "There was an important public policy concern about the energy markets—not just a parochial concern about Citigroup's exposure—and I felt that if a modest intervention by Treasury could potentially make the difference in avoiding a significant economic shock for the country it was worth raising the idea with an official there."[11]

Saving the system in which the best of bad choices always seem to benefit the economic class whose members make the choices is a bipartisan, bi-ideological affair. When Rubin and Clinton needed help to pass NAFTA, they turned to Henry Kissinger for advice. When Rubin and Summers needed advice on Indonesia, they brought in Kissinger and Paul Wolfowitz. It made practical sense; Kissinger knows the Republican presidents, and his clients are the world's biggest transnational corporations. Wolfowitz was ambassador to Indonesia. And it makes sense that during the congressional battle over NAFTA, Rubin would ask Newt Gingrich to ask Alan Greenspan to tell Rush Limbaugh to use his right-wing talk show to pump for a trade agreement.

Despite their tactical and partisan differences and their different specialties, they all swim in a pool of professional and personal relationships from which they draw their wealth and sustenance. It is natural that they decide to serve the country in ways that bring nutrients back to the waters that sustain them. The pursuit of class interest is typically not a question of personal corruption. And in most cases those who pursue it are amazed that anyone would question what they are doing.

Several years ago the Shorenstein Center for the Press and Politics at Harvard held an off-the-record luncheon in Washington for the heads of Washington policy think tanks. The purpose was to give journalists advice on how to evaluate the information coming from different sources. One guest suggested that journalists consider the source of the think tank's funding. This brought an immediate outraged reaction from the head of the organization that advocated the most extreme free-market philosophy. He said he was "offended" that anyone would even suggest that professional economists like him could be swayed by the source of their support. Heads nodded in agreement around the table.

Here was the advocate for the proposition that virtually all human behavior is driven by the greed for money, denying that *his* views could ever be swayed by the source of his income.

In one sense, though, he had a point. The governing class doesn't so much pay people to change their minds. Rather, it promotes people to its membership and public prominence whose views reinforce the power structure. It gives those who are "reliable" access to a public amplifier. Those who are not must shout on their own from the margins of the public discussion.

The examples of personal corruption at the top that are occasionally exposed are usually small-time—tickets to a Super Bowl game, a job for a mistress, a paid-for trip worth a few thousand dollars. Why, asks the citizen, would someone jeopardize their career for such small amounts? The answer of course is that if they thought about it, they would not. People of power and influence live in a world of class perquisites. They have been taking tickets, jobs for mistresses, and free trips for decades. This last one, where they got caught, is usually just a piece of bad luck. They drift over the line so often that they don't really think about it.

It is highly unlikely that Richard Cheney ever ordered anyone at the Pentagon to give a huge sole-source contract to Halliburton. He did not have to. Procurement officers already knew the relationship between the company and the vice president. Moreover, Halliburton had already done so much work for the Pentagon that procurement officers could easily, and often quite honestly, justify giving the company noncompetitive contracts. Cheney's promotion of more funds for the military and the war in Iraq in particular was bound to benefit the world to which he belonged—his circle of rich and powerful people who would always be there for him and his projects. No conflict-of-interest laws need be violated.

There is less reason to doubt Robert Rubin's personal honesty. Yet the Wall Street world that nurtured him was enormously enriched by the trade and financial deregulation policies he successfully promoted in his tenure as Clinton's economic policy czar.

Thus, as we have seen, breaking down Mexico's restrictions on foreign investment in its banks was an absolute nonnegotiable NAFTA objective of both the George H. W. Bush and the Clinton administrations. The peso crisis then provided an opportunity to accelerate the schedule.

Rubin tells us that at the time of the peso crisis, "I didn't know much about Mexico's economic problems." The word "much" is of course open to interpretation. But he certainly knew something.

Along with Lloyd Bentsen, Rubin talked Clinton into making NAFTA a more important priority than health care. In the 1980s, Rubin, representing Goldman Sachs, had advised Carlos Salinas, then the Mexican secretary of planning and budget, on using hedge funds to protect against currency changes. The arrangement was hidden from the Mexican public at the time because Salinas did not want to be seen as relying on Wall Street on economic policy. Later, when Salinas became president, Rubin personally and successfully lobbied him to give Goldman Sachs the contract to underwrite the $2.3 billion international public offering of the government-owned telecommunications company, Telmex.

Commenting on the privatization of Telmex, Salinas writes in his own memoirs, "For transactions involving markets in other parts of the world, we selected as bank agent Goldman Sachs & Co. headed by Robert Rubin who would later become U.S. Treasury Secretary under Bill Clinton. Rubin knew the details of the entire Telmex privatization as well as the detailed steps taken to assure the process."[12] When the Clinton White House called him to ask if he wanted to run the National Economic Council, Rubin was on the way to the airport for a meeting with Salinas in Mexico City.[13]

In Rubin's financial disclosure form that he submitted when he went to work in the Clinton White House, he listed six Mexican clients among those with whom he currently had "significant contact." These were: the Mexican government; the finance ministry; the central bank; Teléfonos de México; Cemex, the largest cement company in the Americas; and Desc Sociedad de Fomento Industrial, the country's seventh largest manufacturing conglomerate.[14] Upon accepting the White House job, he wrote to his clients, "I also look forward to continuing to work with you in my new capacity. I hope I can continue to rely on your interest and support . . . and would be grateful for whatever suggestions you would offer."[15]

At the same time that Rubin was negotiating the bailout loan with the Mexican government, then secretary of state Warren Christopher had recused himself from involvement in the administration's dealing with an American oil company doing business with Iran because someone from his old law firm was representing the company. Given the obvious fact that Goldman Sachs, as a major Mexican creditor, would be a prime beneficiary of the Mexican bailout, a Treasury spokesperson was asked what made Rubin's situation different than Christopher's, but declined to answer.[16]

In any event, it is not reasonable to believe that he and Bentsen did not know, at least at the general level, that corruption and crony capitalism ran very deep in the presidential administration of Carlos Salinas. If Rubin was as ignorant as he suggests, he becomes a prime example of the bankers he criticizes for making ignorant investments in order to "reach for yield."

Rubin was right about the Mexican banking system needing reform, but the idea that opening it up to foreign ownership would clean up the crony capitalism was a bit misplaced. Indeed, one might wonder why the Mexican business elite was so enthusiastic for NAFTA if, as the Washington conventional wisdom had it, the purpose was to force the oligarch families to give up their privileged position in the economy. The story of what happened to Mexico's second largest bank, Banamex, suggests the answer.

The banks had been part of the cozy partnership with government before the crisis of 1982. But they had made the crisis worse by facilitating the enormous flight of capital threatening the country's economy. To stem the capital flight, the government of Miguel de la Madrid nationalized them. A decade later, Salinas sold them back again to the private sector, beginning in 1991–1992.[17]

A syndicate organized by Roberto Hernandez Ramirez, a member of Mexico's power elite with close ties to Salinas, Zedillo, and Fox, bought Banamex from the Salinas government for $3.2 billion. Hernandez used his close friendship with Salinas to profit from the privatization of government enterprises that Goldman Sachs had helped underwrite.

But Hernandez and the other well-connected new owners had little competence in managing banks, and the Salinas government had little competence in regulating them. Corruption and self-dealing were rampant. One of the new bankers, Carlos Cabal Peniche, whom Carlos Salinas had praised as a "model" of the new Mexican business leader, was using his two banks to make loans to himself. After the 1994–1995 peso crisis his bank went belly-up and Cabal fled, leaving the government to pick up the pieces.

When Cabal was later arrested in Australia he told police that during the presidential campaign of 1994, he had shoveled $25 million from his banks to the Zedillo presidential campaign. The political opposition charged that Zedillo was bailing out banks that had illegally donated to the PRI. Despite this, Zedillo—who now had replaced the disgraced Salinas as Washington's paragon of reform—refused to make public any of the loans in the government's bailout portfolio.[18]

In 1995, twelve of the eighteen privatized banks were insolvent and the rest were tottering. As part of the bailout agreement, Zedillo agreed to accelerate the NAFTA schedule for allowing majority ownership by foreign banks, and he added special tax breaks for foreign buyers. He then promised the Mexican bankers a subsidy of their own to make the banks even more attractive to foreign investors.

Under the ubiquitous label of "reform," the deal involved the Mexican treasury buying, on credit, massive amounts of the banks' mostly uncollectible loans. The exact cost to the Mexican taxpayers is obscured by complex accounting procedures, but estimates are that it runs to some $65 billion between 1995 and 2003. In 2003, the federal government's interest payment to the banks under the bailout totaled almost three times what it was investing in roads, school buildings, health facilities, and other physical infrastructure.[19] Government statistics suggest that in 2004 some $3.5 to $4.7 billion of government subsidy remained on Banamex's books.[20]

In 2001, shortly after the date by which the Mexican government had agreed to lift all restrictions on foreign ownership of banks, Citigroup bought Banamex from the Hernandez group for $12.5 billion.[21] A chief negotiator for Citigroup was Robert Rubin, who after leaving Treasury had become the chair of Citigroup's executive committee.

None of this is illegal, or even in violation of any formal ethical code. There is no evidence that when Rubin was secretary of the treasury he knew in advance that his next job would be with Citigroup. And after he took that job, it would be odd if he didn't use his knowledge and contacts to enrich his new employer. That, after all, is why they paid him $17 million in cash, stock, and options in 2003.[22] This is precisely the way the economic class system works at the top. It has always worked that way. The difference is that today the class system crosses borders. Roberto Hernandez Ramirez is a member of the board of directors of Citigroup.

Ernesto Zedillo is a member of the board of directors of Alcoa. He became chair of the UN High Level Panel of Financing for Development, co-coordinator of the UN Millennium Development Goals Task Force on the Multilateral Trading System, cochairman of the UN Commission on the Private Sector and Development, and cochairman of the International Commission on Global Public Goods. He is director of the Center for the Study of Globalization and professor in the field of international economics and politics at Yale University.

The story of Banamex is just one example of the many ways in which the Mexican and U.S. elites used NAFTA to trade favors and increase their economic power. Salinas crony Carlos Slim bought the privatized Telmex, and was, in effect, given a protected telephone monopoly. Slim promptly raised telephone rates 170 percent. As Mexican political scientist Lorenzo Meyer commented, "With wage increases of 18 percent and telephone rate increases of 170 percent, you don't need to be a financial genius to make it in the business world."[23] Before the decade was out, Slim would become the richest man in Latin America.

Another Salinas pal, Emilio Azcárraga, owner of the TV empire Televisa that had 90 percent of the Mexican market, was given a twelve-year protection from any competition. And so it goes. Hernandez, Slim, and Azcárraga were part of a close set of business supporters of the PRI. In February 1993, at a dinner at the home of one of them, Antonio Ortiz Mena, Salinas raised an average of $25 million each from thirty businessmen for the 1994 PRI election. As journalist Andres Oppenheimer notes, Mexico's GDP was 5 percent of that of the United States—about the size of Ohio's economy. Yet the thirty guests at Ortiz Mena's dinner raised five times the amount of money spent by the Democratic Party in the entire American presidential campaign of 1992.[24]

Oppenheimer compares Azcárraga, Slim, and Hernandez to the U.S. robber barons of the late 1890s. But despite the neoliberal mantra about bringing competition to Mexico, the NAFTA negotiators had no interest in adding antitrust provisions to their deal. Speaking of the oligarchs, Meyer writes, "They discovered how convenient it was for them to use the government's power in favor of their enterprises, and to thus accumulate fabulous fortunes. Government leaders walk around arm in arm with them, for the benefit of both of them, and for the detriment of society."[25]

Thus it was that NAFTA spread free markets and the opportunity for "high-yield"—for the privileged few.

7

NAFTA:
Who Got What?

By any measure, NAFTA has been a success. The dismantling of
barriers has led to increased trade and investment, growth
in employment, and enhanced competitiveness.

—Joint statement by Robert B. Zoellick, U.S. trade representative;
Fernando Canales, Mexico's secretary of economy; and the
Honorable James Peterson, Canada's minister of
international trade, July 16, 2004

If you are going to improve your life, you need to go
to the United States.

—The neighbor of a young Mexican killed with eighteen others
trying to cross the border

Let me tell you, you find people who have worked there for twenty-five
to thirty years and they're making nine bucks an hour, you know.
And they raised families, bought homes. . . . And to watch that yanked
away, right at the point when this mass of them were getting close
to the end and life started to look good . . . what you thought
was a light at the end of the tunnel is a freaking freight
train coming at you full blast.

—Chris Silvera, union representative, on the closing
of Swingline Stapler, Brooklyn, New York

There is no more favorable place than North America to test the claim that neoliberalism raises living standards in both rich and poor countries. No other developing nation has Mexico's advantage of a two-thousand-mile border with the wealthiest consumer market in the world, where it can export both its goods and its surplus labor. Nor can any other developing country offer its investors a safety net supported by the U.S. Treasury, which in 1995 signaled to foreign investors that it considers Mexico "too big to fail." If neoliberalism can't work in Mexico, it's hard to imagine it working anywhere.

For American investors, Mexico's proximity should make its markets, its laws, and its business culture more understandable than in other emerging economies. Mexico also seems politically stable, and is without the deep anti-Western political or religious movements of the Middle East, Asia, or Africa. Investors can also feel comforted that Mexico is within easy reach of the U.S. military if their commercial interests become threatened, as Washington apparently thought they did when it sent troops to occupy Veracruz in 1914.

For the Canadian transnational class—whose trade and investment with Mexico is growing, but small—the test of neoliberalism must also include the impact of the 1989 free trade agreement with the United States. Here again, compared with other efforts to integrate developed countries—in Europe, for example—circumstances are favorable. Canada and the United States share three thousand miles of undefended border, a common culture and language (Quebec is bilingual), and have not fought with each other since Canada was a British colony in the War of 1812.

We have now had more than a decade of NAFTA and a decade and a half of the Canada-U.S. Free Trade Agreement. This is a reasonable length of time to provide insights into who is likely to get what out of global integration built on neoliberal principles.

View from the Top

On December 9, 2002, members of Washington's governing class gathered in the new Ronald Reagan Building and International Trade Center to mark the tenth anniversary of the completion of the NAFTA negotiations. The morning speakers were the three who had forged the deal—George H. W. Bush, Carlos Salinas, and Brian Mulroney.

The large auditorium was filled with the same sort of crowd, and many of the same faces, that had attended Clinton's White House rally in 1993. Bipartisan camaraderie filled the morning's speeches. Former president Bush praised Bill Clinton for "fighting for NAFTA after I left the White House," and lauded Clinton aides Mack McLarty, Richard Fisher, and other Democrats for their "bravery." Former Democratic congressman Lee Hamilton, who George W. Bush would soon appoint cochair of the 9/11 Commission, introduced the ex-president, who said that "Lee would have made a helluva Republican."

The conferees celebrated NAFTA as a success and all three leaders as heroes who had defied their electorates at great personal cost. Bush had been attacked in 1992 by Bill Clinton for not having protected labor and the economy in NAFTA. In the 1993 Canadian election, Brian Mulroney had been attacked for betraying Canadian sovereignty. In Mexico, NAFTA had widely been seen as having led to the collapse of the peso in December 1994, which ruined Salinas's reputation. In the aftermath of the NAFTA signing, Bush had been voted out of office, Salinas had become the most despised leader in modern Mexican history, and Mulroney's party had been crushed in the next election.

Now, celebrating among friends, the three ex-leaders argued that history had vindicated them. Bush said that NAFTA had created millions of good jobs in the United States. He dismissed critics as parochial, lawless, and anarchist. He brought the mostly male house down with a story of how, while being driven past a group of antiglobalization demonstrators, he was confronted by "a, frankly, unattractive woman—I think 'ugly' was a good word." She carried a sign that said "Stay out of my womb." Bush deadpanned, "Looked over and said, no problem, just—none at all."[1]

Brian Mulroney told the audience that Canada's trade with the United States had increased to $2 billion a day and trade with Mexico was up to $10 billion per year. One in four new jobs in Canada has been created by trade (although not necessarily by NAFTA), and investment inflows had risen by 21 percent. The "fear-mongering" of NAFTA's opponents in Canada had proven hollow.[2]

Carlos Salinas had even more numbers. Mexico's foreign trade with the United States had grown from $88 billion in 1993 to $350 billion in 2002. Investment rose from $4 billion to $11 billion. "The level of trade and type of products that cross the borders," he said, "silenced even the most ardent critics."[3]

The next day in Mexico City a very "ardent" group of protesting farmers pried open the elaborately carved wooden doors of the lower house of the Mexican Congress and rode horses through its lobby, denouncing NAFTA and demanding that the Mexican government renegotiate the treaty. The protestors let loose horses, cows, and other farm animals on the legislature's grounds while they forced panicked members of Congress to listen to their grievances. The event was followed by a month and a half of demonstrations against NAFTA by farmers, teachers, and other workers all over Mexico, culminating in a February 1 demonstration of more than a hundred thousand people in Mexico City's Zócalo, the city's huge main square in front of the National Palace.

They came to vent their anger over the bankrupting of Mexico's small corn and dairy producers after NAFTA flooded their markets with the subsidized produce of American and Canadian agriculture. It was colorful and spirited: families in traditional shawls, skirts, and hats, cooking their meals in makeshift camps in the streets, home-made signs denouncing the betrayal of Salinas and his successor Zedillo and accusing President Vicente Fox of being a better friend to the United States than to Mexico. The sacred images of Emilio Zapata and the Virgin of Guadalupe were waved over the heads of the crowd.

It was the largest rural protest against the government since the 1930s. In a December 2002 poll, conducted to coincide with NAFTA's tenth anniversary, 52 percent of Mexicans responded that their country had been a loser in the free trade agreement.[4] The Mexican polls were echoed in both the United States and Canada.

Low-Wage Sucking Sound

The Mexican demonstrations were largely ignored by the U.S. media. By and large the punditry accepted the view of those in the Reagan center. NAFTA was a success and those who demonstrated against it were irrational anarchists or people exaggerating the sad but inevitable fact that some people had to lose for there to be progress. As for the polls, the people obviously did not have the facts.

But the facts actually supported the popular impressions. George H. W. Bush's jobs numbers were bogus. They were arrived at by adding up the jobs gained by exports without subtracting the larger number of jobs lost to imports. This is like balancing your checkbook by adding in the deposits without subtracting the checks you wrote. Bush and Clinton had claimed that NAFTA would produce *net* new jobs for Americans because the U.S. trade surplus with Mexico would grow. But after 1994, the U.S. surplus quickly became a deficit, and the same logic resulted in a nine-hundred-thousand-job loss by 2002.[5]

The direct impact of NAFTA on American workers was hidden by the boom of the 1990s. Between 1993 and 2000, the U.S. economy grew by a net of sixteen million jobs. But since there was a net loss of jobs because of our NAFTA trade, no portion of the overall net gain can possibly have been generated by NAFTA. In effect, the U.S. economy in the 1990s was like a corporation whose expanding domestic business hid the losses from its foreign operations, that is, the trade deficits with Canada, Mexico, and most of the rest of the world.

Once NAFTA was approved, the corporations whose executives had assured Congress that they were interested in the Mexican consumer not the Mexican worker immediately shifted gears. By November 1998, Eastman Kodak had shed 1,145 jobs by shifting production to Mexico. General Electric had moved at least 5,524 jobs. Allied-Signal, whose CEO had spearheaded the USA-NAFTA lobby, sent at least 1,633 jobs to Mexico. Johnson & Johnson abandoned 410 U.S. jobs to Mexico, and Kimberly-Clark moved 1,327 jobs there.

These numbers are minimums. They are taken from the reports that the U.S. Department of Labor required companies to file, until 2002 when the Bush administration said that the public had no need to know. But the numbers are the tip of the iceberg. They do not reflect the loss of jobs with subcontractors, grocery stores, and local services. When apparel maker OshKosh B'Gosh closed a plant in Celina, Tennessee, to move production to Mexico, unemployment shot up to 35 percent and retail businesses folded. A wave of out-migration followed. The once bustling main square, anchored by an 1870 brick courthouse, became pockmarked by vacant buildings. Said one resident, "The whole county went back 40 years—in three weeks. There were no jobs, no more."[6]

The threat to move to Mexico gave companies a huge advantage in negotiating wages and benefits with American workers and wringing subsidies from local governments. A study by Professor Kate Bronfenbrenner of Cornell University for the U.S. Department of Labor concluded that NAFTA had allowed American managers to more credibly threaten their workers that they would move to Mexico if workers did not meet their demands for financial concessions. She documented cases where companies began to load machinery on trucks marked "Mexico" outside plants where there was a labor dispute.[7]

Mexico soon became a major permanent factor in the production decisions of America's big manufacturers. Not only did the firms outsource themselves but the large retailers and auto, appliance, and other industries let their U.S. suppliers know that they would expect them to meet the price of their Mexican suppliers—which could only be done by relocating there.

NAFTA made a major contribution to the increase in inequality among Americans. It shows up dramatically in the small share of rising productivity that went to workers in manufacturing industries, which make most of the products traded internationally. Between 1993 and 2002 worker productivity in manufacturing rose 57 percent while wages rose 6 percent.

The situation for Canadian workers was somewhat better. Trade with Mexico was small and had little impact either way on the Canadian job market. Since the signing of CUFTA in 1989, the Canadian surplus with the United States had grown, and had generated more net jobs for Canadians. But virtually all serious observers attribute the overwhelming cause of the Canadian surplus (and thus its trade-induced job growth) to the dramatic drop in the Canadian dollar over the decade after CUFTA.[8]

Canada has some basic "structural" problems in its industrial sector, such as too many small, undercapitalized factories and not enough investment in modern machinery, R&D, and training. And in a sense, CUFTA and NAFTA were sold as a way for the government to solve those problems without more direct involvement in the economy that would challenge the privileges and the increasingly conservative ideology of the Canadian corporate class. Peter Nicholson, a former banker and Canadian government adviser, said that CUFTA promoters believed it would "cause Canadian firms to pull up their socks and compete in the North American market." But for the most part they responded "by simply moving across the border . . . taking the path of least resistance."[9]

Not surprisingly, the pain came at the middle and the bottom, not the top. As in the United States, Canadian workers got little of the decade's productivity gains; while real wages in manufacturing between 1993 and 2002 fell, productivity rose 22 percent. Between 1990 and 2000, the share of income going to the richest 10 percent of Canadians rose from 36 to 42 percent. The take of the top 1 percent rose from 9 to 14 percent.

Perhaps more important for most Canadians was the erosion of public social spending. Canadian governing-class politicians and corporate media ads had promised that free trade and investment with the United States would save Canada's social safety net by raising productivity and thereby increasing wages and tax revenues. But the ink was hardly dry on CUFTA when the line abruptly changed. Lower wages and cuts in social benefits were now said to be necessary to compete with the United States, where social spending was much lower.

Like Bill Clinton, Jean Chrétien became Canada's leader by criticizing his conservative opponents for shortchanging social spending. Like Clinton, once elected, Chrétien gave priority to eliminating the government deficit, which would then, he promised, allow the Liberals to make social investments. And like Clinton, he did not deliver. In 1992, Canadian government spending as a share of GDP was 43 percent—15 percentage points more than the share in the United States. By 2001, it had dropped to 34 percent and the gap with the United States shrunk to 6 percentage points.

Clearly, NAFTA failed to deliver on its promises to U.S. and Canadian workers. Still, one might argue that it was a success if it had produced for Mexico—that is, if it raised living standards for the ordinary Mexican and put its economy on the growth path that the promoters of the agreement had projected. It was certainly reasonable to argue that if NAFTA generated prosperity for Mexican workers, workers in the United States and Canada would ultimately gain from this new market for their production.

Rural Poverty in Mexico: NAFTA's Intended Consequence

The farmers who battered down the doors of the Mexican Congress were poor. But they had been poor for generations and survived. In the Constitution of 1917 and the social contract organized by the PRI in the 1930s, their survival was recognized as important to the nation. In exchange for the farmers' political support, the PRI provided them with price supports for corn and beans and subsidies for inputs like water, electricity, and fertilizer. As in the United States and Canada, the subsidies cushioned the natural movement of people from farms to cities.

Many Mexican farmers were understandably suspicious of NAFTA, which called for a steady lowering of tariffs against foreign corn until they were completely phased out in 2008. This put the small Mexican farmers into direct competition with the huge American and Canadian agribusinesses. Subsidized American corn could be exported for 25 to 30 percent below the cost of production.[10] Not to worry, Carlos Salinas told them. The PRI would never abandon them. He promised a huge program of financial aid, technical assistance, and training that would increase their productivity and allow them to grow more profitable crops.

But a year after NAFTA was signed, the PRI "reformers" pulled the rug out from under the farmers. Mexican government funding for farm subsidies, credit, and technical assistance programs dropped from $2 billion in 1994 to $500 million in 2000.[11]

As in the United States, larger Mexican agricultural enterprises have always received larger subsidies; 85 percent of the subsidies go to 15 percent of the farms.[12] But NAFTA has made the disparities worse. Having lost much of their domestic market to U.S. and Canadian agribusiness, small Mexican farms devoted more effort to home production and barter. But the government supports only production for the market, so the small campesino struggling for survival gets less help and the larger farmers get more.

Simultaneously opening up Mexico to subsidized U.S. food imports while withdrawing supports for small Mexican farmers sharply reduced Mexico's ability to supply the basic food needs of its population. Corn and beans are staples of the Mexican diet. NAFTA provided for a gradually expanding supply of tariff-free U.S. imports for these necessities over a fifteen-year period. But within two years, the Zedillo government waived the NAFTA limits on tariff-free corn on the grounds that Mexico could no longer produce enough—a self-fulfilling prophecy. The next year, it doubled the tariff-free quota on beans.

Contrary to the confident predictions, therefore, opening agriculture did not improve the Mexican balance of payments. While Mexican net exports of fruits, vegetables, and flowers from the northern and western parts of the country grew after NAFTA, they could not offset the expanded imports of grain, oilseeds, and meat from the United States.[13] After ten years, Mexico, with 25 percent of its population living in the countryside, now had to depend on the United States for much of its food.

Between 1993 and 2002, roughly two million farmers were forced to abandon their land. Some moved to the cities. Some found a better life in the United States. Many became migrant workers within Mexico.

From November to May every year, a million Mexicans—many of them displaced small farmers—now work as migrant laborers in their own country. Some two hundred thousand of them live in squalor in Sinaloa, where agriculture is a $600 million industry controlled by twenty families, for whom the Mexican government has built roads, dams, and irrigation canals to support their wealth. As one journalist noted, "They do not leave their homes because they are looking for better wages; they leave because they are looking for any wages. Many of these internal migrants earn nothing at all at home—there are no paying jobs around—and survive only on the beans and corn that they manage to grow on little plots outside their tumbledown houses."[14] The families migrate together. Everyone works. There are neither schools nor health care and often not even the most minimal housing.

Vicente Fox, outspoken about protecting Mexican migrants in the United States, has said little about Mexican migrants in Mexico. After his election, enterprising reporters found that children as young as eleven years old were working in his own family's packing plants.

The conventional wisdom of the global economics punditry shrugs off the catastrophic effect of NAFTA on rural Mexico as the unfortunate unintended consequence of progress. But it was not so unintended. Opening up the Mexican market to U.S. and Canadian agribusiness was as much an instrument for government-directed social engineering as it was a commitment to the free market. The Salinas and Zedillo regimes wanted to force farmers off the land and increase even more the supply of cheap labor for foreign capital. Preparing for NAFTA, Salinas had gotten the Congress to rescind the parts of the Mexican Constitution that authorized the wide distribution of land and protected the communal rights of indigenous villages. The *New York Times*'s Tina Rosenberg reported ten years after NAFTA that "Mexican officials say openly that they long ago concluded that small agriculture was inefficient, and that the solution for farmers was to find other work."[15]

Few Jobs in the City

Since NAFTA was supposed to industrialize Mexico, the experience of the manufacturing sector is a key measure of its success. Overall, Mexico gained roughly 450,000 net new manufacturing jobs between 1993 and 2003.[16] It gained 540,000 in the so-called maquiladora assembly plants that export to the United States, and lost 100,000 jobs in its non-maquiladora manufacturing sector.

The maquiladora firms were established in the mid-1960s under an agreement that allowed Mexican firms to manufacture products by processing and assembling imported American components, which could then be exported back to the United States. At first, the maquiladoras concentrated on apparel and low-quality footwear, but eventually production spread to auto parts and consumer appliances. The maquiladora workers are notoriously underpaid and their working conditions dangerous and degraded. The government virtually guarantees docile, company-controlled unions. Wages are roughly one-third those of Mexican industries that serve the home market.[17]

Proponents of NAFTA, arguing that it would create a middle-class market for U.S. goods rather than a supply of cheap labor to produce them, confidently predicted that the agreement would cause the maquiladora industries to disappear. Instead, employment in the maquiladoras more than doubled—from 550,000 to over 1.3 million at its peak in 2001.

The concentration of Mexico's post-NAFTA growth in the maquiladoras demonstrates the problem with the neoliberal development strategies that rely so heavily on exporting goods made with cheap labor. Sustained economic development requires "linkages" between core companies and local businesses that can supply components, materials, and services. But the Mexican maquiladora industries, set up exclusively to use low-wage labor to assemble imported components for the U.S. market, remain unconnected to local businesses, and therefore have not stimulated the rest of the Mexican economy. In 2001, only about one-tenth of the physical components and supplies for maquiladora products came from Mexico.[18]

The Mexican experience is similar to that of many other export zones set up in third world countries around the globe to take advantage of cheap labor. The raw materials and supplies and machinery are furnished by multinational firms and come from outside the country, so there is little transfer of technology. Often the factories are furnished free or highly subsidized by the host country, allowing multinationals to set up shop with limited commitments. When they find another place in the world where labor is cheaper and the subsidies even more generous, they leave. In this environment, there is little incentive for investors to start businesses that might supply the maquiladora-type industry. Nor is there much incentive for employers or workers to invest in upgrading skills. A 2000 report concluded that skilled labor was only 10 percent of the Mexican manufacturing labor force—compared with 14 percent in the overall economy.[19]

Meanwhile, the rest of Mexico's manufacturing sector, which produced largely for the domestic market and where wages were higher, actually shrunk, losing one hundred thousand jobs from 1993 to 2003. Thus, in effect, NAFTA shifted jobs from higher to lower wages within Mexico itself! The ostensible goal of neoliberalism in Mexico was to close the gap between U.S. and Mexican wages. Instead, it has widened it. In 1975, during the "bad old days" of Mexican isolationism and self-sufficiency, Mexican wages averaged about 23 percent of U.S. wages. In 1993–94, just before NAFTA was implemented, they were 15 percent. In 2002, they averaged 12 percent.[20]

In Mexico, as in Canada and the United States, globalization in general and NAFTA in particular shifted the interests of the investor class from supporting the social contract to ripping it up. Individually, of course, businesses are always seeking to lower costs. But as a class, when they depended on selling to the domestic market, they had to support Keynesian policies to maintain the growth in wages in order to provide Mexican consumers with the incomes to buy their goods and services. But to the extent that the customers were now in another country, the prime economic objective of the governing class became keeping wages as low as possible.

The experience also shows how difficult it is to break out of the trap of low-wage competition with the rest of the world. In 2001, the average wage in the maquiladora industries was below 10 percent of the average in U.S. manufacturing.[21] Still, maquiladora wages had risen 7 percent since 1993—enough to prompt the relocation, between 2002 and 2003, of some two hundred thousand jobs to China, where average wages were about 3 percent of U.S. wages.[22] In 2001, after seven years of NAFTA, Mexico became the second largest exporter to the American market, surpassing Japan. In 2003, China replaced Mexico in that role. (Canada is first.)

Two years after it bought Mr. Coffee in 1998, the Sunbeam Corporation shifted production from Cleveland, Ohio, where workers who make electric appliances earned more than $21 an hour, to Matamoros, Mexico, where they averaged $2.36. Three years after that, the company moved Mr. Coffee production to China, where they can hire labor at 47 cents an hour.[23]

One major reason for the post-NAFTA depression in Mexico's domestic manufacturing was that business credit dried up for small and medium-sized firms after foreign banks like Citigroup took over. Neoliberals claim that opening up third world economies to first world banks benefits local business because the foreigners have more money to lend, are more efficient, take more risks, and are insulated from local politics. But when multinational banks move into a third world country, they also tend to elbow the locals out of the best business, which is lending to the rich, the government, and the biggest multinational enterprises. This reduces the resources for local banks, which had used the revenues from their most profitable business to cover the risks and higher costs of lending to smaller businesses. Multinationals, having no commitment to the long-term development of the country, nor much expertise in assessing local risks, tend to skim the cream of the banking business and reduce the availability of credit.

In Mexico, when the ownership of almost 90 percent of Mexico's banking system was transferred to foreigners—largely U.S. and Spanish banks—bank lending to the private sector fell to 10 percent of GDP, compared with 30 percent in Brazil, a similar developing country, 52 percent in the United States, and 64 percent in Chile.[24]

Mexico's manufacturing workers had a similar experience to those in Canada and the United States. Between 1993 and 2001, their productivity rose 54 percent, while their real wages fell by 1 percent. In 1990 the richest 10 percent of Mexicans received 45.8 percent of the country's income. In 2000 they received 50.4 percent.

Models of Unreality

When pushed, NAFTA promoters tend to back off the claims that it brought jobs, higher wages, and growth. They say now that the real benefits from NAFTA flow to consumers as a result of lower prices. The newer version at least has the advantage of being in sync with some economic theory. In 2001, the Office of the U.S. Trade Representative estimated that the combined net benefits of NAFTA and the WTO amounted to $1,300 to $2,000 for a family of four. The op-ed pages of the *Financial Times*, the *Washington Post*, and other parts of the media echo chamber told their readers that this analysis proved the benefits of neoliberal trade agreements. Certainly this would be an impressive benefit—if there were much evidence to support it.

In fact, the claim was based not on a U.S. government study of the actual experience of the trade agreements but, like the studies cited by Bill Clinton at the 1993 White House meeting, an abstract model simulation, which simply assumes away unemployment, ignores the costs of dislocation, and generates nonsensical conclusions.

In this case, the model cited by the *Financial Times* reaches the bizarre conclusion that countries that export textiles and apparel benefit from U.S. and European Union trade barriers *against* their products. As economist Peter Dorman commented, the model's buoyant predictions for free trade "are like the rabbit pulled out of a hat: the trick works only because the rabbit was put into the hat to begin with."[25]

In 2004 the World Bank tried its hand. In a report called *Lesson from NAFTA for Latin American and Caribbean Countries*, the Bank's authors claimed that NAFTA added 0.5 to 0.7 percentage points to Mexico's growth rate. A later revision scaled the estimate back, but still contended that the net impact had been positive, basing it on a complex model of the Mexican economy.

But again, the model was clearly aimed at producing the desired result. Economists Mark Weisbrot, David Rosnick, and Dean Baker showed that the World Bank overestimated the size of the Mexican economy by a whopping 25 percent and chose a measure of the exchange rate of the peso in a way that artificially added 1 percent per year to its estimate of the country's growth. Moreover, and unacknowledged by the World Bank, the model actually predicted that by 2016, NAFTA will *lower* Mexico's per capita GDP by 4.3 percent.[26] Baker, who confronted the World Bank analysts with the critique, concluded that they did not even understand their own numbers. But the World Bank establishment retains control of the microphone of public debate, so the Bank continues to promote this analysis, whose fatal flaws the average journalist, scholar, and citizen have no way of knowing.

No doubt some Mexicans have benefited from cheaper prices of expensive U.S. and Canadian goods. But in a country where the poverty rate is above 50 percent, the basic cost of living for most people seems to have gotten worse. For example, in 1994 the minimum wage (currently $4.20 per day) bought 44.9 pounds of tortillas. In 2003 it bought 18.6 pounds. In 1994 it bought 24.5 liters of gas for cooking and heating. In 2003 it bought seven.[27]

Felicitas Rivera, a Mexico City maid, explained the economics to journalist Susan Ferriss. Rivera collects eight dollars a day, or about eighty pesos—almost double the minimum daily wage. But her earnings are spent as soon as she makes them—six pesos a day for bus fare for each of the three days she works; twenty-four pesos a day for her youngest child's bus fare to school; thirty pesos a day for the oldest child's bus fare to high school. That leaves twenty pesos a day to buy food and clothing and pay for any doctor's bills or medicine, since her family is among the 63 percent of the population with no health coverage."[28] Twenty pesos is less than two dollars per day.

In 1994, the poorest 40 percent of Mexican households earned 10.7 percent of all household income. By 2000 their share had fallen to 9.1 percent.[29] The poverty rate rose from 45.6 percent in 1994 to 50.3 percent in 2000. The share of Mexicans in extreme poverty, defined as people who cannot maintain the bare minimum of nutrition needed to remain healthy, rose from 27.9 to 31.9 percent. Since economic growth in Mexico was almost entirely dependent on exports to the United States, the recession that began in 2001 slowed growth in Mexico to a crawl, increasing joblessness and reducing living standards further.

During his 2000 campaign, Vicente Fox promised that under his six-year term the country would grow 7 percent per year. Three years after his inauguration, growth had averaged less than 1 percent. Growth picked up to 3 percent with the U.S. recovery but was still way below what was needed. Mexico needs a sustained growth rate of 5 to 6 percent just to create enough jobs to keep up with the increase in the working-age population. Not even the most optimistic business forecasters can see even that goal as reachable in the near future.

Optimists point out that Mexico's per capita income might improve as its population growth slows. Even so, at a growth rate of 4 percent per year, it will take two hundred years before average incomes in Mexico reach developed-country levels.

Voting with Their Feet

The most convincing judgment on NAFTA, however, comes from Mexicans themselves, who continue to cross the border in large numbers because they can't support themselves and their families at home.

Between the U.S. Censuses of 1990 and 2000, the number of Mexican-born residents in the United States grew by more than 80 percent.[30] Some half million Mexicans now migrate to the United States every year—roughly 60 percent of whom are undocumented. The numbers are even more remarkable when you consider the massive increase in border security that began in 1993 and was stepped up further after September 11, 2001. In 2004, U.S. immigration officials apprehended 1.1 million people along the border, a 24 percent increase over the year before, and still they come.[31]

The decision to migrate illegally is not one taken lightly. Mexican families are particularly close-knit. Most people everywhere are reluctant to leave their country, and do so only when their lives at home become intolerable. Then there is the cost—$2,000 for a "coyote" to take them across. And there are risks far beyond just being caught by the border patrol. In the past five years, more than sixteen hundred migrants have died on the journey to the north. In May 2002, nineteen Mexican immigrants were found asphyxiated in an abandoned trailer truck near Houston. But even such gruesome events are no deterrent. A Mexican neighbor of one of the dead young men put it simply: "If you are going to improve your life, you need to go to the United States."[32]

The response of the governing classes, in both Mexico and the United States, to the obvious failure of NAFTA to live up to its promise was not, of course, to reflect on the mistaken assumptions of their original argument. Instead, they are now promoting Mexican migration to the United States—the problem that NAFTA was supposed to address—as the new *solution* for Mexico's problems. In Washington think-tank seminars and conferences, the immigration "problem" is how to make it easier for Mexican workers to cross the border and, once here, remain here. Thus the new solution to illegal immigration is to legalize it. Among those making this case is Mack McLarty, one of the prime movers of NAFTA in the Clinton White House, who recently cochaired a prestigious working group on immigration. McLarty now tells us, "Free trade will not substantially moderate pressures for migration as long as the social and economic fundamentals continue to encourage movement."[33] These "fundamentals" are unemployment and low wages in Mexico—exactly the problems that McLarty and company promised NAFTA would solve.

Unfazed by the utter failure of their assurances that NAFTA would resolve the problem of illegal immigration, the governing class now defines the issue as a domestic question. The Bush administration proposes to establish a temporary guest-worker program that would allow U.S. employers to import Mexican workers. Immigrants would become captive labor; bosses could hire them from Mexico to undercut the bargaining position of U.S. workers, and in the event the guests are rude enough to ask for a raise, the immigration service can send them back and get fresh recruits. In opposition, Democrats propose amnesty and guest-worker programs with less restriction.

As always, the rationale is that guest workers would only be available for jobs that Americans did not want. The theory of the market, of course, is that if there are not enough workers for hard or distasteful jobs, employers should raise their wages. After all, everyone accepts that if there are too many workers for a job, it is natural that employers lower the wage. But among the governing class, fealty to the law of supply and demand weakens when it discomforts capital.

Vicente Fox, former CEO of Coca-Cola Mexico and unreconstructed champion of NAFTA, now refers to Mexican migrants in the United States as "heroes" because their remittances to their families ran at perhaps some $17 billion in 2004, constituting the country's second largest source of hard-currency earnings.[34]

It is obvious that Mexico cannot develop by sending its most ambitious and industrious workers to the United States. It is not the poorest and least educated who migrate; it is the working-class risk-takers who, once in the United States, sacrifice to send home their exploitation wages. Mexico needs these people. It paid for the cost of their upbringing and education, in effect subsidizing U.S. consumers of low-wage work.

Precisely because these are ambitious people, keeping them at home might cause trouble for the Mexican governing class. They might become restless in an economy in which the rich are getting steadily richer, the middle class is getting nowhere, and the poor are falling further behind. Indeed, for Mexico's oligarchs, the public focus on the condition of Mexican workers in the United States has the great virtue of diverting political attention from the condition of Mexican workers in Mexico.

NAFTA's Penalty for Mistreating Workers: Nothing

Ten years later it was clear that the NAFTA side agreements on labor, designed to provide Bill Clinton with political cover, were, as Mexican finance minister Jaime Serra Puche said they would be, "meaningless."

Unlike NAFTA's multiple protections of investor rights, the labor side agreement—the North American Agreement on Labor Cooperation (NAALC)—did not establish any labor standards at all. Instead, it set up a complex bureaucratic procedure to respond to complaints that any of the three countries were not enforcing their own labor laws, which they retained the right to alter at any time.

The side agreement classifies violations of labor laws into three groups. Group 1 consists of violations of the right to organize, bargain collectively, and strike. Group 2 includes forced labor, discrimination, failure to compensate for injuries, and protections of migrant labor. Group 3 covers violations of a country's own laws on child labor, minimum wage, and occupational injuries.

The ultimate penalty for Group 1 violations is that the labor ministers meet and talk. That's it. The penalty for Group 2 violations is that ministers talk and a committee of experts evaluate. That's it. On paper, the ultimate penalty for Group 3 violations is a fine or sanctions. But the process of filing a complaint is arduous, expensive, and time-consuming. It is beyond the capacity of the overwhelming majority of workers to even dream of attempting. While each government has the right to bring a suit against another, none has ever done so. By March 2004, a decade after NAFTA went into effect, twenty-eight complaint briefs had been filed to the NAALC, fifteen accepted, and none gotten any further than to be a subject of a chat among labor ministers.

Yet the brutal exploitation of workers in Mexico has been well documented, as has the widespread complicity of the Mexican authorities in suppressing workers' wages as well as their civil rights. The cases that, with great effort on the part of a few brave workers and their lawyers, have even been allowed to be placed in the NAALC filing cabinets are but the tip of a very large iceberg of abuse. Still, they are revealing.

A Mexican worker testified in 1995 that she and others had attempted to organize an independent union because the company she worked for refused to supply filters to protect them from paint fumes and required them to work seven days a week. The Zedillo government's response was to issue an arrest warrant for her. The charge was "destabilizing the maquiladora industry." She fled to the United States and filed a complaint. The investigation concluded that, indeed, the Mexican government had failed to abide by its own law. The investigation resulted in the most severe "penalty" possible—it was put on the agenda when the labor secretaries of both countries had a brief meeting. Nothing was done about the abuses of workers at the plant.[35]

Another complaint was brought against the Han Young factory in Tijuana.[36] Han Young is a Korean-owned firm that supplies chassis to the nearby Hyundai truck factory, owned by Hyundai of San Diego, California, a subsidiary of Hyundai of Korea. Like many firms in Mexico, Han Young's managers had signed a "protection contract" with a labor union allied with the Mexican government. Protection contracts are the rule in Mexico. The union leadership receives generous payments from the company and in return enforces labor discipline, by force if necessary, using its own thugs and the local and national police. Workers often do not know the name of the union that takes its dues out of their paychecks, and when they ask, are told it is none of their business. According to one estimate, less than 10 percent of the labor agreements in the country are actually negotiated, and practically none among maquiladora factories.

In June 1997, working conditions at Han Young had become intolerable, even by Mexican standards. Wages were low and workers were constantly worried about being cheated in their pay. Health and safety problems had become the norm—heavy electrical cables carrying 440 volts snaking through standing pools of water on the factory floor, malfunctioning overhead cranes, no ventilation, and filthy bathrooms alive with pathogenic microorganisms. The managers at Han Young violated Mexico's own labor laws in every category identified in the NAALC side agreement. Mexican government inspectors routinely filed reports detailing the violations that were never acted on. When one worker complained to his "union" representative, he was told, "Well, if you were paying me, then I would help you. But you do not pay me. The one who pays me is the company."

When workers decided to form their own independent union, they were fired, harassed, beaten, and arrested. They finally forced an election, where they were obliged to cast votes openly, under the watchful eyes of their bosses, the local police, and government union thugs. After the government announced that it would not check the credentials to see if those voting actually worked at the plant, truckloads of strangers bused in by the government union showed up to cast ballots. Even so, the dissident union won the election, only to have the government refuse to certify them. When the workers went out on strike the government declared it illegal and police were sent to rip down the strike signs and arrest the leaders.

The publicity finally reached Washington, where Democratic members of Congress David Bonior and Richard Gephardt used it in 1997 as an example of NAFTA's failure during the debate over the renewal of "fast track" authority. As a result, the case rose to the highest level of review provided by the "side agreements"; it was on the agenda during a meeting between U.S. secretary of labor Alexis Herman and Mexican labor secretary Mariano Palacios Alcocer. The penalty? The Mexican government agreed to hold two public seminars explaining its own laws to its citizens. The first, "A Seminar on Union Freedom in Mexico," was held in Tijuana two months later. The room was packed with people on the payroll of the official government union. When the workers on strike from the Han Young plant entered, they were attacked, beaten, and driven outside in full view of four officials of the U.S. Department of Labor. Nothing was done.

The persistent suppression of independent collective bargaining in Mexico is even routinely noted by the passive U.S. Labor Department office responsible for monitoring the labor side agreement. In September 2004, it issued a report in which it concluded, "The continued difficulty for independent unions to gain registration rights, especially in the maquiladora sector, is supported by credible testimony of non-governmental organizations and legal experts within Mexico . . . if [the government of Mexico] has taken action to address the matter, the results are not immediately evident."[37] There was no danger that this would be picked up by the media.

Abuse the Environment and Face Publication of a "Factual Record"

Like its labor counterpart, the environmental side agreement is aimed simply at getting each nation to enforce its own environmental laws through disclosure that the laws are being violated. From 1995 through 2002, thirty-nine complaints were filed. Of these, four reached the final stage of resolution—publication of a "factual record." This of course is no one's idea of environmental protection, and it is no surprise that the side agreements have had little impact.

Supporters of NAFTA had argued in 1993 that the environment would benefit from the agreement because economic growth actually was benign for the environment. Papers circulating at the World Bank and other neoliberal habitats maintained that, after initially making pollution worse, over time economic growth would reduce it.

The evidence for this assertion is at best mixed. Over time, growth does encourage the use of more efficient and thus less polluting machinery and a shift to service industries. But rising income also increases automobile use and sprawl, which generates more greenhouse gases. Environmental consciousness may increase with incomes, or it may not, depending on the willingness of the political system to impose regulation and planning of waste disposal, transportation, and energy systems.

Leaving aside the argument's dubious assumption that NAFTA would increase economic growth, one big problem in applying this theory to Mexico was that the data seemed to show that the threshold above which growth is benign occurs when per capita income reaches $5,000 per year. But Mexico had already reached $5,000 in per capita income in 1985, and few could make the case in 1993 that Mexico had become more environmentally protective during the previous eight years.

Ten years later, Mexico's environment had become more polluted, not less. In fact, the Mexican government's own numbers showed that the increased costs to the national economy from pollution were more than $36 billion per year—far larger than any possible economic gains from overall economic growth from whatever the source. The response? Rather than increase its efforts at environmental protection, the Mexican government reduced its spending, cutting the actual number of environmental inspections by 45 percent.[38]

Neoliberalism did not create Mexico's environmental degradation. Growth there was unregulated before the neoliberal reforms began in the 1980s. But neoliberalism and NAFTA exacerbated the problem by further unbalancing the country's economy. As a result of NAFTA, the border boomed, flooding the area with people and industrial pollution well beyond the capacity of the weak public sector to accommodate it without massive environmental damage. At the same time, worsening poverty forced the desperate inhabitants who remained on the land into deforestation and other abuses.

Bill Clinton had argued in 1993, "If NAFTA is not implemented, incentives will continue under the maquiladoras to locate facilities in the border areas, thus exacerbating environmental pressures on the border, such as loss of habitat, adverse impacts to endangered and threatened species, and reductions in groundwater levels."[39] In fact, NAFTA concentrated more growth on the border, with maquiladora employment doubling in seven years. Migrants from economically stagnant central and southern Mexico overwhelmed the already inadequate housing, health, and public safety infrastructure, spreading shantytowns and water and air pollution. Unregulated by local governments, the new factories dumped toxic waste into creeks and onto the land, contaminating the environment and poisoning the public health. Since NAFTA the incidence of tuberculosis, hepatitis, and encephalitis has soared.

In rural areas, the shift from small farming to large-scale chemical-intensive corporate agribusiness did further damage. Water consumption rose because crops for export like fresh fruits and vegetables take 20 to 30 percent more groundwater than crops grown only for the domestic market. With large-scale farming comes more ground pollution from waste and chemical runoff, and the biodiversity of the land diminishes.

The record is not totally bleak. The shift of production to Mexico often involved upgrading to more efficient—and less polluting—machinery and equipment. For example, energy today is probably used more efficiently by cement firms in Mexico than those in the United States.[40] Cross-border cooperation created by the environmental side agreement has led to some improvements in the collection and harmonization of environmental data, and somewhat greater access by the public. And in all three countries the last twenty years have seen an increase in environmental awareness—which would have been the case with or without NAFTA.

NAFTA's promoters sometimes argue that the agreement is a success because it did not lead to the overwhelming disaster that some opponents predicted—in this case, turning Mexico into a "pollution haven," with firms fleeing the United States for the less regulated Mexico. Like the argument that there was no "giant sucking sound" of jobs moving south, it is a straw man. While for most companies the cost of environmental regulations does not weigh as heavily on location decision as, say, the cost of labor, for some it does. When any company is making a decision on where to locate, it will add up all the costs and benefits involved. The benefits of moving to Mexico where environmental laws are weaker and less enforced may tip the scales or they may not, but like any other costs they will be a factor.

Over the long run, perhaps the most important potential threat to the environment comes from NAFTA's radical Chapter 11, which gives investors extraordinary powers to sue governments over regulations that may be construed as "tantamount to expropriation." This provision was used ten times between 1994 and 2003 to challenge environmental regulations. Among the cases, the U.S. Metalclad Corporation successfully sued Mexico for $16 million when a local government tried to block the construction of a toxic-waste processing plant. A Canadian firm, Methanex, is suing the U.S. government because California banned the company's foul-smelling gasoline additive that contaminated thirty public water systems and thirty-five hundred groundwater sites in the state. The Ethyl Corporation forced the Canadian government to rescind its ban on another gasoline additive.

Democracy Shortchanged

In 1993, Democrat Bill Clinton asserted that NAFTA was "good for democracy in Mexico."[41] A decade later, Republican Robert Zoellick echoed the claim. "Economic freedom creates habits of liberty and habits of liberty create expectations of democracy."[42]

As Catherine Dalpino, a scholar at the very internationalist Brookings Institution, observes, the assumption that market deregulation brings forth democracy leads some members of the first world policy class to claim that they can trick third world authoritarian regimes with "bait and switch" tactics—in other words, that the promise of economic benefits from neoliberalism will lure authoritarian elites into accepting changes that will ultimately doom them. On the question of whether such globalization brings democracy, Dalpino concludes that "the evidence is mixed and will continue to be so for some time."[43]

Does the evidence even matter? No doubt some trusting souls in the American governing class really have thought that they were hoodwinking oppressive ruling elites into democracy by making them richer and more powerful. But it is hard to believe that the relentless drive to open up third world economies by the Republicans and Democrats who have run the federal government over the last twenty years was motivated by such naïveté.

In Mexico's case, the political motivation for NAFTA was to strangle democracy in its cradle—to reinforce the PRI, which was widely believed to have stolen the election of 1988 against the dissident movement headed by Cuauhtémoc Cárdenas. The election that had frightened the elites of Mexico City had also alarmed the elites of Washington. There is no other credible explanation for the massive campaign to sell Carlos Salinas—whose loyalty to the antidemocratic PRI was beyond doubt and whose administration was riddled with corruption—to Congress and the American people as a democratic reformer.

Salinas himself never hid his own disdain for democracy. As Roderic Ai Camp, a scholar of Mexican society, notes, Mexico's "political power elites' emphasis on neoliberal economic solutions to the neglect of democratization was the result of their benefiting from the existing political model. In other words, they were a product of those authoritarian institutions, and instead of rejecting them outright, they hoped to enhance their effectiveness through better-managed economic solutions."[44]

Still, the decade since NAFTA has seen political change in Mexico. The most dramatic, of course, was the election of Vicente Fox, which broke the PRI's seventy-year hold on the presidency. Mexico still cannot be considered a democratic society and the old authoritarian ways remain embedded, but throughout the country in a variety of institutions—the press, courts, labor unions, and schools—there has been an unmistakable opening up of the society to wider participation and a greater willingness to challenge arbitrary power.

In one sense, the opening up of the Mexican economy to the global market did have a positive impact on democracy. But it was not because of neoliberalism's economic success, but its *failure*.

As the *New York Times* reporters Julia Preston and Samuel Dillon observe in their book *Opening Mexico*, resistance to the authoritarian rule of the PRI had been growing since the early 1960s when intellectuals like Octavio Paz and Carlos Fuentes began openly criticizing the regime in newspapers and magazines.[45] The 1968 massacre of several hundred protesting students in the Tlatelolco neighbor-hood of the university and a similar incident in 1971 that killed twenty-nine students revealed the ruthless violence that underlay the perfect dictatorship of the PRI. The resistance spread beyond the rad-ical upper-class intellectuals. By the mid-1970s armed guerrilla move-ments were operating in the mountains of several Mexican states.

So long as the economy was growing, the PRI was able to keep discontent with its harsh rule at bay. It was the long recession that accompanied the neoliberal response to the peso crisis of 1982 that drove the electorate to its 1988 revolt.

The Bush-Clinton effort to keep the PRI in power temporarily succeeded. With the international press lauding Salinas as a miracle worker, the PRI presented itself in the 1994 election as having found the key to permanent prosperity. The election was not clean. The PRI machine in the countryside was entrenched and not ready to give up its habits. This writer personally witnessed police intimi-dation and violations of the secret ballot in several rural polling places on election day, and the PRI used all of its considerable power to control the news and raise enormous sums of money. Still, compared to the previous elections, the 1994 vote was the most open and hon-est in the country's history. Even the losers understood that some-thing was changing, and Zedillo's victory, with 49 percent of the vote, was accepted.

But the engine of democratic change would have continued its slow pace were it not for the failure of the PRI neoliberals to revive the economy. The voters had given the PRI "reformers" one last chance in 1994, and when the subsequent peso crisis drove Mexico into a deep recession a year later, the voters finally turned on them. In the next elections for the Mexican Congress, in 1997, the rightist PAN and the leftist PRD together gained 261 seats in the lower house to 239 seats for the PRI. Several governorships and the may-oralty of Mexico City went to the opposition. And three years later, PAN candidate Vicente Fox, the tall, handsome former president of Coca-Cola in Mexico, won the presidential election, breaking the PRI's seventy-one-year hold on the national government.

Ernesto Zedillo's instincts were hardly democratic. At a news conference in his first year, a reporter asked Zedillo to comment on a rumor that he was going to resign. Zedillo was so angered that he had the reporter fired and refused to give another press conference for the remaining five years of his term.[46]

At the same time Zedillo—a technocrat outsider to the oligarch families that managed Mexico—helped facilitate Mexico's path to democracy by declining to obstruct some democratic advances that previous Mexican presidents would have stopped dead in their tracks, especially those that threatened to erode PRI's monopoly on power. Thus, for example, the agency that monitored elections was able to prescribe a new standard size for a polling booth so that only one person could fit, eliminating the habit of the local PRI official going into the booth with the voter. And the longtime practice of government payments to journalists for favorable treatment was sharply curtailed. For these and other acts, Zedillo paved the way for Fox's historic victory over the PRI in 2000, for which many PRI-istas will never forgive him.

A freer and more aggressive press has further cleared space for the task of dealing with the corruption that pervades Mexican officialdom. But at the same time, the threat to democracy from the corruption and violence associated with the drug trade has grown. As the business grows so does the competition among the narcotraffickers. Scarcely a day goes by without news stories of drug-related murder and mayhem.

Vicente Fox and many American officials downplay the mushrooming violence as something limited to drug traffickers who operate on the margins of society. But, as everywhere, the corruption associated with the drug business undermines the political institutions' ability to keep order and sustain individual freedoms. Crime and corruption are fungible. People who come to, or stay in, power in association with criminals are likely to extend the habit to other parts of their work. And powerful criminals commonly do not limit their influence just to the economic sector that supports them.

For years law enforcement has been hampered by the fact that Mexican police have always been underpaid, with the expectation that they can augment their salaries with shakedowns of small businesses, automobile drivers, and other informal "taxes" on the public. The growing opportunities for extra income from the drug dealers have further undermined the professionalism and credibility of law enforcement.

The corruption of local police has led to a growing antidrug role for the Mexican National Police, whose subsequent susceptibility to bribery led to the involvement of the military, which accelerated under the Fox regime. The United States has been a major supporter of the effort. As one of many reports has concluded: "With U.S. funds, weapons, training and advisors, the Mexican armed forces have taken over the most important areas in the federal justice system under the pretext of the war on drugs."[47] Pitched gun battles have been fought between local police and the armed forces and entire police departments have been arrested.

Not surprisingly, the corruption has spread to the military. Generals and officers have been arrested, and in one case more than six hundred soldiers in an infantry battalion were held, eleven of their officers arraigned for protecting poppy and marijuana crops.[48]

On December 10, 1996, U.S. general Barry McCaffrey, whom Bill Clinton appointed America's drug czar, warmly endorsed the Mexican general Jesús Gutiérrez Rebollo, whom Ernesto Zedillo had appointed as McCaffrey's Mexican counterpart. "From the ambassador and his team we know a lot about General Gutiérrez Rebollo," McCaffrey told the press. "He's a serious soldier. A very focused guy. He's spent most of his life in field command, the last seven years out in Guadalajara. He's a guy of absolute unquestioned integrity."[49]

That very same day, the general and his mistress moved into an expensive Mexico City apartment courtesy of one of the country's biggest drug traffickers. Nine weeks later he was arrested. Drug officials in Washington suspect that, among other things, General Rebollo had leaked the names of drug informants who were subsequently murdered.[50]

But the arrests—many of which seem suspiciously like one drug faction using the law to remove competition from another—have not put a dent in the flow of drugs. Mexico provides two-thirds of the cocaine that enters the United States every year, one-quarter of the heroin, and most of the marijuana. The continued low street prices for all of these drugs indicate that the supply continues to match if not outpace demand.

Moreover, the business of importing drugs into the United States from Mexico has now been joined to the business of exporting guns from the United States to Mexico. Like other shipping firms, narcotrafficking organizations look for opportunities to profitably fill up the otherwise empty cars and trucks and airplanes on the return trip. "Drugs go north and guns go south," reporter John Burnett told National Public Radio in May 2005. "Many of the drug runners who bring narcotics north will then hide a gun or a disassembled gun in a hidden compartment in his pickup truck and then take it south." The weaponry, which includes assault rifles, grenades, and grenade launchers, Burnett explained, then escalates the cartel wars and their civilian casualties—such as a radio crime reporter in Nuevo Laredo who had recently been assassinated.[51]

In the end, Fox, despite the party differences, was a loyal member of the same governing class that Salinas and Zedillo belonged to. Like them, and like Clinton and the Bushes, like Mulroney and Chrétien, his first priority was to the future as defined by his business supporters. So when in December 2002 the desperate farmers came to Mexico City demanding that the agriculture chapter of NAFTA be revised, they were told to shut up, because the Mexican government no longer had control of its economy. In order to change NAFTA they would need the approval of the United States and Canada. On cue, the U.S. and Canadian ambassadors weighed in on the debate and told the Mexican farmers to forget it. For good measure, J. B. Penn, the U.S. undersecretary of agriculture, lectured the Mexican government that any strategy for protecting its farmers "should focus on rural structural reforms and not in constructing barriers to trade."[52] Structural reform, of course, was itself the euphemism for getting small farmers off the land as rapidly as possible.

In the face of this arrogant response, the governor of Veracruz commented that unfortunately NAFTA was now "above the Constitution."[53]

The limits of post-NAFTA democracy were revealed again in April 2005 when the combined PRI/PAN majority in the Mexican Congress brazenly colluded to destroy the presidential candidacy of André Manuel López Obrador, the popular PRD mayor of Mexico City who for more than a year had been leading all other candidates in the polls. The PRI/PAN coalition voted to order the attorney general to indict the mayor on an unsubstantiated and very minor charge. But the effort backfired when almost a million people came to his defense at a dramatic rally in Mexico City. The frightened Fox backed off, broke with the PRI, fired his attorney general, and promised not to deny López Obrador a place on the ballot.

The episode revealed two things about Mexican democracy: first, the determination of millions of Mexicans to keep from returning to the old days, when the PRI ruled through sham elections; second, that the system is still run from the top down. Fox simply annulled an act of Congress in order to protect his political hide. Clearly, the rule of constitutional law in Mexico still needed some refining.

The Mexican people clearly would prefer to live in a democracy. In a 2004 survey, 79 percent supported the statement that while democracy has problems it is the best system of government, and 60 percent responded that they would never accept a military dictatorship. On the other hand, 67 percent said that it wasn't important to them that a government was not democratic if it was solving the country's economic problems. To the question of whether their country was being run by powerful interests for their own benefit, 75 percent said yes. Finally, were they satisfied with the way democracy was functioning? Eighteen percent said they were—up from 11 percent in 1996, down from 36 percent in 2000.

8

The Constitution According to Davos

We are no longer writing the rules of interaction among separate national economies. We are writing the constitution of a single global economy.

—Renato Ruggiero, director-general of the
World Trade Organization, 1995

Renato Ruggiero got the job Carlos Salinas had wanted: head of the new World Trade Organization. Ruggiero had been Italy's trade minister and a member of the board of directors of Fiat and other European and American companies. He later became Italy's foreign minister under Silvio Berlusconi and then chair of Citigroup's Swiss subsidiary; he is obviously a member of the transnational corporate elite in very good standing. So his use of the word "constitution"— with its implication of world government—was a little shocking to his peers, who in public at least like to associate free trade with less, not more government. Like a reference to sex at a Victorian dinner table by an otherwise respectable gentleman, Ruggiero's remarks were resolutely ignored by the global business media, whose public commentary acts as a Greek chorus for free-market fundamentalism.

Yet Ruggiero was simply acknowledging the obvious. The creation of an integrated global economy is a quantum jump from the mere regulation of trade among nations. Integrated markets require common rules and policies that reach deeply into the domestic economies from which they are constructed. Standards must be set in accounting, finance, safety, technological interfaces, the translation of contract language, and thousands of other areas in order for markets to merge efficiently. Macroeconomic monetary and fiscal systems must be established with a worldwide scope in order to prevent capitalist markets' inevitable downturns from turning into panics and depressions. Inevitably, global rules and policies will limit the sovereignty of individual governments over their own internal economies, and therefore the lives of their citizens. In order to give legitimacy to the necessary rules, regulations, and policies, an integrated global market inevitably requires some sort of global constitution.

Constitutions are not interest-free. The Constitution of the United States reflected the powerful economic interests of the time—slaveholders, to name one example. Therefore, we should not expect the people in charge of writing the global constitution to ignore their own interests in establishing the rules for "who gets what."

We Are the World . . . Wide Investor Class

Economic growth under capitalism is a process, as the great economist Joseph Schumpeter put it, of "creative destruction." Expanding businesses feed on the carcasses of contracting ones. If there are winners, there must be losers. So when the governing class tells us that free trade agreements are "win-win," they cannot mean that every *person* or firm wins, but rather that every *country* wins. This, of course, is the famous theory of comparative advantage. When each country specializes in what it does best, all countries benefit from the overall greater efficiency.

The lesson of NAFTA, reflecting economic common sense, is that globalization makes national economies inadequate as the sole or even primary measure of the international allocation of costs and benefits. Both the American, Robert Rubin, and the Mexican, Roberto Hernandez Ramirez, were winners as a result of NAFTA. Aaron Kemp, an American who lost his job at Maytag, and Salvador Chavez, a Mexican who lost his life crossing the border, were losers.[1]

As globalization integrates investors, managers, and professionals across borders, it merges their class interests across those same borders. The negotiations over NAFTA revealed the common interests of members of the three countries' business classes, who also compete against each other. This is not surprising. In the integrated economy of the United States, bankers in New York, Chicago, and Los Angeles certainly compete with each other. But they also work together. They merge, buy and sell each other's companies, and have career paths that include jobs at each other's banks. When they go to conventions, retreats, and seminars of the American Bankers Association they discuss strategies to change the law, to keep labor at bay, to get their men and women into key jobs at the U.S. Treasury, all to promote the well-being of bankers and the large corporate class of which they are a part. The same is obviously true of other industries, professional societies and labor unions, and other interest groups. It would be strange if that were not the case.

The existence of a cross-border corporate investor class implies the existence of a global working class and civil society as well. But the investor class is organized globally. The working class is not. Therefore the corporate investor class is protected in the global marketplace and the working class and its environment are not.

During the debate over NAFTA, promoters argued that unrestricted trade with Mexico was little different from the unrestricted trade among individual American states. Michigan, after all, trades freely with Mississippi, and both benefit. But what made this work is that after years of bitter conflict, the U.S. Constitution has been interpreted to include federal protections for workers as well as capitalists. Minimum wages, health and safety standards, and other rights of working citizens apply in all states. In contrast, the constitution of the global economy recognizes and protects only one citizen—the corporate investor. The rights of other human beings are excluded from the global rules and left to the protection of nation-states, whose authority stops at their borders.

The failure to acknowledge who is protected and who is not confuses much of the public discussion of "free trade" versus "protectionism" among both citizens and the governing class itself. On the one hand, pundits declare that international *economics* has obliterated borders, making national leaders helpless to resist the dictates of a leaderless herd of stateless corporate CEOs, investment fund managers, and rich investors. On the other, they explain international *politics* as relations between sovereign countries, defined in much the same way as they have been since the 1648 Treaty of Westphalia, which established the nation-state as the principal actor in the drama of international relations. The nightly news shows us images of diplomats meeting, presidents holding joint press conferences, and country representatives deliberating at the UN, the International Monetary Fund, the World Bank, and so forth, all presumably pursuing their "national interests" in competition with each other, even as the process of globalization is systematically shattering those national communities of interest.

The lack of a language that accurately reflects the evolving class politics of the global market hardly seems accidental. Just as the discussion of economic class is resolutely ridiculed by the *national* media as some loony "conspiracy theory," the idea of a *global* governing economic class with its own interests is similarly dismissed in the echo chambers of the international punditry. As the experience of NAFTA shows, it clearly serves the interests of the rich and powerful to maintain the impression that those who manage the nation-state and those who manage transnational corporations represent separate, even antagonistic worlds, in which they act as a check and constraint on each other. No conspiracy here, insist the world's rich and powerful, we're all just part of the electronic herd that no one is in charge of—just the market.

Yet, like all suppressed truth, the existence of a global class structure gets revealed in unguarded moments. A few years ago at the Council on Foreign Relations in New York, an agitated retired State Department official shouted at the luncheon speaker. "What you don't understand," he said, "is that when we negotiate economic agreements with these poorer countries, we are negotiating with people from the same class. That is, people whose interests are like ours."

"Anyone Who Thinks the WTO Agreement Expands Free Trade Hasn't Read It"

A year after Bill Clinton drove NAFTA over the bodies of his political allies, and just weeks after the Democratic Party lost control of the House of Representatives for the first time in four decades, the Clinton/Republican coalition convinced Congress to approve a vastly expanded worldwide version of NAFTA—the World Trade Organization.

For a dozen years, the governing classes of the world's major economies had been discussing the transformation of the General Agreement on Tariffs and Trade (GATT) from a forum for negotiating tariffs to a regulator of an integrated global economy. Whether it went forward or not depended entirely on the willingness of the U.S. Congress to approve a diminishment of American sovereignty.

So, fresh from their NAFTA triumph, the transnational corporate networks mobilized to drive the WTO through Congress. The Business Roundtable, the National Association of Manufacturers, and the Chamber of Commerce combined under the banner of the Alliance for GATT Now, run by the chief lobbyist for Texas Instruments. Its members were the nation's biggest corporations in finance, pharmaceuticals, computers and high-tech, autos, chemicals, aerospace, retailers, liquor, furniture, motion pictures, and food processing.

Members of the publishing industry such as Gannett, Times Mirror, Capital Cities/ABC, McGraw-Hill, and Time Warner overwhelmingly promoted the WTO in their newspapers and magazines. The Alliance for GATT Now hired former congressmen Tom Downey (D-NY) and Vin Weber (R-MN) as honorary chairs. As during the NAFTA debate, Downey and Weber were presented by National Public Radio as representing opposing views of liberals and conservatives on a weekly program broadcast.

Within the White House, Rubin and McLarty were the leading players. Democrat Anne Wexler ran the "grassroots" campaign of the Business Roundtable, organizing 220 CEOs to lobby lawmakers from states and districts in which their business facilities were located. Boeing spoke for the aerospace industry and Washington State, Monsanto for chemicals and Missouri, and Warner-Lambert for pharmaceuticals and New Jersey. As with NAFTA, the Democratic administration did the heavy lifting. "You have to imagine the Alice in Wonderland quality of this," a frustrated administration official told the *New York Times*. "Here we are, trying to figure out how to get business leaders to put pressure on Republicans to vote for something Reagan championed and Bush almost implemented."[2]

Once again, the administration promoted the WTO as a means of generating political stability in the world, jobs, and prosperity. "It is critical for U.S. leadership in the world," said Clinton. Added the vice president gravely, "Should Congress fail, history will frown upon us."[3] And they rolled the opposition again.

The WTO agreement was some twenty-five thousand pages long, assuring that no one would read it or understand the entire document to which they were committing the nation's sovereignty and economic future. "The fact is," one government economist admitted to the *Times*, "we are all shooting in the dark."[4]

Some of the special interests promoted in the legislation were blatant. For example, the WTO bill contained a provision to grant operating licenses worth $1.6 billion to a cell phone company 70 percent of which was owned by the fiercely pro-WTO *Washington Post*. Days before the buried subsidy was exposed, one of the *Post*'s many editorials urging swift passage of the bill proclaimed that it "contains no surprises, no provisions that have not been amply discussed."[5]

In the weeks before the vote on the WTO, Ralph Nader challenged any member of Congress to read the agreement and then answer ten questions posed by an independent journalist. He offered to give $10,000 to the member's favorite charity if he answered the questions correctly. Senator Hank Brown, a Republican from Colorado, who was prepared to vote for the WTO, took up Nader's challenge. He scored 100 on the test, and after reading the agreement, voted against it. "Anyone who thinks this agreement expands free trade," he said, "has not read it."[6]

As with NAFTA, there was no pressing problem that needed to be solved by the creation of the WTO. The world already had a system for negotiating freer trade. Under the GATT, trade among the member noncommunist nations had grown steadily since the end of World War II. Rather, like NAFTA, the major purpose of the WTO was to expand the freedom and strengthen the bargaining power of transnational investors.

The WTO restricts governments' ability to regulate the behavior of multinational business and weakens the public sector's capacity to provide protections and services for its citizens. The core principle of the WTO is not free trade among sovereign states. It is, as Peter Sutherland, GATT director, said in 1994, that in every state, "Governments should interfere in the conduct of the economy as little as possible."[7]

The WTO forbids all governments to condition foreign investment on the purchase of supplies from domestic businesses or to
prohibit the entry of certain products that its scientists deem unsafe
or its people believe immoral (for example, produced with child
labor). The WTO protects patent monopolies of multinational corporations and prohibits laws protecting workers and the environment or public health that interfere with the freedom of corporations to invest, buy, and sell. As with NAFTA, disputes are settled by
secret tribunals primarily chosen from the global fraternity of international lawyers and consultants who are not required to reveal any
conflict of interest.

In one instance, the former head of GATT, who was a board
member at Nestlé, was appointed to a WTO tribunal on a case in
which the company had a direct interest. When a conflict of interest
was exposed by the U.S. nongovernmental organization Public Citizen, the Office of the U.S. Trade Representative said it was unaware
of his background.[8]

The language of the WTO, like the language of NAFTA, is "constitutional." It sets up supranational governance with powers to override what had previously been the province of sovereign states. As
professor Stephen Clarkson notes, both NAFTA and the WTO perform the traditional role of constitutions. They entrench certain in-
violate principles or norms that are above the reach of any national
legislature to alter; set limits on the behavior of governments; define
rights of citizenship; establish a judicial system to interpret its own
texts in the case of conflicts; and provide for enforcement of the
court's decisions. The "nullification and impairment" section of the
WTO allows corporations to challenge the laws of any country that
can be shown to impair the benefits that the corporation could
expect to receive under the WTO. Using this provision, the government of Canada, on behalf of its asbestos industry, has brought suit
against France for its domestic ban on the use of asbestos.[9]

While the corporate lobby did not succeed in getting all of its
NAFTA-style privileges negotiated with the 147 countries in the
WTO, it did succeed in excluding from the WTO the fig leaf of the
NAFTA side agreements. In 1996, when Bill Clinton was running
for election and needed all the help he could get from the U.S. trade
unions, his administration proposed at a WTO meeting in Singapore

that the WTO establish a committee to study the relationship between workers' rights and trade.[10] The WTO delegates understood
that the effort was political window dressing. No arms would be
twisted. So, although the WTO already had eighteen "committees,"
four "working parties," five "working groups," and one "body" for
a wide variety of economic issues, the trade ministers refused to find
room for even a committee to discuss labor. Instead, they officially
declared that labor rights were not their problem, but rather were
under the jurisdiction of the International Labor Organization. The
ILO, a tripartite organization governed by representatives of government, business, and labor, is, by its very structure, not an aggressive
advocate of labor rights and has no sanction authority or any other
power to enforce its decisions. The Clinton administration, after the
perfunctory bow to its domestic constituency, signed the resolution
burying labor rights.

Under the WTO, the economic policies of all national governments—no matter how democratically legitimate—are subject to the
approval of a supranational organization established to impose commercial values over all other domestic considerations—including
health, education, justice, and environmental protection. The only
excepted sector was the military.

The exclusion for the military appears to have a certain fundamental logic in that nations must be free to defend themselves. Yet it
is also true that nations must be free to cure their sick, educate their
children, bring their criminals to justice, and protect the public
health. Moreover, for most countries, the military acts as an enforcer
of domestic order as much or more than as a protector of borders.
The reason for the military exclusion is simply that the military
establishments of most nations would not stand for any formal limits
on their freedom of action. They are too important a part of the
elite structure of most countries to be overruled. Moreover, the
military have their own international networks and—like the transnational corporations—were able to work together to keep their
class prerogatives.

The fundamental antidemocratic character of the WTO was captured in a remark made by an official of the organization to the
Financial Times in 1998. The WTO, he said, is "the place where governments collude in private against their domestic pressure groups."[11]

Yet the comment is disingenuous. The people who represent governments are the people who represent the most powerful of the domestic pressure groups. The WTO and NAFTA provide a place for them to permanently escape from the political competition of *less* powerful interest groups.

The WTO meeting in Seattle in 1999 was itself financed by American multinational corporations. Contributors were promised that they would participate in a "process to develop substantive business input to the WTO." For a donation of $250,000, a corporation got to send five people to the opening and closing receptions, five to the ministerial dinner, and four to a special business conference. The spokesperson for the host committee assured the *Financial Times*, "No individual company will be able to say they bought this meeting." He added, "But if you're going to give more than $200,000, you might want more than a cardboard mug out of it."[12]

The Party of Davos

Every constitution generates a politics—conflict over the interpretation of the constitution's words and phrases for power and profit. In the absence of a world government that replicates the political institutions that we associate with a democratic nation-state, the politics of the constitution of the global market are largely hidden from the world's citizens.

Currently, the politics of the global market reflect a virtual one-party system. For want of another name, we will call it the Party of Davos, after the resort high in the Swiss Alps where managers and agents of the world's most important enterprises meet annually among themselves and with political leaders to discuss the state of the world.

Like its equivalent in the United States, this global governing class is much broader than the Marxist definition of capitalists as the direct owners of the means of production. The Party of Davos includes bureaucrats, journalists, academics, lawyers, and consultants who have never been owners or managers of private companies. At its fringes, it includes some labor leaders, important clergy, and the leadership of some of the largest NGOs.

Davos was originally designed as a meeting place for top business executives to talk about political problems common to their class. But as the political reach of transnational corporations grew, so did the invitation list. Currently it includes about three thousand people. As at the conventions of a Western-style political party, the people at the very top come to give speeches and leave. Presidents of the United States send their cabinet officers. Presidents of Mexico go themselves. Most of the CEOs of the larger transnationals also send their aides, although those who like the publicity—such as Bill Gates or George Soros—often show up.

They meet in an idyllic ski resort protected by razor wire, police and soldiers backed up with missiles and tanks. But this is not a secret cabal. It is covered by the media. There are public speeches by famous people, workshops on technical subjects, debates, and endless receptions and dinners. Most people go for the same reason people go to political and business conventions: to renew and make connections, to have a good time, and to have private conversations to learn what the rest of the party is thinking. It was at Davos in 1989 that Carlos Salinas learned that the European financiers were not interested in Mexico.

One Pulitzer Prize–winning journalist wrote of her impressions of the 2003 meeting in a private e-mail to her friends:

> Finally, who are these guys? I actually enjoyed a lot of my conversations, and found many of the leaders and rich quite charming and remarkably candid. Some dressed elegantly, no matter how bitter, cold and snowy it was, but most seemed quite happy in ski clothes or casual attire. Women wearing pants was perfectly acceptable, and the elite is sufficiently multicultural that even the suit and tie lacks a sense of dominance.
>
> Watching Bill Clinton address the conference while sitting in the hotel room of the President of Mozambique—we were viewing it on closed circuit TV—I got juicy blow-by-blow analysis of U.S. foreign policy from a remarkably candid head of state. A day spent with Bill Gates turned out to be fascinating and fun. I found the CEO of Heineken hilarious, and George Soros seemed quite earnest about confronting AIDS. Vicente Fox—who I had breakfast with—proved sexy and smart like a—well, a fox. David Stern (Chair of the NBA) ran up and gave me a hug.

> The world isn't run by a clever cabal. It's run by about 5,000 bickering, sometimes charming, usually arrogant, mostly male people who are accustomed to living in either phenomenal wealth, or great personal power. A few have both. . . . They are comfortable working across languages, cultures and gender, though white Caucasian males still outnumber all other categories. They adore hi-tech gadgets and are glued to their cell phones.
> Welcome to Earth: meet the leaders.[13]

Davos is certainly not the only place the Party of Davos convenes. Members meet at the Council on Foreign Relations in New York, at the various conferences of the Trilateral Commission, the Ditchley Foundations, the meetings of the CEOs of the five hundred largest corporations sponsored by *Fortune* magazine, and so forth. "There are few major cities in any First or Third World (and now Second World) country that do not have members of or connections with one or more of these organizations," notes Leslie Sklair of the London School of Economics.[14]

The annual conference of the Bilderberg Group, named after a hotel in Holland where the first meeting was held, is one of the most exclusive settings. It was begun in 1954 by a somewhat left-of-center Catholic member of the European governing class as a place for European and American leaders to discuss their different perspectives on the cold war. The meetings were also a way for the American oil giant Standard Oil and Royal Dutch/Shell to communicate. Only 115 leaders (80 from Europe, 35 from the United States) are invited to its annual conference. No press is allowed and there is no publicity.

Among the regulars are Henry Kissinger and Richard Perle. In 2004 Democratic senator John Edwards, conservative Republican activist Ralph Reed, and Richard Holbrooke, Bill Clinton's ambassador to the UN, were among the participants. Bill Clinton himself has been to Bilderberg.

Bilderberg is a favorite target of hard-core conspiracy buffs, the people looking for the source of Zionist plots, papist schemes, and the machinations of the devil. Oklahoma City bomber Timothy McVeigh, Osama bin Laden, and Serbian supporters of Slobodan Milosevic are said to have identified Bilderberg as the source of their political afflictions. But given their prominence, neither Davos nor Bilderberg are likely to be selected as the site for a tightly planned conspiracy to take over the world.

Yet there is little doubt that Davos, Bilderberg, and the other watering holes are places where the rich and powerful discuss strategies on the "big issues" to keep and enlarge their wealth and power. Davos represents a conspiracy in the Adam Smithian sense; it is the global equivalent of what his merchants do when they meet. They are, after all, there on business. They don't need to reach a specific consensus. It is enough to sniff out their common interests, to come away confident that their phone calls will be returned, to learn which politicians are considered "sound" and should be promoted.

Alasdair Spark, head of American Studies at King Alfred's College, Winchester, UK, and a student of conspiracy theories, rejects the demonization of Bilderberg as an unnecessary sinister interpretation of normal elite behavior. "Shouldn't we expect that the rich and powerful organize things in their own interests?" he asks. "It's called capitalism."[15]

Just so. But in the past, the fate of the capitalists was largely tied to the fate of their national economies. They organized in their own interest within a framework in which "what was good for General Motors was good for America." That remark was not about patriotism—Jefferson observed that "merchants have no country"—but about the simple reality of capital and labor needing each other when they are bound together in the same economy.

American companies were always trading and exporting. But international commerce remained an activity of trade among separate economies. The combination of globalization and neoliberal politics has allowed the transnational corporate class to rip up the national social contract and is creating a global elite whose bottom-line decisions are indifferent to where they produce, sell, or buy.

American, Global, and Beyond

In thinking about the elite class phenomenon represented by Davos, it is useful to distinguish the development of a transnational governing class from the overlapping phenomenon of American imperialism. For some, the spread of McDonald's, Coca-Cola, and Disney around the world is proof of the appeal of the American Way of Life. For others, it is evidence that "Americans" are aiming to rule the world. But the globalizing corporation is only superficially connected to its place of origin or the location of its headquarters. Thus, while a large part of the world's economy appears to be Americanized, the "American" corporations generating that process are being global-ized. Much of the world's commercial culture was inspired by the U.S. culture, but consumerism—both as a way of life and as a politi-cal ideology—now has a life of its own.

The transnational corporation is not by any means just an Amer-ican monopoly. Of the world's 500 largest corporations in 2004, 199 were headquartered in the United States, 210 had their home office in Western Europe, 47 were based in the developing world, 80 in Japan, and 13 in Canada.[16]

During the 1980s, much was made in the U.S. press of Japanese purchases of U.S. business assets. When the Japanese economy tanked in the early nineties and the yen lost its luster, it was seen as proof of the ultimate superiority of the U.S. economy. But the selling of U.S. assets continued, and by 2004 European corporations owned a huge number of "American" brands—including A&W root beer, Ben & Jerry's, Brooks Brothers, Motown, Quaker State, and the Los Ange-les Dodgers.

In Europe, these acquisitions are well-known and cited as proof of "L'Europe Qui Gagne"—"Europe the winner."[17] But the average European is no more the winner than was the average Japanese a winner when Mitsubishi Estate Co. bought Rockefeller Center or the average American when Citigroup bought Banamex.[18]

Leslie Sklair makes a useful distinction among three types of economies served by corporations. One is a national economy in which production, marketing, and sales take place within national borders. The second is the international economy in which nations trade imports and exports. The third is a global economy in which the various processes of finance, production, and marketing take place freely across porous borders. In the first two, the corporations can claim to represent the national interest of their country. In the global economy, the national interest disappears.

Sklair surveyed the managers of a sample of the Fortune 500 corporations in the late 1990s. They were all asked to respond to the following statement: "Multinational corporations are not really multi-national. They are national companies with units abroad." Sklair reports that the statement was "roundly rejected as old-fashioned and not compatible with the demands of the contemporary global economy. Most Global 500 executives in the sample considered their corporations to be in a transitional state between the multinational corporation and the global corporation, that is, they were to a greater or lesser extent globalizing."[19] Many referred to the "global-izing moment," when they "stop thinking and acting primarily in terms of 'developing foreign markets and meeting competition from abroad' and start to think and act more in terms of 'competitive strategies for global marketing.' "

On the other side of this globalizing moment, the corporation becomes intentionally stateless, breaking from its national culture. Recruitment and career ladders become global. "BP long ago stopped thinking of nationality as a criterion for promotion," said one executive of that company. Even corporations in an ethnocentric culture like Japan's tend toward the multicultural when they get to be a certain size. In March 2005, Howard Stringer, born in Wales, knighted by Queen Elizabeth II, and an American citizen, was made chairman and chief executive officer of Sony Corporation.

Alex Trotman, the late chief of the Ford Motor Company, told Robert Reich in 1995, "Ford isn't even an *American* company, strictly speaking. We're global. We're investing all over the world. Forty percent of our employees already live and work outside the United States, and that's rising. Our managers are multinational. We teach them to think and act *globally*."[20]

Company divisions in other nations are told to cease thinking of themselves as subsidiaries that run down a vertical chain from the home company office, and instead to operate as profit centers in a more horizontal network. The market is the world. Colgate-Palmolive told the surveyors that the "trigger point" for their marketing is when consumers pass a threshold of $5,000 in personal income. Thus in his 1995 annual report, Michael Eisner of Disney ends his explanation of Disney's multimedia global strategy of each division reinforcing each other with, "We did it in the U.S. We did it and do it in Europe and Asia. We will start doing it in Latin America." In the view of this quintessential American company, the United States is a place where they do business—like any other place. Already, 50 percent of U.S.-owned manufacturing production and 45 percent of Japanese-owned production is located in other countries.[21]

Part of the process of shedding the identification with the home country is changing the name. Southern California Edison becomes Edison International, British Telecom becomes BT, Swiss Bank Corporation becomes the deracinated SBC. In 2004, two Harvard Business School professors published a survey of how consumers in eleven countries in the Middle East, Europe, Asia, and Africa perceived seven U.S. brands—Nike, Exxon Mobil, Kraft, Coca-Cola, Pepsi-Cola, Motorola, and Ford. They concluded that the brands were seen as global, not American.[22] Indeed, brands associated with a particular nationality have morphed into global labels and then taken the final step of being integrated into every culture as its own. Coca-Cola, bottled and distributed locally around the world, is an example.

Networking around the Kantian "Catch-22"

The actual work of the Party of Davos is not done at Davos or Bilderberg. It is done through a thickening network of second- and third-tier corporate managers and bureaucrats whose decisions and agreements put into practice the principles of the Davosian constitution, relentlessly developing global relationships.

This network is essential to save the Party of Davos from having its dream of globalization confounded by the paradox described by the philosopher Immanuel Kant, who argued that only world government could rid us of the scourge of war but that world government would be so tyrannical that it would not be worth it. Having found a way to escape the social contract of the national community through the creation of a global economy, the Party of Davos is confronted with the "catch-22" of how to govern that economy in the absence of a legitimate global government:

> Davos needs global rules to promote the freedom of capital.
> Enforcing rules requires global government.
> Global government would restrain the freedom of capital.

Solving this dilemma requires a management structure far more sophisticated than could possibly be handled by meetings at Davos.

So the vacuum created by the absence of global government is being filled by transnational bureaucratic networks aimed at supervising the global market in a way that maximizes corporate investor freedom. These networks mimic the Rubin, Summers, and Greenspan Committee to Save the World. The style is eclectic, informal, and behind-the-scenes. Democracy is kept at bay.

As in the United States, the global class system is nurtured by common educational experiences. A senior IMF official says of the connections between people at the IMF, the World Bank, and the people who run the finance and economics ministries in Latin America, "We are all the same—people who come and go through the Bank, the Fund, and Finance Ministries and Central Banks of Latin American countries. We all studied at the same universities; we all attend the same seminars, conferences . . . we all know each other very well. We keep in touch with each other on a daily basis. There are some differences, such as between those who studied at Harvard and those who studied at the University of Chicago, but these are minor things."[23]

The emerging global political system has also spawned an international industry of consultants, brokers, and connectors who guide the special interests that need favors from this world—much like the K Street lawyers who perform that function in Washington. At the highest reaches of the global lobbying world are people with the best Rolodexes—such as Republican Henry Kissinger and Democrat George Mitchell, both of whom declined to serve as cochairs of the 9/11 Commission when required to disclose their client list.

More and more, the road to professional advancement leads back and forth across borders. For beginners who dream of someday entering the global corporate Valhalla, there are guides like the quarterly magazine *International Economy*. On the magazine's board of advisers are the former presidents of the central banks of Germany, France, and Mexico, former finance ministers of Korea, Italy, and Great Britain, two former vice chairs of the U.S. Federal Reserve, and an assortment of investment firm and policy academics and prestigious journalists. The magazine provides a periodic "Power Tree" of the holders of what it considers the roughly 173 most important policy-making jobs around the world.

Anne-Marie Slaughter, dean at the Woodrow Wilson School of International Affairs at Princeton, has identified more than sixty of these informal horizontal connections that bypass the traditional vertical government-to-government global connections yet are performing governmental functions. She calls it a "disaggregated state" that has the speed and flexibility to "perform many of the functions of a world government—legislation, administration, and adjudication—without the form."[24]

Free from the constraints of accountable government, globalizing bureaucrats can bring others into the network in ways that would be improper or illegal back home. "Government networks have many advantages," writes Slaughter. "They are fast, flexible, cheap, and potentially more effective, accountable, and inclusive than existing international institutions. They can spring up virtually overnight, address a host of issues, and form 'mega-networks' that link existing networks. As international actors from non-governmental organizations (NGOs) to corporations have already recognized, globalization and the information technology revolution make networking the organizational form of choice for a rapidly changing and varied environment. In comparison, formal international organizations increasingly resemble slow-moving dinosaurs."[25]

Naturally, the finance sector is most advanced at global networking, as Rubin, Summers, and Geenspan have demonstrated. Central bankers, securities commissioners, and insurance supervisors have their own international organizations. They have staffs and conferences, but they are not "inter-state" organizations; they have no place in the landscape of the international legal system. Thus they are in a world far beyond the capacity of most legislators—much less citizens—to be aware of their behavior.

Slaughter believes that these interconnected networks of experts are the solution to the Kantian catch-22. "We need more government," she writes, "but we don't want the centralization of decision-making and the coercive authority so far from the people actually to be governed."

But where is the citizen in these informal elite networks? As globalization provides an escape for corporations from the restraints on capital, so it also provides an opportunity for bureaucrats to escape democratic constraints on their own freedom. Officials working with officials in other countries can hide what they do under the traditional secrecy that protects foreign policy from the public's eye. It is harder for legislators, much less ordinary citizens, to find out what is going on behind closed government doors when officials from other countries are present. Just to get briefed on the most superficial aspect of trade negotiations requires a security clearance in the United States, and even historical records dealing with contacts with officials in other countries are easily placed out of the reach of citizens trying to unlock official secrecy under the Freedom of Information Act.

Overlooked in Slaughter's vision of networking is the immense power of corporate interests to dominate international bureaucracies the same way they dominate national bureaucracies—by virtue of their money. A vivid example is the effort to harmonize the international regulation of food and health safety. Under both NAFTA and the WTO, the job of setting standards for trade in food is specifically given over to the Codex Alimentarius, a commission run by the World Health Organization and the Food and Agricultural Organization of the United Nations, headquartered in Rome. The Codex establishes the standards for nutrition, sanitation, and consumer safety that all nations presumably must adhere to if their exports are to be traded freely.

Having common rules for trade in food is obviously a good idea. But as Leslie Sklair points out, the organization is dominated by transnational agribusiness. In the 1989–91 session of the Codex, 105 governments and 140 transnational food and agribusiness companies were represented on the twelve working committees. Of the nongovernment representatives to the entire session, 660 were from transnational corporations and 26 were from public interest groups. In the U.S. delegation, 112 people were from government, 119 from industry. It was not just an American phenomenon. Sixty percent of the Swiss delegation was from industry, 44 percent of the Japanese, 40 percent of the French, 31 percent of the British, and so on. Nestlé had thirty-eight delegates, more than most countries.[26]

A decade later, reports Sklair, "despite some well-publicized and costly failures in the global food system (in terms of both human and animal health and industry profits) nothing much has changed."[27]

The Party of Porto Alegre

Protest against Davos is widespread. Peasants in Bolivia block roads to stop the privatization of water. Workers in China riot against mistreatment by the capitalist commissars who now get rich exporting socks to America. Teachers in Guatemala strike against austerity budgets forced by the World Bank. Virtually every day, somewhere in the world, rocks are being thrown, demonstrators are being tear-gassed and clubbed, and someone is likely being killed.

But dissent from Davos, while passionate, is scattered, disorganized, and far from internally consistent. It can harass, but not challenge, Davos's control over the governance of the globalizing economy.

The most visible and dramatic opposition network might be called the Party of Porto Alegre. Porto Alegre is a bustling city in the flat, cattle-raising landscape of southeastern Brazil where the World Social Forum was founded in 2000 as a counterconvention to the Davos January meetings. The Porto Alegre forum began in 2000 with about four thousand "delegates" from environmental, trade union, university, women's rights, and religious groups, tribal communities, small farmers, and other hubs of local and leftist social activism. In January 2005, some 150,000 attended.

In contrast with the controlled, barbed-wired, and exclusive Davos, the convention of the Party of Porto Alegre is diverse, participatory, and expressive. There is street dancing, folk singing, and the spontaneous socializing of a much younger and certainly less well-heeled crowd than you'll find on the slopes at Davos.

The Party of Porto Alegre lives in the Internet. One can imagine the existence of Davos without the World Wide Web. Business and government elites have airline tickets and expense accounts and the incentive of financial rewards to do business with each other. In contrast, the institutions of Porto Alegre are often short-lived, resource-poor, and very dependent upon young people who dedicate enormous energy to the movement and quite often burn out.

The Seattle demonstrations against the WTO in November–December 1999, which put forty thousand people in the streets, was the catalyzing event for the Party of Porto Alegre. Taking full advantage of a surprised and untrained local police department, they stuck a wrench in the usually well-oiled machinery of the world's formal and informal governing class. The shouting, blocked streets, and screeching police sirens outside the meeting halls frayed the tempers of the officials inside, encouraging some third world elites—who detested the demonstrators—to make some demands of their own. After four days, a stunned WTO leadership saw its meeting break up without an agreement.

Over the next few years, protesters dogged the international meetings of neoliberal institutions across the globe—in Quebec, Prague, Genoa, Miami, and, above all, Washington, at the annual meetings of the World Bank and the IMF.

But Davos recovered. Police were trained to handle the crowds more effectively, and the WTO began to meet in settings that were harder to get to and easier to defend—places like Qatar on the Persian Gulf, or Cancún on the Gulf of Mexico. Demonstrations dissolved into street theater and the core institutions of the Party of Porto Alegre spent less time trying to organize them.

The Party of Porto Alegre is a reaction to the failure of neoliberal globalization to trickle down enough benefits to make up for the pain of its creative destruction. And it has inspired a steady stream of proposals for reform of the global economy, including global enforceable worker and environmental rights, a decentralized World Bank and a sensitized IMF, a tax on financial flows, global antitrust, transparency, and so forth. Many are reasonably thought-through ideas.[28] But the intellectual gatekeepers of neoliberalism are under no pressure to engage them, so they do not.

There have been a few victories. The British-based Jubilee 2000 helped put sufficient public pressure on the world's major creditor governments to forgive some of the debt of the poorest nations in Africa. Most, if not all, of the debt was uncollectible, and the promise has yet to be completely fulfilled. Nevertheless it provided some marginal economic relief.

And in 1998 a group of NGOs mobilized to defeat a proposal within the Organisation for Economic Co-operation and Development (OECD) for NAFTA-style protections for private investors. By exposing the Multilateral Agreement on Investment before it was approved, they managed to generate enough suspicions among national business interests in France, Canada, and a few other countries to force their governments to abandon the effort for the time being.

But the Party of Porto Alegre cannot mount a serious sustained challenge to Davos. It is too diverse, too disconnected from the core culture of the global working classes, and without a political vehicle to contest for global political power. As a result the more politically ambitious wings of the Party are often coopted by the offers to dialogue with Davos on issues of interest to its corporate members. Thus the CEO of the pharmaceutical giant Merck graciously compliments the NGOs he met in Davos who have stopped pestering him about the drug company's monopolistic practice and are willing to focus on "what's required to get the medicine to people—building infrastructure," i.e., getting Merck's products into poor countries that have few drug stores.[29]

Workers of the World

In most advanced societies organized labor is the major antagonist to organized capital. Labor was the backbone of the development of social democracy in Western Europe, North America, Oceania, and the other outposts of modern capitalism. In the United States, labor unions remain the core electoral support of the Democratic Party.

Global trade unions would, therefore, seem to be a logical response to global corporations in a global marketplace. But labor unions, always the junior partner to capital in national market societies, have been left far behind in the class struggle over the rules of the global economy.

Part of the problem is resources. Unions barely have the money to combat corporations within their own domestic economies, much less to finance an organized global effort. Even when labor was at the peak of its power in the advanced nations, in the years after World War II, it never had the strength to carve out an independent global-level institution of its own. The IMF, the World Bank, and the WTO, which reflect the perspective of transnational capital, have the power of money and trade sanctions to enforce their writs. In contrast, the International Labor Organization—where labor unions, business, and government each have one-third of the seats—has no power of enforcement.

By their very nature, unions are rooted in local communities, mandated to protect a defined group of people with restricted mobility. This makes it especially hard to become an effective challenger to global capital. Transnational corporations have the flexibility to abandon workers, middle managers, and communities as soon as they do not serve senior management's purposes. Labor unions cannot follow.

Nor do they have the flexibility of most NGOs, who either have no membership constituencies, or whose constituencies are attached through an impulse of charity. Only in the most abstract and indirect sense does a member contribute to the Sierra Club or Save the Children in order to protect themselves or promote their own living standards. But union members pay dues to unite for mutual economic survival. So despite an historical attachment to the notion of workers of the world united in solidarity, and the widespread use of the term "international" in the names of labor unions, their leaders must concentrate their energies on parochial issues.

Moreover, many of the world labor unions are not independent instruments of their members, but arms of the government or company unions, acting as extensions of the corporations' personnel departments.

Yet despite the many difficulties, the world's trade unions have no choice but try to mount a collective response to global neoliberalism. The International Confederation of Free Trade Unions is the largest network; it includes most of the world's unions that are independent of their governments and corporate class, and many that are not. At 150 million workers worldwide, it represents one-eighteenth of the world's wage earners.

Over the last decade or so, the ICFTU and its affiliated networks of unions in the same industry have nurtured cooperation among workers' organizations on various continents. They share information on transnational corporations, give each other advice on how to deal with certain corporate executives, and work to encourage unionism in developing nations. In 1997, transport unions in Belgium, France, Holland, and Germany threatened a walkout against the United Parcel Service to support the strike of the American Teamsters union against the company in the United States. In another instance, American cement workers stalled in their bargaining with a French-owned company brought in the lead negotiator for the French union to lead their negotiations. Turkish rubber workers stopped work for a half day to support a U.S. strike against Bridgestone-Firestone.

Service workers unions, whose work is not normally involved in international trade, also have begun to organize across borders against common transnational employers. In August 2005, unions representing cleaners and security guards in a variety of nations met to plan a campaign against two global corporations who employ over six hundred thousand people at a hundred companies. A first step was to demand that the International Olympic Committee disqualify firms who mistreat their workers for maintenance and security contracts.

American and European unions were critical to the support of organized black workers' struggle against apartheid in South Africa. They have also created an international network for helping get workers out of prisons in Africa, Indonesia, Mexico, Colombia, South Korea, Nigeria, and Brazil, among other places. One successful campaign protected Luiz Lula da Silva, a metalworker jailed by the Brazilian military.[30] Lula went on to form the Workers' Party of Brazil and became the country's president.

But violence and state-sponsored terrorism against unions in many of the world's countries persists. The ICFTU's annual survey of the violation of labor rights is a depressing catalog of assassinations, beatings, and official intimidation. Colombia, whose business/military government is heavily subsidized by the United States, leads the world in the assassinations of labor union members. In 2002 alone documented cases include 184 murders, 189 death threats, 9 disappearances, and 27 kidnappings. In addition, 80 trade unionists were forced into exile and 139 were the victims of arbitrary arrests. Roughly 90 percent of the assassinations and death threats occurred in the midst of some labor–management dispute and most of the evidence suggests that the killers are from the paramilitary groups linked to the army, subsidized by the U.S. government, and controlled by the Colombian economic elite.[31]

In Asia in 2003, three hundred thousand workers were imprisoned for union activities. Saudi Arabia has a total ban on unionization. China, Zimbabwe, Pakistan, Argentina, Costa Rica, Guatemala, Burma, and Indonesia were among the many places in the world where to attempt to form a labor union risked ending up in a ditch with broken bones or even a bullet in your head.

But it is not just the opposition of the world's governing classes that has thwarted efforts to organize a global trade union movement. The assumption of most trade unionists continues to be that their economic interests are entirely bound up with the success of their nation-state in international competition for capital.

The conflict between the appeal of class solidarity and the appeal of nationalism for the political loyalty of working people is of course an old story. Despite the famous exhortation of Marx and Engels for workers of the world to unite, nationalism has usually won the struggle. When the interest of both a nation's workers and its capitalists—however they may fight over the distribution of wages and profits—was in maximizing a nation's economic growth, there was a certain logic to this. As the largest and most politically powerful investors seek their profits in global markets, their fellow citizens are left to resist international wage competition by themselves.

9

America Abandoned

If something can't continue forever . . . it probably won't.

—Herbert Stein, chair of the Council
of Economic Advisers, 1972–1974

In the global class conflict over who gets what, it would not seem smart to bet against Davos. The movement of corporations through Sklair's stages of growth from national company to global enterprise liberated from democratic constraints appears unstoppable.

But although the world is globalizing, it is not yet global. Davos's busy, informed networks are a long way from constituting a global government. Thus its agenda depends on support from the governing classes in the strongest nation-states. For Davos, Madeleine Albright was correct: the superpower United States is indispensable. Its elites have provided the vision and the resources necessary to organize the bailouts, the military defense of neoliberal governments, and the engine of economic growth through its expanding markets for other nations' goods. It's not that the world could not grow without the U.S. engine. But the leverage of the American market, American military aid, and American influence at the IMF, World Bank, and WTO have been essential for giving the global economy its present neoliberal shape.

The ability of American elites to support the Davos agenda, in turn, has depended on the willingness of American citizens to accept the erosion of their economic security and on the willingness of the rest of the world to keep lending the United States money in the face of its mounting debts. The support of the American people and the support of foreign creditors are connected. The borrowing has created an illusion of prosperity, which is hiding the real price Americans are paying to keep their governing class in the international lifestyle to which they have become accustomed. How long can this go on?

The China Price

The emergence of China, with its virtually unlimited supply of cheap labor and an authoritarian government dedicated to keeping it that way, is a challenge that troubles all but the most ideologically blinded free-market fundamentalists. Between 1980 and 2004, China's per capita GDP rose 8.2 percent. The comparable figure for the United States during its rise to world economic power, in the nineteenth and early twentieth centuries, was 1.5 percent. On its current rate of growth, China will supplant the United States as the world's largest national economy in roughly a decade.[1] (If the European Union is counted as one economy, the United States will drop to third.)

China's capitalism is not modeled after the United States. Like Japan, its market operates in the context of state planning, export-led growth, and little pretense of a separation between big business and big government. But the size of China's labor and potential consumer market and the ability of its brutal regime to suppress labor costs give the Chinese elite a much more powerful economic weapon than the Japanese governing class has.

China is so large that it can grow along a wide range of industries, from apparel and shoes on the low end of the technological ladder, to plastic moldings, electrical machinery, and computer hardware on the other. It's now moving up to even more sophisticated production, building new plants to make silicon chips and data-communications switching systems. China is graduating 350,000 engineers a year who are willing to work twelve-hour days and weekends for a fraction of what they would cost in the United States.

Among others, Microsoft, Hewlett-Packard, Verizon, and Intel have opened up research laboratories there.

A few short years ago, it was said that shipping distances prohibited China from becoming competitive in any product "larger than a breadbox." The breadbox is expanding. U.S. suppliers making larger—and more sophisticated—products are being told they have to match the "China price." A manager for one U.S. furniture manufacturer showed a business journalist a knockoff dresser that the Chinese were wholesaling in the United States for $105, which was below the world price for the wood it was made of. Such furniture is built in massive factories that can put out a volume that dwarfs anything in North America. The U.S. company's productivity rose 600 percent between 1995 and 2004 and still it cannot compete. "The first wave is shock and awe," said the company president. "American industry has never encountered [such] production."[2]

When Clinton and the Republicans promoted China's entry into the WTO in 1999, they assured the nation that their transnational clients were interested in China's consumers, not its workers. As with NAFTA, it didn't turn out that way. In 2004, the United States sold $35 billion worth of goods to China. It bought $197 billion.[3] "Today," says one trade lawyer, "China overwhelms a market so quickly you don't see it coming."[4]

In January 2005, when the world agreement that limited textile and apparel imports to the United States expired, shipments from China surged almost 60 percent from the previous January. In January 2004, China sent 941,000 cotton shirts to the United States. In January 2005 it sent 18.2 million. In that same month, the U.S. industry laid off ten thousand workers.[5]

As usual, the language misleads. It's not "China" that is swamping the world's markets. It is Chinese labor combined with the capital of "American" and other first world transnationals who persuaded a Democratic president and a Republican Congress to approve China's entry into the WTO, and therefore the U.S. market, with no protections against China's virtually limitless supply of exploited labor. Today, some 60 percent of China's exports are shipped by foreign firms.

In 2004, the sectors where China ran the largest surpluses with the United States were computer hardware and parts for electrical machinery. The largest U.S. exports to China are in the subsidized

U.S. sectors of oilseeds and grain. The United States also has a small surplus in aircraft. But the Chinese require that Boeing—the largest U.S. exporter—give contracts locally to build up its own industry. The Chinese strategic model is automobiles, where China used imported cars to build up its own capacity, so that it is now beginning to export cars. At the marketing end, Wal-Mart, JCPenney, Target, and other retailers provide the outlets that Chinese companies could not provide for themselves.

And alongside China is India, whose similarly large but more educated labor force has carved out niches in pharmaceuticals, computer programming and design, radiology services, and a variety of research and development functions. And then there is Russia, still recovering from its cold war collapse, but with large numbers of engineers ready to work for fractions of what they would get in the United States. And spread farther around the world are tens of thousands of locations in which transnational firms can now produce goods and services thanks to the new global constitutions without the annoying interference of government protections for people and the environment.

Again, Jeffrey Garten—a major designer of the policies that opened the world to China's capitalist dictatorship—is instructive. China, he notes, is now emerging as a "technological superstate." He writes that Washington must "figure out how to deepen basic R & D in America when so much is dispersed abroad. *And it must adapt to the reality that U.S. multinationalists' goals may no longer dovetail with the national interest*" [italics added].[6] Suddenly, the light is dawning.

The Outsourcing Canary

We do not know how long the American people will be willing to pay the cost of our elites' global agenda. But we do know that the cost will keep rising, and that it cannot keep rising forever.

Throughout the 1990s, millions of Americans listened to Bill Clinton's call to embrace the global economy. They were encouraged to invest their dollars and time to go to school and/or get trained in the special high-tech occupations of the future. Young people took out loans. Older workers' families sacrificed so the

breadwinner could go back to school. Poor rural communities borrowed money to furnish facilities for credit card processing and call
centers to make up for the apparel or shoe company that picked up
and went overseas.

The point was to go out and get the "good jobs" that the pundits told them would be there for them if they got the right skills
and created a friendly business climate in their community. People
without college educations would work in New Economy service jobs
such as call centers, bookkeeping, drafting, and computer maintenance. Others would fill the demand for programmers, accountants,
financial researchers, medical technicians, biochemists, technical writers, and many lucrative niche occupations that would line the global
economic stairway to a better and more secure future.

As it turned out, the outsourcing of production did not stop
with blue-collar workers. The neoliberalization of investment and
trade, coupled with the technology of the Internet, allowed enterprises to outsource virtually any occupation, in whole or in part, to
places in the world where labor was substantially cheaper.

In December 1992, at a call-in segment of a conference on the
economy organized by the newly elected Bill Clinton, a woman from
Brighton, Massachusetts, got on the line. "I have a master's degree
in communications," she said. "I've been looking for a job for three
years, since May of 1990. I've held freelance positions. I've done
internships for free without school credit." Clinton felt her pain. His
secretary of labor, Robert Reich was optimistic. He said that people
with college educations "are going to do pretty well in this new
economy, this global economy over the long term."[7]

A few years later, President Bill Clinton appeared in Hazard, Kentucky, where the state government had contributed $7.6 million to
a company bringing a call center to town. "I came here to show
America who you are," he said. "Sykes Enterprises is making a major
commitment—listen to this—to construct two information technology centers in eastern Kentucky that will bring hundreds of new jobs
in Pike and Perry counties. Thank you, Mr. Sykes."

A few years after that, Sykes Enterprises cleared out for India and
the Philippines, leaving Hazard in debt and the people out of work,
again. "We were blindsided," said Johnny Napier, a worker who lost
his job.[8]

People who had invested years of their lives and gone into debt to get the credentials to enter the New Economy as radiologists, auditors, and animators found themselves subject to the callous disrespect they thought only blue-collar workers had to suffer. Computer programmers, software engineers, and other professionals were told to train their replacements in Asia.

Twelve years after the 1992 Little Rock conference, Reich appeared on a CNN program with yet another unemployed professional—a computer programmer who had a degree in physics and a degree in engineering. Her brother, also an engineer physicist, was also looking for a job. "We went to college," she said. "We paid our dues. What do we do now?"[9]

In fact, the overall skill level of American workers has risen rapidly since the country started running trade deficits in the mid-1970s. The share of the workforce with college degrees has almost doubled from 15 percent in 1973 to 29 percent in 2003, while high school dropouts have shrunk from 29 to 11 percent. Yet the demand for jobs that require a college education has not accelerated as the promoters of free trade promised it would. Indeed, the U.S. Bureau of Labor Statistics projects that of the thirty occupations that will grow the most over the next decade, only eight will require a college degree.[10]

Outsourcing has now ratcheted up to design research and development that only a few years ago Americans assumed would always be theirs. "American" transnationals are locating their R&D in India, Taiwan, and China where the skills are high and come cheap. Boeing, Motorola, Procter & Gamble, and GlaxoSmithKline are just a few companies shifting R&D to Asia. According to one estimate, 80 percent of engineering tasks in product development can be "easily outsourced."[11]

In response to the worries about outsourcing, professional defenders of the neoliberal faith tended to minimize the problem. Most jobs, they pointed out, were not being outsourced. It was true. Just as it had been true when the apparel and shoe industries began to move out of the United States, and then appliances and consumer electronics left, and then routine back-office work was transferred to places where labor was cheaper. The offshoring of white-collar and professional work—the jobs that those laid off blue-collar workers and their children were supposed to get—was like the dying canary in the mine shaft warning of approaching catastrophe. If you wait until the gas explodes, it's too late.

The economic consulting firm of Forrester Research projects that by 2015, 6 percent of white-collar jobs existing in 2004 will be outsourced, including 20 percent of computer jobs. Forrester's numbers are probably an underestimate. Only one-third of large U.S. firms in 2002 did any white-collar outsourcing at all because the infrastructure necessary to make outsourcing available to all firms was still being built. Successful outsourcing relies on an industry of facilitators—lawyers, financiers, fixers—who can lead the outsourcing corporation through a thicket of other countries' laws and cultures. Like any industry, it takes time to develop the contacts, the infrastructure, and the procedures. Large companies like IBM are just now coming into the market as providers of offshore services, and the business schools are starting to teach it. With the infrastructure, the potential for outsourcing widens to just about any jobs that can be digitalized, where actual face-to-face interaction is not absolutely necessary—which means just about anything short of a barber, a waiter, or a nurse's aide.

"Outsourcing is just a new way of doing international trade," said N. Gregory Mankiw, the chair of George W. Bush's Council of Economic Advisers, in February 2004. "More things are tradable now than were tradable in the past. And that's a good thing."[12] Mankiw was hammered by Democrats and disowned by Republicans for the remark, but his equation of trade and outsourcing was correct. You cannot logically believe that one is good and the other is bad. Like free trade, the major impact of outsourcing is not on the number of jobs as much as it is on the wages they pay. Thus Forrester's modest numbers imply a cut in the wages of white-collar workers over the next decade. Even Yale's Jeffrey Garten, who had ardently championed globalization as undersecretary of commerce, acknowledged that Forrester's numbers were likely to be an underestimate. Garten wrote in a *Business Week* column, "As U.S.-based employers consider the cost of adding either one American or, say, one Indian to the payroll, the alternative of offshoring will put downward pressure on middle-class wages throughout the U.S. And in a broadband world that allows overseas work to be supervised in real time, the sheer speed at which large swaths of the service sector can be moved to another country will create far more disruption for workers and communities than we've seen so far in the slower-moving manufacturing sector."[13]

It is thus gradually dawning on the more thoughtful members of the American governing class that the China price is moving rapidly up the ladder of sophisticated products and production to areas that had been assumed to be the monopoly of the United States and other advanced nations. Countries like China and India are large enough that their governing classes can maintain huge supplies of labor willing to work for subsistence and at the same time graduate scientists, engineers, and technicians in greater numbers than the United States. With the appearance of low-wage/high-tech economies, the comforting traditional economic models that postulate high-wage nations maintaining their prosperity by virtue of their superior technology lose what is left of their relevance.

Garten, like fellow Democrats Clinton and Reich, and unlike Gingrich and George W. Bush, smells the gas, and would like to see something done about it. But commitment to corporate-driven globalization keeps them from dealing with this reality. Instead of trying to get the workers out of the mine, they propose emergency help after the explosion. So for two decades they have been suggesting that the "losers" get more retraining, more "adjustment" programs, more flexible unemployment compensation, schemes for wage insurance, and so forth.

Democrats reasonably complain that Republicans are unwilling to spend the money for adequate programs. True, yet when the Democratic Party's leaders had the opportunity to force Republicans to accept decent adjustment programs as the price for the trade agreements that big business wanted, they refused. The Clinton White House never had a full-court press for even these modest efforts to strengthen the safety net. There was no "war room" for programs to help globalization's losers as there was for NAFTA and the WTO and the agenda of globalization's winners.

Over the last twenty-five years, the money for federal training programs has been slashed from $27 billion to $4 billion. The few programs for the "special training" of workers laid off because of trade agreements provide $250 per week—hardly enough for a family to live on while its breadwinner gets trained to be a computer programmer, only to watch his or her new job move overseas.

Except for the golden parachutes at the top, winners in the brave new world of global competition do not compensate the losers. That is the point of winning.

Abandoning America to the Competition

In a modern economy, competitiveness depends on investment. Because living standards in the United States are higher than in most countries, that investment must be larger and continuous in order to sell more and better products in the global economy. A governing class that had gambled on Americans' capacity, as Clinton put it, to "compete and win" would be making such investments to accelerate the quality and the spread of the workforce's skills and would be providing them with privileged access to cutting-edge technology. Yet little of this is happening. In fact, over the last twenty years, America's leaders have presided over the dramatic erosion of the ability of the citizens to maintain their living standards in the brutally competitive world that the leaders have created.

The United States has already lost its once formidable lead in key indicators of competitiveness. Today, the Japanese are building robots that can act as receptionists, night watchmen, and hospital workers. The Japanese government estimates that by 2015, every household will have at least one robot, and it is establishing guidelines for consumer safety and legal responsibility.[14]

The Europeans are now further along in fuel-efficient cars and appliances, interactive television, and wireless technology—there are more cell phones per person in Western Europe than in the United States. By 2007, Europe will have the world's largest atom smasher, and by 2008 it will have the world's premier global positioning satellite in orbit. European space probes have already found methane—a sign of life—on Mars.

While the governments of Japan, Canada, Korea, and other nations are using their powers of regulation and subsidy to spread broadband infrastructure, the U.S. governing class remains paralyzed by a conflict between the Bell systems that own the phone lines and ATT and MCI that want to use them to compete on broadband services. One result is that a 1.5 megabyte-per-second connection costs thirty-five dollars or more per month in the United States while the Japanese pay twenty-five dollars for 26 megabytes.[15] By 2003, the United States had dropped to tenth place among the world's advanced nations in the share of its economy penetrated by broadband.

The United States no longer leads the world in the share of the workforce with the equivalent of a two-year college education. We rank tenth in the world in the share of twenty-four-year-olds with engineering or natural science degrees. Our high school students rank behind at least nine other industrial nations in math and science scores. And in 2000, only 44 percent of high school students were enrolled in a foreign language course.[16]

The problems in U.S. education are not hidden; hand-wringing about them has in itself become a mini-industry. But the debates have been trapped in mindless ideological arguments brought on by religious and social conservatives over sex education, creationism, and the claim that parents are better equipped to educate their children than professional teachers.

If national competitiveness was important to the American governing class and its business clients, these attacks would not be tolerated. Business would be demanding higher achievement and imposing a world-class system of teachers and facilities to get it. "Oh, but the teachers' unions won't let us," the political agents of the business class complain. The charge is largely untrue. With some exceptions, most teachers' unions have supported serious plans for higher quality in their profession. But even if it were true, the idea that unions could thwart anything that a united business community was determined to do is not credible.

Neither would a corporate business elite that saw its fate connected to the future competitiveness of America stand by while its own party led the attack on stem-cell research. Religious fundamentalists would be elbowed out of the way, just as they were when blue laws that respected the Sunday sabbath were removed because they were obstacles to profitability. Instead, the corporate class has abetted the attacks on public education as part of its political alliance with the radical right.

Neither would big business look on indifferently at the decline in national investment in research and development. Research and development spending as a share of our GDP has been declining over the last three business cycles as the federal government's support for basic research has shrunk. The share of American-authored scientific papers has dropped from 61 percent in 1983 to 29 percent in 2003, with the absolute number of papers dropping 10 percent since 1992. European and Chinese researchers now produce more scientific papers than do Americans.

Public investment is the act of society shaping its own future and has always been a generator of private investment opportunities; America's history is studded with grand economic sectors opened up by government to the profit of business. Early in the Republic's life we built canals and highways and provided land for schools and housing in the territories. Government financed the first assembly lines, subsidized the railroads to settle the West, and developed long-range radio technology. It created the suburbs with housing and highway programs. And it took the entrepreneurial risk in developing the jet engine, the computer, and the Internet, and provided the basic research upon which thousands of pharmaceuticals have been produced.

Today, business elites that cared about America's future would be demanding new government investments in renewable energy technologies, biomedical research, and nanotechnologies (the science of manipulating molecules to produce materials that last a lifetime and computers the size of a grain of sand). Instead, they send their lobbyists to demand more tax cuts, now.

Even as dogged a promoter of global laissez-faire as *New York Times* pundit Thomas Friedman has become anxious about the lack of interest in America's CEOs in the country's looming disasters in health, energy, and technology investments. "When I look around for the group that has both the power and interest in seeing America remain globally focused and competitive—America's business leaders—they seem to be missing in action," he writes.

Friedman offers three reasons why CEOs are missing in political action. One is that they are "culturally Republican," which apparently makes them afraid to challenge George W. Bush. Another, even odder explanation is that the Enron and other scandals make them want to keep their heads down—a fear that does not prevent them from lobbying for tax breaks, deregulation, and the privatization of public assets and services. Finally, Friedman gets to the most obvious cause: "In today's flatter world, many key U.S. companies now make most of their profits abroad and can increasingly recruit the best talent in the world today without ever hiring another American."[17]

However, Friedman, like Garten, does not seem interested in exploring the startling implications of this admission. Rather, he goes on to scold "us" to get "our" act together, oblivious to his own responsibility in promoting the policies that destroyed incentives for America's corporate investors to care about America.

Payback Time

Yet the citizen who looked around in the first few years of the twenty-first century certainly had the impression that Americans were doing fine. The stores were stocked. The roads were crowded. New houses continued to be built. Americans traveled abroad. Although the average worker was spending more hours on the job and was less secure than his or her parents were, the country still looked prosperous. Moreover, the U.S. economy continued to grow—and seemed to be pulling the rest of the world's economy along with it.

So if things are so bad, why did they look so good? The answer is that the American economy was living on the rest of the world's credit. Over the last twenty-five years, America has been buying more from the rest of the world than it has been selling, a fundamental measure of the lack of competitiveness of the economy.

Transnational corporations with American names may be competitive, but the U.S. *economy*—the collection of workers, businesses, and infrastructure that produces in America—is clearly not. No business that bought more than it sold for twenty-five years and had to borrow more and more in order to cover its debts could be said to be competitive.

Given our shop-till-we-drop culture, we do not save enough out of our domestic income to cover the growing losses from our international trade. So in order to raise the extra money needed to import from abroad, we've been borrowing more from foreigners and selling them our assets (U.S. stocks and other property). The result has been a growing annual trade deficit, reflected in the key measure of a country's financial relationship with the rest of the world, the "current account."[18]

There is nothing intrinsically wrong with borrowing money. It depends on what you use it for. If you borrow to buy a house or start a business or get an education you hope to end up with an income-producing asset or skill that will help you pay off the loan. If you borrow to go on a vacation or to buy a house full of electronic gadgets you really can't afford, you accumulate debt with no increased income to pay it off. At times over the past twenty years, Americans borrowed to invest. But for the most part, we have been borrowing to consume—which is what keeps fueling the domestic economy and has provided an expanding market for other countries to send us their imports.

One result is the extraordinary rise in consumer debt, which during the 1990s surged some 53 percent. Consumer debt now amounts to 80 percent of GDP and totals more than the disposable income of all families. Middle-income families' credit card debt rose 75 percent, and for low-income families it rose an extraordinary 184 percent. Personal bankruptcies soared to $1.6 billion by 2001, double the number ten years before. As one report observes, "More children today will see their parents go through bankruptcy than divorce."[19]

Economists do not all agree on the macroeconomic causes of the trade deficit. For some it is Americans' unwillingness to save. For others it's an overvalued dollar. Still others blame the rest of the world for growing too slowly and therefore not taking in enough of our exports. There is a little truth in all of these explanations. But there is no getting around the brutal fact that the American economy is living beyond its means.

Under the circumstances of a chronic trade deficit, whatever its causes, the engineered opening up of the American economy to more trade through NAFTA and the WTO has been extraordinarily reckless. Each new trade agreement encouraged more imports, provoked more outsourcing, and required more debt. A 2000 study concluded, "A 10% increase in the level of U.S. direct investment in an industry in China is associated with a 7.3% increase in the volume of U.S. imports from China and a 2.1% decline in U.S. exports to China in that industry."[20] The promoters of expanded trade acted out the old story of the street vendor who bought apples for a dime and sold them for a nickel, intending to make it up on the volume.

The U.S. "current account" deficit climbed to 4 percent of GDP in 2002, 5 percent by 2003, and more than 6 percent by the end of 2004. As a share of its GDP, it had not been as high as 4 percent since 1816. At its present rate of growth it will be almost 8 percent by 2007. The International Monetary Fund considers a nation at serious risk when it runs a current account deficit of 5 percent.

In the space of two decades the United States went from being the world's largest creditor to the world's largest debtor. By the end of 2004, our debt to foreigners equaled about 25 percent of our gross domestic product. On this trajectory, the U.S. debt would hit 40 percent of GDP by 2008. This was roughly the foreign debt burden of the Argentine economy just before that country's financial collapse in 2001.

A country like Argentina that runs a trade deficit will see the value of its currency decline relative to other currencies. Because foreigners will have sold more to Argentina than they have bought from her, they will have an oversupply of the country's pesos. As the value of the currency falls, foreign imports become more expensive so people buy less. Its exports become cheaper so foreigners buy more. When the currency drops low enough, its trade will be balanced.

But the United States is not Argentina. Or rather, the dollar is not the peso. Since the end of World War II, the dollar has served as the world's basic store of value. It is the reserve currency for most of the world's central banks, that is, their supply of dollars backs up the money they issue.[21] It is also used to settle most international transactions; when the Brazilians buy oil from the Saudis, they pay in dollars. And its general accepted value made the dollar a "safe haven" for investors worried about instability in other parts of the world. Thus they were willing to send their excess dollars—earned from their exports to the United States—back to America by purchasing stocks and bonds. The high demand for the dollar allowed the United States to borrow to finance the trade deficit without paying the price of a decline in its currency.

Among the losers in this game were the businesses and workers engaged in exports and competition with imports. Among the winners were American tourists, consumers who had access to cheap foreign goods, and the twin pillars of the governing class—transnational corporations and the military. A highly valued dollar allowed transnational corporations to use their American profits to buy up foreign factories, banks, and other assets cheaply. A highly valued dollar also made it cheaper for the U.S. military to lease and operate its bases around the world and to pay for arms and the training of foreign soldiers.

But not even the United States, protected though it is by the unique status of the dollar, can continue forever with its debt rising faster than its income. By 2002, nervous foreign investors and banks slowly began to shift out of U.S. government bonds and other dollar-denominated securities. To keep their currencies from rising against the dollar, foreign governments, particularly the Chinese and Japanese, bought more. By 2004, foreigners held almost 50 percent of outstanding U.S. Treasury bonds. The deft Alan Greenspan, who had blessed and encouraged the economic excesses that were leading to a crisis, began to distance himself from his own handiwork, warning that foreigners were signaling a "diminished appetite" for American securities.

At the same time, the dollar's virtual monopoly as the world's currency standard has eroded. Euros have begun to replace dollars in international transactions and as central bank reserves. On the list of Washington's complaints about Saddam Hussein was that he was beginning to accept payment for oil in euros. The Saudis have since begun to do so. At the end of 2004 the dollar's share of global foreign exchange reserves had slipped to 65 percent.[22] In February 2005, the dollar plunged when the Japanese prime minister suggested that his government might consider reallocating some of its huge reserves away from the dollar. He quickly said he'd been misinterpreted, calming the markets—for a while.

The failure of the European countries to agree to a constitution in 2005 weakened the euro and led to gleeful speculation among many American editorial writers that the U.S. dollar would regain its virtual monopoly as the world's reserve currency. But the European Union has had harder bumps than that along the road to integration, and there is little chance that it will be derailed. With the current expansion to another ten nations and the eventual accession of Great Britain, the euro zone will at some point be twice the size of the U.S. economy. Its balanced trade will help the euro maintain stability over the long haul, and it is on track to become at least the equal of the dollar as the world's core currency.

In any event, there was no question that the dollar would have to fall further. The question now was when and how much.

In the winter of 2004, the *Economist* suggested, "If the dollar falls by another 30% as some predict, it would amount to the biggest default in history: not a conventional default on debt service but a default by stealth, wiping trillions off the value of foreigners' dollar assets." Indeed, "A fall in the dollar sufficient to close the U.S. current account deficit might destroy its safe-haven status."[23]

The dollar will have to fall much further than that. The *Economist*'s estimate was based on getting the dollar's value back to where it was in 1995, when the current account deficit was a mere $100 billion. But the trade deficit has fed on itself. As more production is outsourced, the U.S. economy becomes more dependent on goods made overseas. This import addiction puts us into a vicious downward cycle; as American incomes rise, the trade deficit expands faster.[24]

Stephen Roach, chief economist at Morgan Stanley, told a closed meeting of investment fund managers in Boston in late 2004 that the United States had a one-in-ten chance of avoiding an economic "Armageddon."[25] A little earlier ex Fed chair Paul Volcker said that there was a 75 percent chance of an economic crisis over the next five years, which "could be fueled by a decision by other nations to reduce their purchases of U.S. securities."[26]

It is not that the governing class could not have seen it coming. Over the years, a number of voices raised alarms over the chronic trade deficit. But the majority of Washington's political leaders took their cue from the corporate-financed policy networks that did not want anything to interfere with their neoliberal agenda.

Whenever Rubin addressed the problem it was to first insist that lowering the value of the dollar and any interference with free trade and investment were nonstarters. His answer was to run a federal surplus to increase national savings, and, somehow, to raise productivity even more. Yet Rubin and Clinton ran budget surpluses and productivity rose while the trade deficit continued to rise.

Rubin and Clinton were reflecting the conventional wisdom of their day. Similarly, the fabled financier Warren Buffett dismissed the trade deficit as a problem at a conference in December 1998, insisting that the United States had many assets to sell before we needed to worry. But by 2003 he had become alarmed, and by the beginning of 2005 he sounded panicked. Instead of Bush's "ownership" society, he wrote to his investors, America's external debt was making us a "sharecropper's" society. By 2015 he projected Americans would owe the rest of the world $11 trillion, which would cost $550 billion a year just to service. It was a level of financial burden that Buffett believed "would undoubtedly produce significant political unrest in the U.S."[27]

The Republican response was to ignore the problem all together. George W. Bush's first treasury secretary, Paul O'Neill, blithely dismissed the current account deficit as a "meaningless concept." The *Economist* responded that the consequences of a declining dollar would bring sleepless nights to "a Treasury secretary who knew what he was talking about."[28] Nor did such worries furrow the brow of U.S. trade representative Robert Zoellick, the administration's Doctor Pangloss, who insisted that only exports should be counted when measuring trade.

Most members of Congress were clueless. When Senator Byron Dorgan (D-ND) asked his colleagues on the floor of the Senate what share of the GDP the trade deficit had to get to before they'd start to worry, the answer was dumb silence.

In Washington, the divine right of multinational corporations to have access to the world's cheap labor trumped any concern for the resulting red ink. The indifference to an out-of-control foreign debt is in striking contrast to the fretting about projections that the Social Security system might have to start borrowing money forty years from now. On the present path, accumulating trade deficits will touch off a serious economic crisis long before the Social Security trust fund needs a modest tax to cover its obligations.

Most in Washington policy networks believed that the United States was so important to the ruling classes of other nations that they would not permit the dollar to crash. After all, they argued, Japan, China, and South Korea, who hold a substantial share of U.S. Treasury bonds, had based their current growth strategies on continuing to sell to the U.S. market. They had an interest in keeping this financial "balance of terror" going as long as possible before the U.S. market for imports would be forced to shrink.

Indeed, the governing classes of Europe and Japan did just that in the 1985 Plaza Accord that guided down the overvalued dollar of that era without any major diminishment of American living standards or their elites' power in the world. But George W. Bush or his successor is not likely to be so lucky. Europe and Asia no longer need U.S. military protection from the Soviet Union and their leaders do not share their American counterparts' fixation with a worldwide war on terrorism. Even if they themselves would be willing to bail out their U.S. partners, they will be under enormous domestic pressure to maintain economic growth at home—and from publics who have little respect and affection left for the U.S. government.

This, in turn, makes it less probable that our trading partners' elites will act against their own political interests by running trade deficits in order to get the U.S. governing class off the hook. It's hard to imagine that the rulers of China, for example, whose economic growth and political stability depends on rising exports, will be easily persuaded to cut their exports and increase their imports from the United States to help out a United States whose military planners regularly exercise with China as the target.

History and human nature rather suggest that the rest of the world is just as likely to respond by attempting to keep their own currencies low or by turning to protectionism. At the very least, they are unlikely to rescue the United States without political compensation. China, for example, might want the United States to withdraw its military commitment to defend Taiwan as the price for increasing its imports of American goods and decreasing its imports. In any event, as one Wall Street economist observed, "The adjustment to the dollar that . . . we need to reduce the current account problem is in the hands of the Chinese. It is not a U.S. call, and that is a profound change."[29]

As for the world's poor countries, their elites will certainly feel abandoned by America as the dollar drops. Thus, for example, the decline in the dollar in 2003–2004 wiped out some ten thousand jobs in the desperately poor African country of Lesotho, whose T-shirt industry had been selling almost all its output to the United States. The cost of paying and equipping a sewing machine operator went from $56 to $109 per month.[30] Lesotho's plight will become a familiar story. And while such nations' elites have little leverage over the United States, they are not likely to give political support to some international accommodation that forces them to further tighten their belts in order to save the country that shoved neoliberalism down their throats.

Even if the governing classes of America's trading partners do agree to have their populations absorb the pain of a huge transformation of the U.S. trade deficit into a surplus, it will take time for any growth of exports to add jobs in America. Thirty years of a shrinking industrial base will not be reversed quickly. Many products are no longer made in the United States. These include telephones, color TVs, and many consumer appliances. Investors must be convinced that manufacturing in the United States is a good bet before they will make the long-term commitment to invest in new factories. Workers must be persuaded to get trained and educated in the technical skills needed to work in modern manufacturing. And, of course, they must agree to keep their wages low.

However smooth and orderly the path to a lower dollar, the result has to be a substantial drop in living standards for the average American. An economic exercise by the economist Wynne Godley and a team of economists at the Levy Institute at Bard College concluded that by 2008 in order to keep employment from falling, the U.S. government would have to substantially increase its deficit spending, on top of a projected federal deficit of $2.3 trillion over the decade. As Godley concludes, this "would send the internal and the external debts hurtling toward 100 percent of GDP, with more to come after that."[31]

Neither Godley nor anyone else can predict the future. And no one knows precisely when the crisis will start and how it will play out. But we know the basic laws of economics will demand that the U.S. trade balance eventually be reversed and that this will cause a great deal of economic pain for the majority of American working families. American consumers and businesses will be forced by inflation (in part caused by rising prices of imports and higher interest rates) to spend less. Spending less will slow growth and reduce employment and wages. Indeed, the income growth in the United States will have to fall below that of its trading partners and remain below for a substantial period in order to depress our imports and increase our exports.

The American family is unprepared for this coming economic storm. It is already deeply in debt. The fixed costs of running a family—items that cannot be legally or easily cut back, such as mortgage payments, health care, the cost of sending children to school, transportation, and insurance—now come to about 75 percent of family income compared with 50 percent in the 1970s.

For a large number of families, keeping financially afloat already depends on a continuing housing price boom—which cannot, in fact, continue. Home equity loans and mortgages with no down payment, interest-only payments, and variable interest rates are extremely vulnerable to a combination of a flameout in prices and higher interest rates. The stock market drop did not affect the average American family because they have little or no stock. But a housing price dive will be a prolonged disaster. For another comparison, the Japanese housing market has still not recovered from the price bubble that burst in 1991.

The Japanese were able to cushion their domestic housing price collapse with continued trade surpluses and government spending supported by a high saving rate. The American governing class will have less ability to alleviate the domestic economic pain. In addition to the mountainous external debt, the domestic financial burdens on the American economy over the next few years will be enormous. Begin with the $150 billion or so in the cost to the public for expenses related to Hurricane Katrina. Add a major costly rescue of the Medicare program. Further on, the federal government will need to pay back the money that it borrowed under Reagan and the Bushes to the Social Security trust fund. The education system will need large infusions of funds in order to bring it to the world-class levels needed to compete. New investments will be needed in research and development as the probabilities of a meltdown of the private pension system grows. As the emerging giant economies of China and India bid up the price of oil, a serious expensive national program for energy alternatives and efficiency will at some point have to be financed.

U.S. imports from the rest of the world rose $780 billion between 1991 and 2003. They will not just have to slow down, they will have to decline.[32] Whether the domestic politics moves left or moves right, the governing class will not be able to use access to the U.S. market in order to induce the rest of the world's elites to join the Party of Davos. With U.S. imports from the rest of the world flat and probably declining, the economic ties that bind the world's elites to American leadership will be strained.

Without the U.S. market, transnational capital's interest in the developing world will surely diminish. So long as transnationals could promise the third world elites a share of the growing profits from the exploitation of the U.S. market with cheap labor, their loyalty to Davos was assured. But with the neoliberal system weakened by the shrinking of the world's most important market, local elites will have to start recalculating their own situation. Certainly, many will resist trade agreements that allow the United States to continue to protect its agricultural sector. At the same time, given that agriculture is one of the few areas in which the United States is earning a surplus, the pressures to keep those subsidies will not diminish.

Without a robust U.S. import market, the motor of neoliberalism is likely to sputter, if not to stall out. The European Union will have to give priority to maintaining enough internal demand to integrate Eastern Europe and will not want to run large trade deficits with the rest of the world. The Asian economic giants—China, Japan, and India—have built their economies around exports, not imports. As a result, the neoliberal nightmare—protectionism—may well become the policy of necessity. Indeed, the logic leads economist Godley to suggest that, even on the basis of his modest scenario, the United States will have to impose some sort of import surcharge (tariff) in order to protect itself against a massive flight from the dollar. Richard Nixon did it in 1971 and the rest of the world stood still for it. But that was during the cold war, when the United States was the capitalist West's protection against communism. Today, much world opinion does not see America as a protector against terrorism, but rather a provoker of it.

The economic crisis will certainly not spare the military side of the governing-class agenda. A weak dollar will make overseas military bases, especially in Europe and Asia, more expensive to maintain. And the federal budget squeeze will substantially diminish the enthusiasm of Americans for assuming the role of the world's policeman. Commitments to Iraq's reconstruction will be less popular with an American public tightening its own belt for, among other things, the rebuilding of New Orleans. Issues like the continued membership of the United States in NATO, which Washington elites are unanimous in supporting, will be raised by younger entrepreneurial politicians. "Why should we pay to defend people who are richer than we are?" will be the question in America. And in Europe, it will be, "If the Americans aren't going to pay most of the bill, why do we need them?"

In the rhetoric of empire, the neoconservative wing of the governing class has often compared itself to the heroic leaders of British imperialism who maintained an empire for close to a century. Overlooked is the mundane fact that the British Empire, upon which the sun never set, was supported by a national economy whose current account was in balance and which was the world's largest creditor nation—not the world's largest debtor. It thus never faced a currency crisis. However one feels about the analogy between Cecil Rhodes and Donald Rumsfeld, it clearly helps, when setting off to control the world, to have your bank account in the black.

The Party of Davos, along with American public, is in for a shock.

10

After the Fall

*Democratic nations care but little for what has been, but they
are haunted by visions of what will be; in this direction
their unbounded imagination grows and dilates beyond all
measure. . . . Democracy, which shuts the past against
the poet, opens the future before him.*

—Alexis de Tocqueville, *Democracy in America*

There is no great secret about what Americans will have to do to
escape the economic dead end of debt and diminishing competitiveness into which their governing class has led them. The logic is
straightforward: Americans will have to save more and spend less,
export more and import less.

But the transition out of debt under the best of circumstances
will be hard. For decades those who have managed the American
economy have defied the basic rules of financial responsibility, while
relentlessly insisting that the rest of the world accept the dictates of
laissez-faire economics. When the inevitable moment for settling up
comes due, the market is likely to be an unforgiving creditor.

Saving more means spending less than our income. But spending more than our income has supported the American economy for
the last quarter century. So spending less will mean that the economy
will grow more slowly, as will average incomes—if they grow at all.

The problem of course is that average incomes need to grow *faster* if families are to pay their debts, afford the spiraling cost of health care, and educate their children to compete in the dog-eat-dog global marketplace. Average incomes also need to grow faster in order to generate the tax revenues to finance the required bailouts of the health and pension systems, and to make public investments in education, infrastructure, and technology needed to regain national competitiveness—which are necessary to rebalance our foreign trade.

Thus, whether it happens sooner or whether it happens later, a long-term stagnation, if not decline, in American living standards is inevitable. The cards have already been dealt. And the longer the governing class keeps the game going by bluffing and raising the ante, the larger will be the eventual loss.

The market will certainly take its revenge, although under present arrangements it is not likely to fall heavily on the rich and powerful. Recent history provides us with plenty of images of ex-dictators and civilian politicians enjoying villas in the south of France while the bankers squeeze the less mobile citizens left holding their debt back home. So we can expect the elite to land on their feet, protected by diversified portfolios and gated communities—in America or elsewhere.

On our present path, the vast majority of Americans who must work for a living will end up competing with the rest of the world at least in part on the basis of price, that is, the price of their labor. Real incomes will fall as wages are cut and prices of imported goods that cannot be easily substituted for will rise. As the Mexicans found out, there will always be someone in the world willing to work for less. The gap between worker productivity and wages will widen.

Limiting the damage and reversing the downward spiral will require a sea change in the way the American economy has been managed over the last three decades. Building a political climate for that change must begin with a public discussion that makes clear the distinction between the interests of stateless transnational corporations on the one hand and the people whose economic fate is bounded by the nation on the other.

Because those interests diverge, management of the national economy requires a competent, aggressive, and accountable government. The reader is entitled to skepticism, but there is no choice. The lesson of the recent past is clear. Strong government leadership is essential for a country, as distinguished from a corporation, to participate successfully in the global market. Indeed, a good case can be made that the decision to embrace free-trade demands more, not less, government intervention in the market because only a democratic government has the power and moral authority to organize the resources and systems to allow its people to compete on the basis of something other than the world price of their individual labor. Those who seek prosperity through laissez-faire and weak government at home are better advised to resort to protectionism. The Clinton/Gingrich package simply does not hold together; given the open global markets, the era of big government cannot be over.

A reasonable definition of a nation effectively competing in the world would be one that has a balance of trade and a level of productivity that allows living standards to rise without having to expand the hours of work. Given this definition, the people of the United States cannot effectively compete against the rest of the world unless their government invests heavily in education, infrastructure, and technology. They cannot compete effectively unless their government reorganizes our disastrously inefficient health care system that takes 15 percent of our GDP, compared with 10 percent in France and 8 percent in Japan, and provides less longevity, greater infant mortality, and generally less health than that of any other developed nation. They cannot compete effectively unless their government is willing and able to manage trade so as to balance the nation's accounts with the rest of the world.

But any serious effort to make the health care system more efficient, or to redistribute wealth and opportunity, or to generally define American economic interests in terms of those who produce in America, will trigger fierce ideological and political resistance from the corporate clients of the Washington governing class. The CEOs and principal owners of corporations who have disconnected, or are in the process of disconnecting, their fate from America's have no interest in paying more taxes to make the society they are abandoning more competitive.

Thus, as market forces lower the veil of debt-bloated prosperity that has hidden the widening and hardening of class differences, more explicitly class-based political conflicts are likely to follow. For example, the debate over taxes will go far beyond the question of whether to extend George W. Bush's tax cuts. Large new revenues will have to be raised, and old government programs cut to make room for others. The politically easy part—the starving of programs for the poor—has already been done. The politics of the last two decades that pitted the poor against the middle class and the rich cannot continue because there is not enough money to be gained there. The governing class will therefore have to confront the explicit division between the interests of the middle class and the rich. And the sinkholes of government spending—subsidies to corporate farmers, hidden military budgets, and tax favors to upper-income Americans—will move out from the newsletters of marginal populist NGOs and be forced onto the front pages of the hometown newspapers, despite their conservative ownership.

There will be major battles over education. The contradictory attack on the public schools, which for the past two decades has demanded maximum local control over content and at the same time maximum national standards, can no longer be indulged if the country is to regain and sustain international competitiveness. National standards and massive federal investment to attract, train, and keep first-rate teachers will be needed. And at some point, a national decision will have to be made to alter the priorities of an economy that pays the average teacher $45,000 and seven digits to people who execute trades for Wall Street speculators.

The biggest battle may be over trade policy. As the economy goes through an economic squeeze, the issues of outsourcing and low-wage imports will dig the class lines that emerged in the NAFTA debate even deeper. Americans are now more aware of the costs they pay for "free trade." Corporate investors more aware of the benefits they get. And the governing class is even more sensitive to the loss of its leverage in the world should the United States stop offering the world its market.

Just as the Washington governing class is a network of Republicans and Democrats, the populist side of the class conflict over the distribution of economic pain may well also cross partisan lines. In 2005, despite George W. Bush's electoral triumph and Republican control over both houses of Congress, significant numbers of Republicans backed away from his effort to dismantle Social Security because the public had reacted against the threat to the most important working-class safety net.

How these conflicts will play out and get resolved we obviously cannot tell. But as the days of easy credit disappear, the American economy will not be able to sustain the minimal living standards demanded by the public without dramatic changes in tax, health care, education, trade, and budget policies.

Democratizing the Debate

For a constructive resolution to emerge from the coming economic crisis, American politics will have to return to the subject of our common future—a subject that was banished from political life after the election of 1980.

Politics in a democracy is almost always about the future. Bill Clinton understood this when he sold NAFTA as "the center of the effort that we're making in America to define what the future is going to be about." But he never defined that future.

In one three-paragraph section of his speech, Clinton used the word "change" eleven times. Change to what? Neither Clinton nor Bush, Mulroney nor Chrétien, Salinas nor Zedillo, could be specific. The reason was that NAFTA was not a way to build a new world for "us" *as a society*. NAFTA was spawned from a Reagan-Thatcher view that assumed no "us," that is, no society at all—just individuals competing with each other in the marketplace, with the profit-making corporation as the only constitutionally protected legitimate collective institution.

Again, the individuals at the 1993 White House rally, and those whom they represented, understood what NAFTA meant for *their* future: a career of riding the rising tide of international investment. More clients, more deals, new friends and partners among the business elite; suites at the Four Seasons, meetings in the world's best restaurants with the charming and interesting, vacations in places that the middle class has never heard of.

NAFTA, like the Reaganite economics that inspired it, was an attempt to privatize the shaping of the future by the governing class and its corporate clients under the cover of a nihilistic faith in the market's creative destruction for which no one is responsible. We are all on our own, except of course for those with "access."

It was not always the case. Before Reagan, America was in fact slowly developing an infrastructure for democratizing the debate over where we were going together. City and transportation planning spread in the 1940s and 1950s. When he was president, Dwight Eisenhower created a National Goals Commission. In the 1960s, the process was opened up to the general public; the right of citizens to participate in decisions that were previously made behind bureaucratic doors was established, even for the poor. Officials now had to respond to citizen questions in open hearings. Under Richard Nixon the process was made routine and the federal government made many of its programs contingent upon a locally approved plan for the future to spend the money.

The process moved further along in the mid-1970s under both Jerry Ford and Jimmy Carter. Around the time of the bicentennial celebration of the American Revolution, citizens and officials in a large number of cities and states engaged in public dialogue about their common future through meetings and discussion groups. Many came up with specific plans—a vision of California, or Atlanta, or Maine in the year 2000. For some, the focus was on land use planning and transportation systems. Others became engaged in the issue of environmental sustainability and energy efficiencies. Still others moved to more difficult questions of the relationship between races, genders, and classes. Some of the efforts were of high quality. Some were little more than civic boosterism. But most supported a public dialogue that enriched the quality of local citizenship.

Most of these activities stopped dead after the election of Ronald Reagan in 1980, when the conversion of public purpose into private profit became the dominant definition of progress.

The coming financial crisis—whether an economic meltdown or a long period of hard times—could provide us with an historic opportunity to reexamine and reject the Reagan-Thatcher ideologies that still dominate American politics. It could, if we are lucky, return us to the task of democratizing the future, building a political economy that is prosperous, equitable, and sustainable and that reflects the interests of America's citizens, not just the corporate clients of its governing class.

The Continental "We"

We can start again, but we cannot start over. The world has changed dramatically since Reagan's election. And so has the definition of "us." NAFTA has permanently merged the economic geography of the United States, Canada, and Mexico. Our domestic economy now stretches not just from the Atlantic to the Pacific, but from the Arctic to Chiapas. Despite U.S. homeland security policies, anti-immigrant sentiment in border states, and bursts of nationalism in Mexico and Canada, the toothpaste of NAFTA cannot be put back into the tube. Bankers and brokers now deal with each other in a seamless web of finance. Car makers and food packagers are dependent on supplies and markets in all three countries. And the movement of people back and forth across the borders cannot be stopped. Cultures are mixing, and new common rules will be needed. Like it or not, we are building a continental society.

The North American common market now contains more than 430 million people with an annual GDP of close to $20 trillion. In 2003, Canada was the world's eleventh largest economy, and Mexico was number twelve.[1]

When the American governing class is finally forced to come up with a strategy for the country to work its way out of the debt trap, it will find itself hung by its own petard. Twenty-five to 30 percent of the entire production of Canada and Mexico is now dependent on sales to the U.S. market. The elimination or even substantial reduction of the U.S. trade deficit could thus do them substantial damage, as well as disrupt American businesses with cross-border production and marketing. It could plunge Mexico into an explosive social crisis, which, given the level of social and economic integration, would be a political nightmare.

Both Canada and Mexico, weaned from their traditional policies of economic independence, now depend on the American market for growth, with 85–90 percent of Canadian and Mexican exports now going to the United States. Between 1994 and 2001, American investors supplied 58 and 46 percent respectively of the foreign direct investment into Canada and Mexico.

The process has gone way beyond trade and investment relations. Every day, more intracontinental connections in finance, marketing, production, and other business networks are being hardwired for a seamless North American market.

Increasingly, the national economies are not simply selling each other goods and services, but producing together. A large share of U.S. trade with Canada and Mexico occurs within the same or an affiliated firm. The auto industry, which makes up some 25 percent of U.S.-Canadian trade, is the most dramatic example. Ford pickup trucks are now assembled in Mexico's Cuautitlán, with engines coming from Canada's Windsor, Ontario, and transmissions made in America's Livonia, Michigan. A car made in North America may, in its separate pieces, cross the borders dozens of times before it is finally sold.

As the report of a conference sponsored by Canadian, Mexican, and U.S. business schools in November 2003 concluded, "Americans do not buy Canadian cars and they do not sell American cars to Canada. Americans and Canadians (and Mexicans) make North American cars together in the same companies, in cross-border continental production networks. We also share increasingly integrated energy markets, service the same customers with an array of financial services, use the same roads and railroads to transport jointly made products to market, fly on the same integrated airlines networks, and increasingly meet the same or similar standards of professional practice."[2]

The process of economic integration takes time. Businesses in one country have to learn how to outsource to another. A manufacturer of refrigerators cannot simply shut down a plant in Iowa one week and open up in Mexico the next. Except for the very largest, most businesses cannot make such shifts by themselves. So an industry of lawyers and plant locators and accountants and fixers has to develop. It also takes time for the experience of the first pioneers to feed back to the second wave of industrial firms wanting to relocate. Where companies own the factory and land, they cannot easily pull up stakes. Typically, the company lets the old facility wear out, laying off small numbers of workers slowly while it prepares to relocate. Often the decision is made at the moment of expansion, or the shift to a new product line.

It is nevertheless relentless. To accommodate trade, transportation links are bending north-south. The Canadian federal government's two-hundred-year transportation policy of linking Canada east-west, and later north to the undeveloped north, is now shifting to widen the routes to the U.S. market. It is not the federal government in Ottawa that is driving this change; the provinces are shifting their road plans in response to the increasing demands from exporters and importers. Mexican, Canadian, and U.S. transportation companies have made plans for a seamless rail system through the continent. Kansas City Southern and its Mexican subsidiary call their service NAFTA Rail.[3] By 1997 Canada and the United States had the most air connections of any two nations in the world. More than fifteen million passengers flew between the United States and Mexico in 2003, an almost 40 percent increase since 1994.

The financial markets are perhaps the most fully integrated. Banks, insurance companies, and securities firms operate continent-wide under the protection of NAFTA. Mexican and Canadian firms sell stock on the New York Stock Exchange, and Mexican investors can now buy U.S. stocks for pesos on the Mexican exchange.

As the economic relationships proliferate, cross-border political connections have grown among the states and provinces, outside the formal foreign policy apparatus of the three governments. Earl Fry, professor of Canadian Studies at Brigham Young University, observes, "only a small minority of the 200 nations around the world has a federal system, and three of them are concentrated in North America."[4]

Some eighteen American states now maintain offices in Mexico. Another twelve have offices in Canada. The large Canadian provinces have permanent commercial representation in the United States and Mexico. Ontario and Quebec are associate members of U.S. Council of State Governments. The governments of the New England states and eastern Canadian provinces have a formal association, as do British Columbia, Alberta, the Yukon, Washington, Oregon, Idaho, Montana, and Alaska. The governors of the Great Lakes states and the premiers of their provincial counterparts meet regularly on regional problems. On the southern border, the Border Governors Conference holds annual meetings between the heads of California, Arizona, New Mexico, Texas, Baja California, Chihuahua, Coahuila, Nuevo León, Sonora, and Tamaulipas. Formal commissions exist between Sonora and Arizona, Chihuahua and New Mexico, and Baja California and California.[5]

Along the frontiers, despite the restrictions of homeland security and the backlash against the cost of supporting immigrants in Arizona and other states, many people already ignore the legal boundaries of their country and think of themselves as living in one environmental and economic society.

Each year, well over half a billion legal trips are taken across the northern and southern borders of the United States. Canada and Mexico are the top destinations for U.S. travelers and 90 and 85 percent, respectively, of those countries' visitors are from the United States. For professionals from the United States and Canada—and increasingly from Mexico—career ladders are continental. At the other end of the labor market, migrant workers from Mexico have spread northward to virtually every U.S. region and Canada as well. Roughly one-quarter of Mexico's working-age population is now in the United States.

Tightened post–September 11, 2001, security notwithstanding, U.S. officialdom accommodates the porous border. Illegal immigrants now furnish much of the labor forces important in U.S. economic sectors—from meatpacking to hotels and casinos to construction to agriculture. As one Californian noted, "There are no immigration service roundups at harvest time." The expanding share of illegal migrants in low-wage industries led the AFL-CIO to support amnesty for them, believing that they would be easier to organize into unions if the boss couldn't threaten to have them deported. The provision of undocumented immigrants' services, drivers' licenses, and even the right to vote in local elections has become a major political issue in many states and localities.

Twenty years of heavy migration have created formal and informal political integration between Mexicans in the United States and Mexicans in Mexico. The government of Mexico finances an organization called the Institute for Mexicans Abroad in a number of U.S. cities. Its purpose is to provide assistance to immigrants, from English classes to help in getting the deceased back home for burial. Local advisory committees are now elected, and the members from various parts of the country now meet periodically in the United States or Mexico, creating a space for Mexican politics in the United States.

Because of their remittances, Mexicans living in the United States have gradually achieved influential status in their home communities.

Mexican politicians regularly visit Los Angeles, Chicago, and New York to raise funds and get the endorsements of immigrant leaders. In the Chicago barrios, it is said that you can't throw a rock without hitting a Mexican governor.

In many cities and towns, migrants from a number of Mexican states (Michoacán, Guerruero, and Zacatecas, to name a few) have formed clubs whose members contribute funds to hometown projects such as schools or playgrounds or health clinics. The leaders of these organizations wield increasing power back in Mexico, and some have already won election to several of Mexico's state legislatures, where the complex system of voting allows Mexicans living in the United States to run for office. The expected extension of the vote to Mexicans living abroad will increase their influence. Indeed, given the dual citizenship between the two countries, some of the same people could vote in the Mexican presidential election of 2006 and the American presidential election of 2008 without changing their residence or citizenship.

Music, art, sports, popular entertainment, eating habits, and daily routines have become more alike throughout North America. Much, but not all, of this has to do with the appeal of American mass entertainment. With the Canadian population crowded along the U.S. border, its attention has long been captured by the alluringly packaged images and high-decibel sounds to the south. The Canadian cultural establishment—both English and French—fights a constant battle to protect its native artists and writers and moviemakers. But even so, much of the content produced by those artists and writers and filmmakers is hardly distinguishable in style from that of their U.S. counterparts. In early 2005, the *New York Times* reported that Montreal was the hot town for Anglophone pop-rock music.

Popular Canadian cultural nationalism is having an even harder time. For a while, the Canadian beer company Molson ran ads featuring Joe, a Canadian patriot with an aggressive attitude toward all things American. The actor who played Joe became a Canadian icon. As a result of his success, he left for Hollywood. In January 2005, Molson merged with Denver-based Coors, a name associated with one of the most militantly right-wing American business families.

Mexicans, whose culture is more distinct, have more confidence in their culture to survive. But the cultural dynamics work in both directions. Mexican migrants, their Spanish amplified by Latinos from the Caribbean and South America, are clearly changing food, music, and styles in the United States. They are also bringing American culture back home—fast food, basketball, and U.S. movies. This Americanization has driven deepest in the border cities of Tijuana, Ciudad Juárez, and the business centers of Monterrey and Mexico City. But throughout Mexico the rhythms of Mexican life are steadily being altered to fit first world—American—patterns. This includes the traditional more casual sense of time. In urban areas the siesta is disappearing, and in 1996 Mexico adopted daylight savings time to conform to the workday in the United States.

Continental Politics, Post–September 11, 2001

When two ex-corporate executives, George W. Bush and Vicente Fox, became presidents of the United States and Mexico, they were ready to do some more business. Fox had come to Washington and Ottawa in September 2000, after his election as Mexican president. Brimming with confidence, he suggested to lame-duck Bill Clinton an expanded "NAFTA-Plus" along the lines of the European Union—specifically, Mexico would be given the equivalent of the European "cohesion" funds, transfers from rich countries to poor ones for infrastructure development. He also proposed that, like Europe, the NAFTA countries open up their borders to unrestricted labor mobility among the citizens of the three countries.

Clinton, who had sold NAFTA on the basis that free trade would keep Mexicans at home, and who had seen the protests in the streets of Seattle the previous winter, was not interested. Fox then went to Ottawa to propose a single currency for the continent. Jean Chrétien, whose country was benefiting from a weak currency relative to the U.S. dollar, responded with an icy "no thanks."

When Bush became president, Fox whittled down his expectations to making a deal on immigration. Bush, whose constituencies included many of the growers in Republican rural areas who wanted a more dependable supply of labor from Mexico, was willing to talk.

Their public relations people dubbed them the "two amigos," and they tramped around each other's haciendas in Texas and Guanajuato, seemingly bonded by a shared landscape and a shared faith in unregulated markets. The bureaucracies in both countries began to negotiate new deals involving a guest-worker program and more access for U.S. companies to Mexico's nationally owned oil.

But in the immediate wake of the September 11, 2001, terrorist attacks, encouraging immigration from anywhere was a political nonstarter in U.S. politics. The White House put Mexico on its back burner. For a while, continental economic integration itself seemed to unravel. Tightened border security caused trucks to back up for miles into Canada and Mexico, and sudden new immigration restrictions fouled up thousands of cross-border business trips that had become routine for Canadian and Mexican businesspeople.

But commerce prevailed. More customs agents were sent to the border to break the bottlenecks. New "smart border" systems were initiated to allow Mexican and Canadian goods bound for the United States to be checked by American customs officials stationed at the factories, electronically sealed, and sent without interference into the United States. Plans were developed for "NAFTA Express" immigration lines at airports for citizens of the three North American countries. Ultimately, the war on terrorism is more likely to constrict the freedom of Americans under the Bill of Rights than the freedom of money and goods to cross borders under NAFTA.

Fox, who had staked his presidency on his relationship with Bush, saw his popularity at home plummet along with the Mexican economy, which was now tied to the United States in recession. Feeling abandoned, and faced with huge majorities of Mexicans who opposed the invasion of Iraq, he had Mexico side with France and Russia in the dispute over the wording of the United Nations resolution on Iraq. At an international conference in October 2003, an angry Bush cold-shouldered his old pal.

The invasion of Iraq split the business classes from the public in both Canada and Mexico. Businesspeople, fearing that the U.S. government would somehow retaliate economically against them, demanded that their governments support the U.S. action. But the publics were overwhelmingly and passionately against the war. In the end, Fox and Chrétien held back. The reason they could was that the economic integration of the two countries with the U.S. economy had gone so far that the neoconservatives in the Bush administration did not have much leverage to force them to get in line.

Although on the whole Mexico and Canada are more dependent on the United States than the United States is on them, hurting Canadian or Mexican businesses by shutting the border would hurt important American businesses as well. Indeed, they were often the same business. The corporations who now depended on Mexican low-wage labor were, after all, among the strongest supporters of George Bush.

The late Adolfo Aguilar Zinser, who was Mexico's ambassador to the UN at the time, recalled asking the Mexican businesspeople who were pressuring the Fox government to support the United States how, in fact, they thought the business-oriented U.S. government would retaliate. "They couldn't tell me," he said.[6]

Still, while unwilling to take the political risk of sending their soldiers to fight the unpopular Bush's unpopular war, both governments gave support in less visible ways. Chrétien increased Canada's participation in the occupation of Afghanistan and maintained navy patrols in the Persian Gulf, which freed up U.S. forces for Iraq. Canada also made substantial contributions to the Iraq reconstruction program and overall gave more support to the U.S. operation than all but Great Britain and Australia in Bush's Coalition of the Willing. In Mexico, Fox redeployed some thirty thousand police and national military to the borders and the defense of American-owned assets in Mexico in order to accommodate U.S. security concerns. And both Mexico and Canada reorganized their own government agencies to make it easier to cooperate with the homeland security program of the Bush administration.

Bush, of course, remained out-of-sorts with both Fox and Paul Martin, who succeeded Chrétien as prime minister. But Bush or no Bush, and despite the war on terror, the three countries are now on an irreversible path to further economic integration.

NAFTA II: By Stealth and Panic

The citizens of each of the nations were led to believe that NAFTA was simply a "free trade" agreement, not a new constitution. So the economic and political governance of North America has been developing through the informal networking of bureaucrats, lawyers, and lobbyists that Anne-Marie Slaughter describes. Making incremental obscure agreements and understandings on environmental, military, judicial, transportation, energy, agricultural, tax, regulatory, lumber, water, and hundreds of other issues, government officials are setting precedents outside of the political radar screen, obligating their governments and connecting the three societies together knot by knot.

But as the countries' economies have meshed, it has become obvious that many of the interfaces do not connect and cannot be patched through bureaucratic back channels. The courts are filled with cases ranging from American disputes with the Canadians over softwood lumber to conflicts with Mexicans over truck drivers and the death penalty for Mexican citizens convicted in U.S. state courts. American state governments are making contracts to buy Canadian medicines while Washington is trying to stop them, and Canadians are worried that there won't be enough left over for their needs. On the one hand, American growers want the U.S. immigration service to look the other way so they can employ more cheap immigrant laborers. On the other, conservative populists are demanding a crackdown on undocumented workers. Meanwhile, Latino voters are pressing for more services and rights for immigrants, from drivers' licenses to health, education, and social services. At some point the informal arrangements have to be made legal so they can be understood and enforced.

So negotiations among the governing classes to expand NAFTA continue. The Mexican elites want a deal to make it easier for people to migrate. The U.S. elites want cheap labor and access to Mexican and Canadian oil for "American" oil companies. The Canadian governing class wants to eliminate U.S. laws on "antidumping." But the discussions are held in secret through the extended informal networks. As one journalist noted in March 2005, "Officials have been quietly negotiating the initiative for a year and a half, avoiding public comments as election campaigns were being conducted in Canada and the United States."[7] The voting public of course could not be trusted with the knowledge that their countries were to be further merged.

The NAFTA Trap

The unstoppable integration of the North American economies will make the coming U.S. financial adjustment much more difficult. In effect, the United States government will have to rebalance the country's huge trade deficit without doing damage to its largest and third largest trading partners.

Canada's social safety net, although frayed, is still relatively strong and, up to a point, would help cushion the blow from a loss of U.S. markets and give the economy time to diversify some of its exports and to build up stronger domestic demand. Even so, it will face a much more competitive world market. With Canada exporting roughly half of its GDP, living standards will most certainly stagnate, if not fall. The bitter disputes between American and Canadian producers over softwood lumber and North Atlantic fishing would spread and the Canadian governing class would have to reflect the anger of the citizens. An American government need not be worried about hordes of unemployed Canadians coming across its northern border, but the United States is now very dependent on close Canadian collaboration and goodwill for air defenses and homeland security.

Mexico's economy, which is much less flexible and has half of its population already living at rock bottom, would be hurt much more. The border region, almost entirely dependent on the U.S. market, would face crushing unemployment. Even larger numbers of Mexicans will be crossing the border illegally. The U.S. governing class could at a great expense build even taller and longer walls between the United States and Mexico, but the effect would be to shut off the safety valve of migration that has protected its Mexican partners against a left populist takeover—not to mention the alienation of Latino voters.

An economic crisis in Mexico caused by an effort to turn around the U.S. balance of trade would be widely seen by virtually all economic classes in Mexico as a huge betrayal of trust. This would threaten Washington with the election of an anti-U.S. government, right on the border. Already the failure of neoliberalism to make life better for most people in Latin America had by early 2005 brought leftist governments of varying degrees to Venezuela, Brazil, Argentina, and Uruguay. The U.S. elite would not want to let that happen in Mexico. After all, preventing the left from coming to power after the disputed election of 1988 was a prime motive for Washington's commitment to NAFTA in the first place.

The problem, therefore, will be how to cut the U.S. trade deficit with the rest of the world without causing major political crises in

Mexico and Canada. Given that the rest of the world—the Chinese, the Japanese, the Europeans, the Latin Americans—is unlikely to sit back and give up markets in order to pull the American governing class's chestnuts out of the fire, this will be no small task.

Already the looming competitiveness problems are worrying the policy intellectuals and the business think tanks in all three countries. Thus U.S. Council on Foreign Relations, the Mexican Council on Foreign Affairs, and the Canadian Council of Chief Executives set up an Independent Task Force on the Future of North America. It is composed of corporate directors and lawyers, ex–high government officials, and a sprinkling of business-oriented academics from the three NAFTA countries. In March 2005, its principal chairs— former Canadian finance minister and deputy prime minister John Manley, former Massachusetts Republican governor William Weld, and former Mexican finance minister Pedro Aspe—released a statement calling for NAFTA's next stage, including a shared military security perimeter for the continent, a common tariff with the rest of the world cut to the lowest level on each product, common energy and natural resource policies, and an investment fund for Mexico.[8] Overseeing it all would be a nonelected North American Advisory Council "to prepare and monitor" decisions that would be made in summit meetings by the heads of the three countries.[9]

The task force report is a good indication of the bind that the governing classes of the three countries have gotten themselves into. The call for a common tariff, Mexican development, and a continental energy policy hints at the sort of activist government intervention in the economy that NAFTA was supposed to make impossible. It implicitly acknowledges that free trade abroad and limited government at home are incompatible.

Just a few years before, one of the prominent members of the task force, Wendy Dobson, business school professor and former head of the business-backed C.D. Howe Institute in Toronto, had defended NAFTA's restrictions on regulating business as a way of assuring that governments would never engage in "industrial policy." "States are the architects of their own restraints," she wrote approvingly, using the same logic that defends people's right to sell themselves into slavery. Of course, it wasn't the "states" that voluntarily restrained themselves; why would any institution voluntarily give up its own freedom and sovereignty? Rather, it was those in charge of the governments at the time. The result was that the freedom of states to invest in even the most traditional of public enterprises like postal service, education, and health care have been undercut. Moreover, the deliberately intensified competition among localities for new business assured that governments' tax revenues would be restricted and their stomach for regulation greatly diminished.

But the role of government being suggested by the task force's somewhat tortured language is far from restrained, indicating that the members know that it will take more than free trade to rescue their capital invested in the hemisphere from Chinese competition and American financial vulnerability.

A "common tariff" is a euphemism for a customs union, that is, a joint trade policy against the rest of the world, and the removal of all trade barriers internally. This could protect Canada and Mexico from U.S. policies aimed at cutting its trade deficit. But the governing class's class interests have been in opening up their nations to the world, not just the United States. If the United States is going to resolve its trade deficit problem, it will have to erect more trade barriers against the rest of the world. This would result in the raising of prices for Mexicans and Canadians in order to bail out the United States—not exactly something to make a politician popular. Yet, because Mexico and Canada are dependent on the United States, a customs union with America would give them some protection against the "China price."

One of the members of the task force was asked, on the assurance of anonymity, what was discussed during their sessions.

"China," was the response.

What else?

"China."

11

Imagining North America

Having lost the comfort of our geographical boundaries,
we must in effect rediscover what creates the bond between humans
that constitutes a community.

—Jean-Marie Guéhenno

As long as the people of Canada, Mexico, and the United States see their political interests as separate from one another, while the elites of these same nations see their interests as joined, the gap in wealth and opportunity between the Party of Davos and the rest of us will continue to grow in all three nations.

But the elites of North America are also caught in their own trap. The glib assertions of the American governing class about miracles of free trade and investment and of the immunity of America to the laws of credit and debt will come back to haunt them. It turns out that their transnational corporate clients meant what they said about preferring to rule their world from a faraway island. In turn, the Canadian and Mexican business people are finding that the American wagon to which they have hitched themselves is both politically erratic and increasingly economically unstable.

The process of globalization is incomplete, so the transition of many large firms to full transnational operation is also incomplete. Some will not make it. But in the culture of business, the smaller and more numerous firms take their political cues from the larger ones. Thus, members of the U.S. Chamber of Commerce, the National Association of Manufacturers, and the various trade associations follow the lead of the transnational CEOs whose free-trade and investment agenda undercuts the long-term interests of the modest-sized businesses that are stuck in America. In part this is because of the peer pressure that enforces ideological solidarity. In part it is because the larger firms have the resources and clout to make sure the associations pursue their interests.

The same is true in Canada and Mexico, where businesspeople support U.S. foreign policy, even when it is against their interests. At a meeting of business and political leaders in Mexico City in early 2003, this writer asked why Mexican businesspeople favored the extension of free trade with the United States to Central and Latin America, given that it meant reducing Mexicans' special access to the U.S. market. After being assured that the answers were "not for attribution," the chairman said that he didn't think anyone there doubted that it would hurt the Mexican economy. Heads nodded around the table. The question of why they didn't oppose it was answered with a shrug.

The fact that most business assets in North America cannot be shifted overseas suggests that at some point at least a portion of the businesspeople will begin to see that their interests are distinct from those of the larger transnational corporations. Those who see that they cannot easily fly across the seas may come back to earth. Already there are stirrings of dissent against free trade in the U.S. Chamber of Commerce and the National Association of Manufacturers.[1]

At the same 2003 Mexico City meeting, some of the Mexican businesspeople grumbled that they had been somewhat mistreated by their American counterparts. They had been led to believe that NAFTA represented a partnership between themselves and American big business. Together, they would compete against the world, with Mexican business supplying the low-wage labor and the U.S. business supplying the capital. Some of this of course occurred. But shortly afterward, the U.S. government embraced the World Trade

Organization and actively encouraged the entry of China into the world market, which then undercut Mexico's low-wage strategy. The proposed extension of NAFTA to Central and South America further undercut the strategy. When I mentioned this to people who had promoted NAFTA in Washington, I was told that the Mexicans had been mistaken, or naïve. Anyway, "things changed."

What these Mexicans did not see was that the motivation for NAFTA was not to improve the competitiveness of the United States, much less North America. It was to sever the competitiveness of the private corporations from the competitiveness of *any* particular country or continent. Once NAFTA established that principle, there was no need to be restricted to North America.

But "things" are changing again. Given the integration of North America, the coming traumatic adjustment of the U.S. economy will require the American governing class to give priority to the question of how North America as a whole is going to compete and prosper in this new world. While U.S. governing class will be forced to pull back from its pursuit of neoliberal globalization, it cannot extract itself from NAFTA. Neither can the Mexican or Canadian governing classes. They have created a continental economy, to which the economic fate of the working-class majorities in the three nations—as opposed to their globally mobile investors—is now tied.

As we have seen, governing-class intellectuals in all three countries are thinking about NAFTA's next stage. But that next stage can no longer be marketed as "free trade." It will require a much more intense level of integration among the three nations than even the people at the Independent Task Force on the Future of North America will publicly admit. Thus, in order to make a customs union effective, a whole host of economic policies have to be in some way harmonized—taxes, product standards, and eventually currency. To say the least, this will raise a huge number of complicated and contentious issues, including those of sovereignty and the fate of what is left of each nation's social contract that cannot be avoided by repeating the mantra of "free trade," and for which the electorates of the countries—particularly in the United States—are not prepared.

Certainly for many Americans, Canadians, and Mexicans a new North American political and economic democracy will seem to some a wildly utopian idea. It is a common assumption of our geopolitical language that independent nation-states are the natural outgrowth of separate cultures—deep ethnic and social forces that have evolved through the centuries, using and casting off various forms of organization around the tribe, the religious sect, feudal systems, and the absolute monarchy to arrive finally at the nation-state that reflects their unique community.

But the evidence suggests that all modern nation-states are somewhat arbitrary creations. Most began as "imagined communities," as the influential sociologist Benedict Anderson calls them.[2] Established seemingly permanent nations often originated as political abstractions, financed by narrow economic interests, and helped along by the accidents of history. Had the French fleet not been in the right place at the right time outside of Yorktown, the American Revolution might not have ended with a separate nation at all.

As for culture and language, the historian Ernest Gellner notes that there are at least eight thousand separate languages in the world, but fewer than two hundred countries, and many of those contain separate languages and cultures. The cultural differences *within* nation-states are often much greater than the cultural distinctions *between* them. Thus, "Dialectical and cultural differences within Germany or Italy are as great as those between recognized Teutonic or Romance languages. Southern Russians differ culturally from Northern Russians, but, unlike Ukrainians, do not translate this into a sense of nationhood."[3]

This is not to underestimate the importance of nationalism, which is by far the strongest secular political force in the world. Nor is it to make the case for one single North American nation. It is simply to remind us that human beings have the power to recreate their own political institutions, including the definition of who is a fellow citizen. It is also worth noting that the present political boundaries of the three nations of North America—and the internal configuration of their states and provinces—are themselves less than two hundred years old.

The European Model

In contemplating the future integration of North America, it is the experience of the European Union that most comes to mind, just as the founders of the EU—originally dubbed the United States of

Europe—had looked to the United States to help think through their model of federalism.

The European Union, created in the ashes of a massively destructive half century of European history, reflected an understanding that simply expanding trade among nations was not enough to prevent war. World War I and World War II were in effect two parts of the same war. In the two decades before World War I, trade between Britain and Germany rose substantially. This led many of the businesspeople on both sides to declare that war between the two was impossible, because each nation was the other's best customer.

But expanding trade actually aggravated nationalist rivalry. Economic competition was the "soil out of which the great questions at issue between the two nations grew," wrote one historian. "It was a source of fear for alarmists to exploit, and it gave nourishment to suspicions, jealousy, and hatred."[4]

Given that experience, the framers of post–World War II Europe did not make the mistake of thinking that simple free trade was the answer to war. Only a much closer economic interdependence could blunt the edges of the excessive nationalism that plagued the continent for so long. Nor, despite their commitment to market economics, did they make the mistake of thinking that if markets are socially useful it makes sense to turn society into one big market. The European Union was grounded on a generally shared social model in which citizens are not alone. They take for granted a high level of social solidarity and public investment in people—and they have been willing to pay the taxes necessary to support it.

There is no one model European social contract. Each has its own variation. The Scandinavians have strong safety nets and less government enterprise. The Mediterranean nations, with a Catholic tradition, have more government enterprise and build their social system around the family. The "Rhenish" model in Germany, Austria, and the Benelux countries is built more explicitly around labor–management partnerships. But their citizens and elites (the latter sometimes grudgingly) all share the conscious assumption that the market is an instrument to serve social values. Indeed, the term "welfare" does not have the offensive connotation it has in the United States: in Europe it is used as it is used in the preamble to the U.S. Constitution, which states that its purpose is to "promote the general Welfare."

Because the European Union was a merger of nations with different levels of development, initially there was widespread fear that allowing workers to move across borders would mean flooding the richer nations like France, Germany, Britain, and Holland with migrants from Spain, Portugal, Greece, and Ireland. So the EU was constructed with a conscious "cohesion" policy. The wealthier countries provided loans and grants for investment to the poorer ones, designed to close the economic gap between them. The funds were important both for their investment value and as an incentive for modernizing the archaic economic policies of the poorer countries.

In order to get political support at home in the advanced economies, many of the funds were designated for impoverished "areas" rather than impoverished countries, so that poor sectors of rich countries were eligible as well. But most of the money went to the four laggard economies of Spain, Portugal, Greece, and Ireland.

The system was a resounding success. Unlike with NAFTA, the poorer nations grew faster than the richer ones and the gap between them narrowed. In the case of Ireland, it disappeared. Indeed, by the dawn of the twenty-first century, Ireland's per capita GDP was above the EU average. The country whose people had been leaving in search of a better life for centuries became a net importer of migrants. Most stunning of all is what did *not* occur—the feared mass migration of the unemployed. As it turned out, when decent opportunities were created at home—even if the jobs were not as lucrative as in the richer nations—people stayed home. In 2001, only 2 percent of Europeans were looking for work in other EU countries.[5]

The cohesion funds were not the only reason for the success of the EU in closing the gaps between the rich and poor. Governments reduced interest rates, encouraged labor–management cooperation, and modernized education. But there is little doubt that the transfer of funds for public infrastructure played the vital role.

The process of European integration has been—and is—painful and difficult. Every major step forward has been subject to fiery public debates over the rules, particularly over the balance between individual rights, democracy, national sovereignty, and market efficiency. Britain, among others, has so far refused to take the step of joining the euro zone. Nationalist resistance to rule by bureaucrats in "Brussels" has at times been fierce, giving rise to chronic complaints about a "democratic deficit." The elected European parliament is weak. And the labor, environmental, and other social movements, which are not nearly as organized as the business world, have to work hard to keep Europeanization from becoming another way for corporate elites to escape the social contract.

After half a century, that Europe is not as integrated as the United States is not surprising. The difficulties of overcoming differences in language, culture, and national identity are immeasurably greater than was the problem of joining the thirteen colonies and their western territories in 1789. Even so, the question of union in the United States was not finally settled until the Civil War ended in 1865.

It also remains to be seen whether the decision to expand to the ten poorer economies in Eastern Europe may be more than the EU can successfully swallow at this stage of its evolution. The rejection of the proposed new EU constitution by the French and Dutch voters in the spring of 2005 showed how far Europe's elites had gotten away from the interests and concerns of average citizens—mostly the threat that jobs and wages would be undercut by lower-paid workers from the East.

Western European voters had been willing to take the risk with the original union of fifteen nations for two reasons. One was to avoid plunging the continent into another war between France and Germany. By 2005, no one was worried about war between Eastern and Western Europe. The other reason was the protection against low-wage competition provided by the cohesion fund strategy. But the new eastward expansion of the European Union would provide little of the compensatory funds for the poorer nations. Indeed, the priorities of the governing class on that score were reflected in the defeated constitution's 174 references to economic competition, 78 markets, and 3 to the subject of social protections.

Popular resistance has delayed the process of European integration, as it has on occasion in the past. Europe's elites will now have to take the time to modify their program for a neoliberal makeover of the European Union. But the European project is not likely to be derailed. Over the years the sense of being a citizen of Europe has certainly grown, especially among the young, who are the greatest supporters of a united Europe. In virtually every referendum on

Europe in every country, it is the youngest voters—Generation "E" (for Europe)—who vote for more and faster integration. They are the reason that it is just a matter of time before the British—and the Swedes and the Danes—accept the euro.[6]

Imperfect, plagued with the confusion of having to communicate in multiple languages, along with all the other difficulties of integration, Europe nevertheless represents the world's most advanced effort at resolving the mismatch between political democracy and globalizing economic boundaries. Its people are engaged in dealing with the immense question of reconciling accountability and cultural diversity with the necessity of developing larger institutions.

The vastness of the enterprise of building a new Europe absorbs the time and energies of the elites. Their attention is concentrated on projects to unify: Airbus, space missions, the "Chunnel." Compared with their American counterparts, the European governing class is more inward-looking, less aggressive internationally, and less able to throw its weight around in the world. Rather, it is forced into an ongoing conscious and transparent political debate—open to all—across national boundaries over the continent's future. From the perspective of American elites, this insularity and self-absorption of the European governing class is a weakness. From the perspective of America's ordinary working people, if clearly understood, it is a blessing.

Newlanders?

North America is not Europe. NAFTA is not the European Union. But the European experience is a useful reminder of the potential for people—not just elites—to cast off deep-seated nationalist feelings in order to build a future in their common interest.

One obvious difference between the integration of Europe and North America is that the latter will not, of course, be motivated by the fear of war. Another difference is the imbalance of power between the United States and its neighbors. California's GDP alone is roughly the size of the Canadian and Mexican economies combined. And the U.S. location as the huge filling of the North American "sandwich" means that economic integration of North America is not as much trilateral as it is two sets of bilateral relations. Trade and finance relations between Canada and Mexico are expanding but still relatively small. The elites of Canada and Mexico are becoming closer, Mexican immigration to Canada is growing, and Canadian vacationers in Mexico are increasing. But the way the people of these two countries have interconnected is largely through the United States.

Yet in many ways, obstacles to the political integration of North America are less formidable than those faced by the integration of Europe. The European Union now encompasses twenty-five separate nations with twenty different official languages. There are a dozen more nations on the European continent that could logically be absorbed, before one gets to the huge question of Turkey.

NAFTA is only three nations. Counting Quebecois French, it involves three principal languages. And although the settlement of North America has its own violent history, it pales beside the deep-rooted hatreds and blood feuds of Europe's past.

As yet there is little consciousness of being North American among the people of the three nations. Once the history books have covered the earliest European explorers, they quickly settle into the separate stories of Canada, Mexico, or the United States. The question of whether Mexico is in fact in North America (Mexicans still refer to people living in the United States as *Norteamericanos*) has only been answered recently—by NAFTA. Despite common struggles with industrialization and discrimination, there are few histories of the North American labor movement, North American race relations, or the North American women's movement. A search of the U.S. Library of Congress finds no citation for a history of North America.

Yet there is some broad commonality in the collective experience of the three societies: the original human settlement by nomadic Asians, the conquest of the Europeans, the throwing off of the colonial yoke, and the oppression of the indigenous population. Most of all, perhaps, is their common status as nations of the New World. Anthony DePalma, an American journalist who wrote a survey of Mexican and Canadian politics and culture, suggests that citizens of North America might be called "Newlanders."[7]

Certainly they are all young countries and, in different ways, are kept young through migration. The back-and-forth movement of migrants to the United States has been the way in which many Mexicans get real-life contact with the wider outside world. Both Canada and the United States have grown through inmigration: in 2000, the share of their populations that are foreign-born was 19 and 12 percent respectively. In Mexico it was less than 1 percent, although in the twentieth century the country was a haven for refugees from the Spanish civil war, the Holocaust, and unrest in Central and South America.

The history of each nation is different, but the large historical framework within which they developed is similar. All three countries' political systems are the products of "creole" culture—people of European descent born in the colonies, who freed themselves from imperial authority in London and Madrid. In Mexico, the indigenous population had already created several civilizations, which the Spanish destroyed. But the culture remained, and modern Mexico—which celebrates its mixed, or mestizo, heritage—has a strong indigenous character missing from its northern neighbors whose creoles decimated the native population.

The U.S.-Mexico War of a century and a half ago is the biggest conflict in our collective historical relationship. While most Americans have, at best, a vague notion that their country seized well more that 40 percent of Mexico's territory in 1848, the event is embedded in Mexico's collective memory.[8] Every schoolchild knows the story of the gallant student-soldiers of Chapultepec Castle in the heart of Mexico City, defying the U.S. Army to the death. Mexicans are acutely aware of other U.S. interventions—including the occupation of Veracruz in 1914—that are hardly blips on the radar screen of what Americans consider U.S. history. But few Mexicans harbor illusions of regaining the territory. There are no politics in dreaming of reconquest in Mexico.

In the early days of the American republic, Canada was also considered up for grabs. After the British conquest of New France in 1760, the American revolutionists made several attempts to convince the French settlers in Quebec to join them in their rebellion against Great Britain. But the British had promised French Catholic leadership cultural autonomy, and the Quebecois trusted the English "high church" Episcopalians more than they did the fundamentalist Protestants who dominated New England just across the border. So they sat it out.

In the wake of the American Revolution, some forty thousand Tories fled the thirteen colonies to Canada, reinforcing resistance to

U.S. northward expansion. Still, many in the new United States assumed that sooner or later, all of British North America would become one nation. The first American constitution—the Articles of Confederation of 1781—specifically preapproved any future application from Canada to become a state. The last significant armed conflict between the United States and Canada (or the British in Canada) was the War of 1812.

After the American Civil War, the U.S. government had a million-man army. Strong voices in Congress, still smarting from British support for the Southern cause, wanted to send it north. The British, who had been fought to a draw in the War of 1812 when the United States was much weaker, avoided the challenge. With the British North America Act of 1867, Britain recognized Canada as an independent confederation resting on a delicate political agreement between the leadership of the English- and French-speaking populations.

The U.S. Civil War was also a turning point in Mexican history. For four decades after its independence, Mexico was wracked by internal wars, economic decline, and social chaos. In 1864, a group of Mexican conservatives invited the Austrian archduke Maximilian to begin a new Mexican monarchy. He was backed by an army sent by Napoleon III of France, who had been convinced by his advisers that the Mexican people would welcome the return of European rulers with open arms. But many Mexicans rebelled. Two years later, with the U.S. Civil War over and a huge American army threatening to march south to dislodge the French, Napoleon III withdrew his troops. Maximilian went to the firing squad, ending Europe's last claim on the country. With the U.S. purchase of Alaska from the Russians in 1867 the entire North American continent became formally under the control of its residents—or at least its resident elites.

The latter part of the nineteenth century saw the industrialization of all three nations. Manufacturing, railroads, the telegraph and telephone were sources of great profit, jobs, and urbanization. In the United States and Canada, the working class moved from the farms to the factories, and the divide between labor and capital widened. Throughout the continent, the governing classes declared war on efforts to challenge their economic prerogatives. The history of all three nations of North America is studded with instances where workers risked beatings, mass arrests, and murder for the right to ask for better wages and working conditions. Historic confrontations occurred at mines in Cobalt, Ontario; Ludlow, Colorado; and Cananea, Sonora. They occurred at textile mills in Río Blanco, Veracruz; Valleyfield, Quebec; and Lawrence, Massachusetts; on the Mexican National Railway, the Canadian Pacific, the Pullman Company.

Mexico's industrialization was particularly brutal, directed by the dictator Porfirio Díaz, a general in the war against the French who then ruled Mexico for thirty-five years. In 1910, Mexicans revolted against Díaz. The revolution became a civil war that continued off and on for two decades, ending with the compromise that established a broad national social contract with the Partido Revolucionario Institucional as its protector. In the 1930s, the oil industry was nationalized, land given to peasants, and public social services initiated.

The 1930s also saw an expansion of left-of-center politics in the United States and Canada, with the triumph of the Democratic Party's New Deal in 1932 and the Canadian Liberals in 1935. Over the next forty years, the U.S. Democrats and Canadian Liberals were the engines of political change in their respective countries. They introduced Keynesian economics, Social Security, unemployment compensation, health care programs, and quality public education. The elites of both nations turned their attention to shaping the future with ambitious investments. American political leaders created the Tennessee Valley Authority, the great western dams, and the national highway system. Canadians developed the nation's immense hydroelectric potential, built the St. Lawrence Seaway, and created a strong east-west highway and rail system.

In Canada especially, efficient compassionate government was a source of pride and national cohesion, which was increasingly at risk. As immigrants from all over the world swelled the Canadian population, the special minority status of Quebec weakened. The great compromises of the eighteenth and nineteenth centuries seemed obsolete to the newcomers. At the same time, a demand for more autonomy and, if not, independence arose in a modernizing and increasingly secular Quebec. Provincial referenda proposing that the province become an independent nation narrowly lost several times.

As we have seen, business elites in all three nations organized a counterrevolution in the 1970s. Conservatives invested in think tanks, university economics departments, and the media to change the public dialogue. The first wave of conservative victories produced Reagan,

Mulroney, and de la Madrid, all of whom began the process of tearing up the social contract. In Canada and the United States, the ideological shift was reflected in deepening fissures between the major political parties. In Mexico the conservative triumph took place within the one-party rule of the PRI.

A decade later, the second wave of continental neoliberalism swept into power. Clinton the New Democrat was in Washington. Chrétien the New Liberal was in Ottawa. Salinas, the leader of the New PRI, was running Mexico.

Who "We" Are

Is it credible to think that the non-elite majorities of Canadians, Mexicans, and Americans would respond to a call for a common social agenda to fit the emerging continental market?

Polls show that they have different political attitudes, but not as different as many stereotypes suggest. Canadians and Mexicans expect more out of government than do Americans. A 2003 poll of people in all three countries asked whether it was more important for government to guarantee that no one be in need or for people to be free from government to pursue their goals. Fifty-eight percent of Americans, but only 43 percent of Canadians and 46 percent of Mexicans, opted for less government as a priority. On the other hand, the same poll showed that 71 percent of Canadians, as opposed to just 55 percent of Americans and 51 percent of Mexicans, believed in the separation of church and state. Sixty-nine percent of Canadians, but only 51 percent of Americans and 54 percent of Mexicans, felt that homosexuality should be "accepted" by society.[9]

Canadians of course take much of their national identity from their social democratic values. In addition to their stronger social safety net, their drug laws are more progressive, same-sex marriage is accepted, and while gun ownership is high and Canadians watch many of the same violent shows that Americans do, the rate of violent crime is about one-tenth that of the United States. Mexico has more guns per capita and more violent crime than even the United States. But like Canada, it bans the death penalty.

Much is made of these differences, especially in the Canadian press, which reflects the national preoccupation with their relationship to the United States. A best-seller in Canada, *Fire and Ice*, by

Canadian pollster Michael Adams, amassed an array of statistics to prove that the social "values" of Canadians and Americans were diverging.[10] In the space of a decade, characteristics like openness and tolerance that once were associated with Americans are now more characteristic of Canadians. Yet it is mostly the Americans who have changed. Thus, on one key measure of community, whether one discusses local problems with others, Americans dropped from 66 to 34 percent. Canadians also dropped, but only from 52 to 47 percent. So while Adams's description may be accurate, one has to wonder how much these values show permanent differences and how much they might change back under different circumstances.

The American polling analyst Ruy Teixeira and his coauthor, journalist John Judis, offer convincing evidence that the demographics of the American electorate point to a much less conservative future.[11] They suggest that American political values will become more liberal "blue state," that is, more like Canada, as a result of shifting demographics—which, by the way, includes a large and growing Latino population. Already it is clear that the majority of the American people are more liberal than their elites on questions of government responsibility. Consistent majorities think that the government should be responsible for assuring access to affordable health care for every citizen and for making sure that there is a job for everyone willing and able to work. As an old adage of American politics explains, Americans tend to be ideologically conservative but operationally liberal—and on many key questions not too far from the average Canadian.

Certainly neither Mexicans nor Canadians say they want to be absorbed by the United States. But when asked in a 2000 poll if they would be willing to form a new single country if it meant having a higher quality of life, majorities in *all three countries* said yes.

The events following September 11, 2001, had a substantial impact on the attitudes of Americans, Canadians, and Mexicans toward each other. At the end of the last century, 70 to 80 percent of Mexicans and Canadians had favorable views of the United States, and a similar percentage of Americans felt positively toward their neighbors to the north and south. In the immediate aftermath of the September 11 attacks, there was a huge outpouring of sympathy for the United States from Canada and Mexico. But, as in the rest of the world, it began to dissipate after the invasion of Afghanistan, and fell dramatically with the attack on and occupation of Iraq. By the fall of 2004, the percentage of Canadians and Mexicans with a favorable view of the United States had fallen considerably.

In both countries, overwhelming majorities opposed George W. Bush's reelection in 2004. Yet when Canadians were asked about their opinion of "Americans," as opposed to their opinion of "America," the favorable share remained high, at 77 percent.[12]

On the other hand, given the aggressive nationalism pumped up by George W. Bush and the media, Americans' views of both neighbors fell after their refusal to support the war in Iraq. Favorable views of Canada fell from 83 to 65 percent. Americans' regard for Mexico dropped to 54 percent.[13]

The major issue that isolated the majority of Americans from their neighbors was the Iraq war. Yet by March 2005, two years after the invasion of Iraq, a majority of Americans had joined most Canadians and Mexicans in believing that the war was a mistake.

Despite the divisions over September 11, 2001, there is still openness for more integration, even among the more wary Canadians. In 2002, when asked whether the three countries should integrate more, the same, or less, a plurality of Canadians wanted closer ties, a plurality of Americans wanted economic integration to remain where it was, and Mexicans were split between wanting more and wanting less.[14]

When Canadians were asked in 2001 if Canada would become part of a North American Union in ten years, 75 percent said it was moderately (30 percent chance) or highly (45 percent chance) likely. On the prospect of actually becoming part of the United States, 40 percent said it was moderately (23 percent chance) and 17 percent thought it was highly (30 percent chance) likely.[15]

Opinion polls are treacherous. We all know that a skilled pollster can design a question to elicit any desired answer. Moreover, in this case, questions of further integration immediately conjure up Canadian and Mexican fears of being dragged further into the imperial agenda of Washington's governing class. Certainly the only model that people have—NAFTA—is not popular, and was designed, not to encourage solidarity among the continent's citizens but to undercut their social contract.

234 GLOBAL CLASS WAR

Given all of that, the ambiguous results of most public opinion surveys suggest that at the very least, a substantial share of the people in each of the countries might be open to an alternative vision of a continental union. And that such a vision, reflecting a commitment to make life better and more secure for them, might have some cross-border political traction.

The people of the three NAFTA countries will continue to consider themselves Americans, Canadians, and Mexicans for a long time—perhaps forever. But there is no reason to assume that under conditions of increasing shared economic stress, they could at the same time begin to consider themselves—and act politically—as North Americans.

12

Toward, and Beyond, a Continental Democracy

We must all hang together,
or assuredly we shall all hang separately.

—Benjamin Franklin

Franklin gave his advice to a group of revolutionaries breaking away from the British colonial system—an earlier version of globalization dominated by an elite whose interests were disconnected from the typical citizen. The experiment in democracy that followed proved down through the years to be an inspiration to others in Europe, South America, India, Mexico, and Canada and elsewhere.

The political system that manages today's global economy is more complex than that of earlier empires. It is not so much based on the control of territory as it is on the manipulation of the electronic symbols of wealth, which increasingly mock the electoral democracy that Franklin and the others risked their lives to establish.

The problem of democratizing the North American economy is a regional-scale version of globalization's catch-22: how to regulate a market that expands beyond the mandate of national political institutions. It is also a microcosm of the problem of how to integrate rich countries and poor economies in ways that widen the distribution of wealth, political power, and personal freedom.

At this time in history, it is obvious that we do not have a credible model for the political organization of the global economy in a way that provides for these outcomes. There are plenty of ideas, certainly—for global central banks, for the UN to make fiscal policy, for direct elections to the International Monetary Fund, and so forth. But creating a politics to make the global economy of two hundred nations and more than six billion people work for the world's people is at present beyond our collective capacity. Scaling down the effort to the world's regions appears to have a much greater chance of success.

A North American Model?

Economic integration usually takes place through mergers of nearby markets. Most advanced economies grew out of a consolidation of smaller subnational regions. Villages traded with villages, cities with surrounding rural areas, cities with cities, forming marketing webs that sometimes did and sometimes did not become nations.

Unlike elites, who have wider access to the world, ordinary citizens in countries in the same region tend to have more in common with each other than they do with people half a world away. Culture and language are closer, and trading relations are usually the strongest. From a development perspective, regional clusters of nations can provide the economies of scale for small economies to take advantage of new technologies. From a political perspective, a path to global integration built on expanding regional markets could eventually provide a more accommodating political path to a global social contract.

Failed efforts at regional mergers are of course scattered through the graveyard of history. And many of the successes are likely to have been produced by military coercion rather than democratic deliberation. Still, a series of regional political arrangements working out the class tensions that arise from the expansion of market economies across borders may have a greater chance than a regime imposed by a governing class of a superpower whose people are ultimately unwilling to sacrifice themselves for empire.

As sociologist Amitai Etzioni observes, there is logic to the building up of a global system from regional blocs: "It is difficult to imagine that a world community could evolve out of bonding among some 200 nations. . . . However, if these nations first formed a number of regional bodies—a United States of Europe, a Union of Latin

American States, a Union of Southeast Asia, and so on—it would be easier for the regional communities to develop shared policies, and it would make possible the formation of a more encompassing community, a global community of communities."[1]

This makes perfectly good sense. It is not hard, in the abstract, to imagine building a global social contract on regional foundations. The hard part is imagining a politics that would support such a project in North America, where the governing class of the United States remains intoxicated with its imagined mission to rule the globe, and its elite clients in Canada and Mexico are committed to the agenda of Davos.

But as we have seen, the economic support for the present post–cold war order will certainly weaken if not crumble. Already we are reaching the limits of political tolerance for the costs of both the Sixth Fleet and the Wall Street pillars of empire. As the economic constraints tighten around the globalist visions of both Rumsfeld and Rubin, we can expect the rise of an inward-looking politics that gives more priority to New Orleans than to Baghdad. Whether such a politics is channeled to the left or to the right or in some new direction is unknowable. But it is likely that it will provide opportunity for their parties' corporate clients and be more concerned with the eroding living standards of their voters at home.

The question of how those left to live and work in America compete in the global market *and* maintain their living standards will inevitably become a much more important topic of U.S. popular political discussion than it is now. Given the integrating North American markets, it is a reasonable bet that the political discussion will expand beyond the country's northern and southern borders. At least some parts of the electorates of all three nations will see the question of competitiveness as inseparable from the questions of democracy and equality, in continental as well as national terms. Under these circumstances it is credible to imagine a cross-border class conscious politics developing—a politics in which citizens of the three nations of North America see themselves together, not just in a contest with other nations and regional blocs, but with the Party of Davos that currently dominates their political institutions.

Democratizing North America's future does not require a leap to a new single continental nation, any more than the creation of the European Union meant the disappearance of Britain or Germany or

France. Nor is the EU *the* model, any more than the United States was *the* model for European integration. The North America Project would certainly be something different—the yet unknowable product of much trial and error in a continuous effort at establishing a continental social contract in three parts. Its political foundation would be wide public acknowledgment that the economies of the three nations are irrevocably integrating and that its citizens have a right and responsibility to shape their shared economic future.

A cross-border politics motivated by these assumptions would aim at a continental agreement among the people of the three different nations *and* between the people of the three nations and their governing classes. The trinational bargain between the two first world nations, the United States and Canada, and the poorer nation of Mexico would trade substantial assistance for needed public investment in exchange for political and social reforms in Mexico. The bargain between classes would provide corporations who produce in North America with world-class infrastructure education and technology research and protection against imports produced under sweatshop and other oppressive conditions. In exchange, enforceable labor and environmental protections with high standards (adjusted for Mexico's level of development) would apply throughout the continent.

An initial "platform" for a movement for a democratic North America might thus include:

1. A continental economic Bill of Rights
2. "Cohesion" funds for Mexico
3. A common competitiveness agenda
4. A citizens' Continental Congress

1. A Continental Economic Bill of Rights

Establishing common protections to citizens and the environment parallel to the protections of capital investors is clearly justified on its own moral and political terms. If enforceable social protections make sense in the domestic economies of the three nations, they should make sense in the single continental economy. But in addition, such protections are essential for producing faster growth and a better distribution of income.

Mexico will not grow enough to close the income gap with the United States unless the infections of widespread corruption and crony capitalism are removed from its political system. Despite the valiant efforts of brave and able individuals, the Mexican government is unable to cope with street crime and narcotraffickers and with widespread graft. Nor is it able to force the rich to pay their share of taxes. The result is a public sector that is both starved and bloated at the same time.

Crony capitalism and the distribution of wealth and opportunity are clearly connected. A government that will not or cannot prevent its officials from taking bribes from drug traffickers is unlikely to be able to prevent them from taking bribes from employers in labor disputes. Indeed, in February 2005, a high official in the Mexican Labor Department admitted that there was "neither compliance nor respect" for Mexico's labor laws.[2]

These problems are not unique to Mexico. The United States and Canada have their own class systems that are creating more inequality. The gap between productivity and workers' wages is growing in all three nations. A 2000 report by Human Rights Watch concluded that "workers' freedom of association is under sustained attack in the United States, and the government is often failing its responsibility under international human rights standards to deter such attacks and protect workers' rights."[3] Policies to regulate against crony capitalism and human rights abuses must be applied continent-wide.

But in Mexico the scale and the economic and social consequences of these problems are much greater—as indicated by the testimony of the people themselves. A 2002 poll asked respondents in all three countries what they thought were their country's biggest problems. Crime was cited by 26 percent of Canadians, 48 percent of Americans, and 81 percent of Mexicans. Corrupt leaders were cited by 31 percent of Canadians, 46 percent of Americans, and 78 percent of Mexicans.[4]

Given these conditions, simply providing more development funds is not likely to put Mexico on the path to sustainable and widely shared economic growth. Workers and taxpayers in the United States and Canada cannot be expected to support investments to make Mexico more productive if the result is simply to make a few more people south of the border rich.

Each of the three nations has elaborated a list of basic rights of its citizens in their constitutions—Canada's Charter of Rights and Freedoms, Chapter 1 of the Mexican Constitution, and the U.S. Bill of Rights. These cover basic freedom of speech, the press, the right to peaceably assemble, trial by jury, due process, equal protection, and the fundamental protections for a free citizenry. These rights should be merged into a Continental Bill of Rights and made enforceable in every part of the continent. A Canadian, Mexican, or American access to these rights would be jointly guaranteed by the judicial systems of each of the three governments.

All of the governments would agree to codify into their law the International Labor Organization's several articles covering four core workers' rights: (1) the guarantee of the right to organize and bargain collectively free from interference by government or employers, and the prohibition of (2) forced labor, (3) child labor, and (4) discrimination on the basis of race, sex, religion, political opinion, or social class.

The issue of labor rights is particularly important. Free trade unions are essential to bring some balance to the natural advantages of business under capitalism, because they have the power to bring profit-making to a halt. Unlike other institutions of civil society, unions do not have to rely on the charitable impulses of citizens or foundations set up with tax concessions to the rich. Within the industrial nations, unions have been the most powerful force in building social protections, not just for their own members but for all society.

Every worker in North America now has a stake in the treatment of workers everywhere else on the continent. Suppression of workers' rights in one place undercuts workers in all places. Unless the Mexican working class has more bargaining power, the bargaining power of workers in the United States and Canada will be dragged down. An express goal, therefore, of a Bill of Rights ought to be the encouragement of labor unions that can operate as freely across borders as corporations.

Mexican unions are still trying to learn how to be independent, self-sustaining institutions. Many remain in thrall to the PRI and/or the corrupt guardians of sweetheart contracts with employers. In any sensible vision of the future continental economy, the rights of workers to advance their interests through collective bargaining must be made at least as strong as the rights of investors to advance their interests though collective corporate ownership. Some trade unions already straddle both Canada and the United States—the United Steelworkers, the United Food and Commercial Workers, the Service Employees International Union—and there have been episodes of cooperation among U.S. and Canadian unions and the emerging independent Mexican unions. In 1999, for example, American longshoremen refused to unload Volkswagens in Newark, New Jersey, in support of a strike at the VW plant in Puebla, Mexico. And Canadian, Mexican, and U.S. unions have jointly filed a legal action charging that the Fox government's proposal to change Mexican labor law violated the NAFTA side agreement, even as weak as it is.

Rebalancing the power between workers and investors in North America would also require an extension of the rights of citizens to minimum levels of health, safety and conditions of work, transparency in government, minimum levels of education, food free from contamination, and minimum levels of clean air and water as well as other fundamental environmental conditions.

Given the unevenness in the income of each of the three nations, such protections would distinguish between rights and standards. Rights are fundamental and belong to all workers. Standards would differ according to the level of development. Thus, each nation's minimum wage would not be specified, but each nation's workers would have the right to a minimum wage that is set by the legislature and adjusted upward as the average wage rises.

Enforcement of these rights would be guaranteed. Just as investor rights were continentalized, so would these citizens' economic rights be. Where governments fail to enforce these rights, citizens of any other NAFTA country would be able to take that government to court, and seek remedies and penalties.

Finally, the right of each nation's citizens to allow government to regulate the markets and to establish public enterprises would be affirmed. The notion that "states are the architects of their own restraints" would be rejected. Thus, Chapter 11 of NAFTA, which gives corporations extraordinary rights that do not exist in the domestic legal systems of the individual countries, would be rescinded.

2. "Cohesion" Funds for Mexico

Accelerating economic growth in Mexico, which NAFTA failed to do, is absolutely necessary for any continental development program. There are two major obstacles to creating enough jobs and income to bring prosperity to Mexico's people. One is economic; the lack of investment in infrastructure and education needed to support an expanding economy. The other, a corrupt and ineffective public sector, dominated by private business oligarchs, is addressed below.

One result of the lack of infrastructure is that while the border areas of Mexico are growing on the basis of exports to the United States, the rest of the country cannot participate because the roads, communications, energy, and other systems are inadequate. Indeed, since NAFTA, the share of Mexico's GDP devoted to public investments has declined—in part, as we have seen, as a result of competing demands for public funds, such as the bailout of the large commercial banks.

Accelerating Mexico's growth therefore requires the equivalent of the "cohesion" investment funds that the rich countries of Europe provided to the poor ones in the original formation of the European Union. In Europe, the funds were primarily financed by tax revenues in the rich countries. But a large share of the North American investment monies could be raised through government guarantees of private business loans. The projects would be required to adhere to environmental and labor standards and rules to maximize the purchase of machinery, supplies, and technical personnel from North America.[5] As part of the bargain, Mexico's governing class would have to agree to finance more of its own infrastructure spending by raising taxes on the undertaxed rich.

Economist Raul Hinojosa has estimated that providing Mexico with funds at a rate equivalent to the European Union program would cost the United States $100 billion per year—about $1,000 per person in Mexico—for ten years. Given the importance of a healthy, growing Mexico to the people of the United States, it would be a bargain. In one sense it would amount to a payback of the investment that Mexico made in the care, support, and education of the Mexicans who then migrated to the United States as adult workers.[6]

Sustained, accelerated, and widely shared growth in Mexico is the only way in which the prospect of more forced migration from

Mexico to the United States can be avoided. The process will obviously take a while. But the expansion of economic opportunities in Mexico will make it much easier to resolve existing conflicts over Mexican migration. It will, for example, be much easier to argue for amnesty for undocumented Mexicans who have lived and worked in the United States for some time if it is seen as a one-time adjustment, rather than—as opponents argue—an incentive encouraging more illegal immigration.

3. A Common Competitiveness Agenda

Through NAFTA, the governing classes of each nation gave away their capacity to manage their own foreign trade. The people need to take it back. Given integration, there is no returning to pre-NAFTA conditions of three separate national trade regimes. But a North American Union—like a European Union—could present a single unified trade policy to the world. The task is to create a continental customs union in the service of continental economic development—not the "free trade" ideologies that cover the interests of mobile transnationals.

One way or another, Americans will have to balance out their trade with the rest of the world by selling more than they buy. This will require more than a temporary adjustment. The days of the world indulging U.S. financial profligacy are numbered, and the world will not accept the kind of American arrogance reflected in Jimmy Carter's reference to "markets that are rightfully ours."

The idea that the majority of Americans and Canadians can compete in a free market where computer engineers and radiologists can be hired in India and China for one-tenth of their cost is clearly false. Increasingly, this is also true of Mexicans, whose low-labor-cost advantage is being blown away in Asia and south of their own border.

Many Canadians and Mexicans will, understandably, object to having to help the Americans work out their financial imbalances. "We don't trust the Americans" is a phrase commonly heard in Canadian and Mexican political circles. Canadians complain about the United States' lack of good faith in disputes over trade and fishing rights. Mexicans complain about what they consider U.S. perfidy in dealing with migration and truck services under NAFTA. The charge is that the "Americans" use their size and power to get "their" way. But if the reader gets anything from this book, it should be that—whatever the merits of the specific complaints—economic relations among the three nations are a product of collusion at the top.

Salinas and Zedillo, Mulroney, and Chrétien pulled the wool over the eyes of many of their people, but it is absurd to think that they did not make their deals with Bush and Clinton with their own eyes wide open. Disconnecting their elite corporate constituencies from the social contract was in all of their interests. Professing to be "shocked" that the American government would then attempt to gain advantage for some politically powerful national constituency is political playacting.

Unfortunately, given the increased dependence on the U.S. market engineered by their governing elites, the citizens of Canada and Mexico do not now have much choice. Ultimately, either they engage in a hopeless trade war with the United States, or they become partners with Americans in competition with the rest of the world. Surely, if the adjustments are planned to minimize the impact on their economies, the damage to the average citizens of all the nations will be less than if they were left to the mercies of a "free" market dominated by their large neighbor.

But trade policies should not just be managed to deal with the American balance-of-payments problems. They should be driven by the economic development strategies and priorities of the three societies. To begin developing these strategies and priorities, the three nations would establish joint commissions, composed of business, labor, government, and civil society and holding open meetings in each nation, to discuss the future of economic sectors important to all of them.

A commission on industry might begin with the question of how to preserve, integrate, and make more competitive the steel and auto industries of North America. A commission on technology development would engage the future of telecommunications, cutting-edge science, and the acceleration of research and development in ways that channel the resulting products into production in North America. A commission on health and education would address the question of social safety net standards—minimum levels of education, health, and training in all three countries. Transportation, energy, and natural resources are other areas in which commission-type hearings should be held around the continent and ultimately strategies developed for the future.

The initial function of the commissions would be to get people thinking in continental terms. Thus, for example, only in the context of a common plan for sustainable economic growth would it ever make sense for the people of Canada or Mexico to share their energy, water, and other resources with the people of the United States. And only if the people of Canada and Mexico have some say in the pattern of energy consumption of the people of the United States can they be assured of that. In the absence of transparent, continental energy and resource planning, the ongoing pressures for privatization of those countries' natural resources makes it almost certain that they will be sold off and end up serving wasteful and uncontrolled development in the United States and elsewhere.

4. A Citizens' Continental Congress

Nowhere is the contempt for democracy on the part of the framers of NAFTA more evident than in the absence of any way for citizens to become informed about—much less participate in—the management of the economy that NAFTA created. Indeed, there is not even one single office where a citizen of North America or a legislator or a journalist can go to speak to whoever is in charge. The government of this continental economy is not only out of reach, it is out of sight.

The closed system is further protected by the notion that the relations between the three countries are matters of foreign policy. Citizens who are not in the elite government and business networks must get their information from the foreign policy apparatus of their country, which by its nature is secretive. The purpose of keeping such information hidden is clearly not national security, but to keep the citizen from knowing what goes on.

The governing classes have little incentive, and therefore little interest, in opening their activities for inspection. Openness will only come when forced by the demand for information generated by a public that considers the economic relations between Canada, Mexico, and the United States to be domestic issues, rather than matters of foreign policy.

To this end, a conference, or congress, of North American civil society, state and local officials and representatives of labor, and small businesses should be held every year. One of its functions would be to do a public review of the state of continental integration and to discuss, debate, and make proposals for the future.

A North American Congress would not have to wait for a new treaty. An informal version could be organized immediately and financed by unions, foundations, and enlightened business groups. Later, a more elaborate version with a formal role in the emerging continental political systems of all three nations could be supported by pooled funds from the three governments and administered by an independent organization with experience in putting on conferences.

As a viable assembly of the people of all three countries, the Congress would help make the public aware that they are citizens of North America. As this awareness seeps in through the media, Internet blogs, and the dialogue within civil society, business, labor, and political parties, we could expect to see more joint activities, for example, campaigns around environmental issues, union organizing, and public health. Eventually, members of the three national legislatures would start introducing similar bills to solve similar problems.

Geographically, people would represent not countries, but regions of North America that would be defined by economic, social, and other criteria. For example, one such region might include Southern California and northwest Mexico. Another would include Saskatchewan, Manitoba, Minnesota, and the Dakotas, or Ontario and the upper U.S. Midwest.[7] The political boundaries of much of North America no longer reflect the way in which people live and work and commute—and think. So providing an alternative map of North America could be a useful tool in helping people look at the continent in a different way.

The Congress could establish the right of the citizens of one country to attempt to influence the important policies of the two other North American countries. Mexicans and Canadians who are being asked to commit and risk themselves to a continental security system made necessary by the foreign policy of the United States ought at the very least to be able to participate in a continental discussion over American foreign policy. Americans and Canadians whose living standards are affected by Mexico's lax enforcement of its worker protections ought to have something to say about that.

The purpose of the Continental Congress would not be to govern by plebiscite, but to balance the power of big money that will certainly not disappear with the emergence of a continental union. It would provide a place where citizens can have an ongoing participatory discussion on the values that ought to inform the government.

In a sense a Continental Congress is an effort to make real Joseph Nye's notion that the public interest is simply what citizens, "after proper deliberation, say it is." The statement, as we have discussed in chapter 3, is either naïve or disingenuous, because there is no forum for the public—in any of the three nations—to properly deliberate on the future. The legislatures are broken into committees whose work is overwhelmed by the special interests. The executive branches are likewise divided into sectors and become vacuums that soak up money and influence. At the top, presidents emerge from campaigns that are such a confused jumble of personality and double-talk that, once elected, they can pursue the opposite of what they promised with impunity.

Democracy is imperfect, of course, and people who have money will always have more influence than those who do not. But today their economic interests have so clogged the systems that there is little room for any proper deliberation by citizens. Thus, for example, the governing class of the United States has decided to manage the economy in such a way that the average American worker puts in ten, nine, and three weeks more on the job a year than the average worker in Holland, Germany, and Great Britain respectively. According to the punditry, this is what Americans want—it is the national interest. Yet when and where have American workers, whose constant complaint is that they have no spare time, come to that conclusion? In what national forum have the ordinary citizens been able to discuss and ponder the question of how much of the benefits of higher productivity we want to take in more goods and how much in more leisure—or greater health care or early retirement?

There is no forum. The decision not to reduce work time has been made with no discussion by a political class that represents the interests of employers, and then has been wrapped up in the American flag and justified as *our* exceptional national work habit.

Decisions on work hours would remain with national governments. The purpose of the Continental Congress would be to force the question of policies that influence the trade-off between leisure and work into the open.

The growth of the illegal drug business is another issue that could benefit from a citizens' forum outside the constraints of official institutions. Every serious student of crime in Mexico knows that it has grown to massive proportions since the country became the center of the drug business. Every serious student of the drug business also knows that its growth depends not just on political corruption in Mexico but on the relentless demand for illegal substances in the U.S. consumer market. The "war on drugs" has failed in both the United States and Mexico, and the cost in lives and money has been enormous. The only rational way to deal with the demand side is some combination of decriminalization, taxation, and serious rehabilitation.

By themselves, the U.S. elites are incapable of dealing with the demand side: conservatives are trapped by prohibitionist hysteria in their fundamentalist base, and liberals are paralyzed by the fear of being charged with immorality. By themselves, the Mexican elites are incapable of dealing with the supply side: politicians are cowed by the power of the drug cartels. The result is a politically convenient arrangement in which American politicians blame Mexicans for selling drugs, Mexican politicians blame Americans for buying them, and the taxpayers are assuaged with the occasional capture of a "narcotrafficker kingpin" whose incarceration makes no dent at all in the flow of drugs.

An honest and open public discussion generated by civil society on both sides of the border, and perhaps brokered by Canadians whose views on this issue tend to be more rational, might be the only way to break out of this impasse.

Another issue is taxation. The competitiveness of North America's working people—in addition to their well-being—requires a tax base that can support more public investments in education and health and job career ladders. Thus, representing the interests of the cross-border working-class majority, the Continental Congress could be a place to push for tax accords that guarantee a minimum share of each country's GDP going to critical public investments.

Continental Class Politics

The ideas sketched out here represent one way of thinking about the democratic development of our continental economy. It is meant to begin a discussion, not to end it. Many in North America's governing classes and their transnational clients will not want to have the conversation at all. The point of their NAFTA, after all, was to escape the constraints of democracy, not to recreate them on a continental scale. For them, privatization, deregulation, and the freedom to pursue profit anywhere in the world will continue to trump the cause of building a just society at home. American elites especially will resist any threat to their ability to swagger into the world's conference rooms where heads turn and deference is paid because they—like the British and the French and the Spanish and the Chinese and the Indians and the Romans and the Greeks and the Egyptians before them—represent the current superpower.

Most of the ruling elites of Mexico and Canada will likewise be implacably opposed. Their role as interpreters and emissaries of the United States to their populations has been a valuable asset in consolidating their political and economic power. Democratizing that relationship is a threat to the current concentration of wealth and power that suits them just fine. In Mexico especially, where violence remains an instrument of politics, democratizing NAFTA is simply unacceptable to most of the oligarchs.

Some on the left in all three countries will also resist the political blurring of the border. In all three nations, nationalism has been an important card in the otherwise weak hand of those trying to stop the takeover of their society by transnational Davos. John Kerry's complaints about "Benedict Arnold" corporations were an awkward attempt to tap into the patriotic anger that for the most part nurtures the conservative cause. In Canada and Mexico, the left has used resentment of the United States as a major weapon against NAFTA and the Americanization of their economy and culture. But nationalism has not been sufficient to blow up the bridges of continental integration—and is not likely to be in the future. Without making common cause with their counterparts across North America in civil society, trade unions, local governments, and other institutions, they will be left with defending the people's sovereign right to lower their living standards in the cause of national competitiveness.

North American integration is inevitable. On its present trajectory it will continue to be an extension of the Party of Davos's constitutional agenda—the corporate investor as the uniquely protected citizen. It may continue along this path. But the power of the American governing class to shape the world is changing, and it is a reasonable bet that American politics—and therefore North American politics—will change with it.

As real wages decline, as the cost of energy and other essential products rises, as interest rates go up, as the burden of inadequate health care and pension protection spreads, the public tolerance for the outsourcing of jobs and the expense of empire will surely weaken. Like it or not, the American governing class will have to retreat from its post–cold war dreams of world domination and concentrate on the defense of middle-class living standards. Among other discomforts, its cozy partnership with the transnational corporations will be strained.

It is a reasonable bet that this will send major tremors through the already shaky structure of American politics. The conservative columnist David Brooks believes that the fallout from the rising costs of entitlement programs alone threatens political instability. He speculates that the benefit cuts and tax increases needed will dissolve the glue that now holds the parties together—programs for the Democrats, tax cuts for the Republicans. "Both parties will lose their reason for being," writes Brooks. And, by the way, "It would mean the end of the United States as a great economic power."[8]

Brooks misstates the entitlement crisis, which at least in the case of Social Security is not a function of rising costs but of the Reagan and Bush administrations' borrowing from the trust fund to finance tax cuts and military spending. But, by leaving out the current account deficit and the competitive threats from China and elsewhere, if anything he underestimates the wrenching economic adjustments that lie ahead.

Others, smelling the trouble ahead for neoliberalism, are looking for a more explicitly class-based politics. Joe Klein of *Time* magazine wants a new "Party of Sanity" led by business and professional elites. Thomas Friedman of the *New York Times* sees a future alliance between the business wing of the Republican Party and Democratic Hollywood social liberals against globalization's losers—labor unions and the *Passion of the Christ* crowd.[9]

Their projection of a majority of wealthy "haves" realigned against a minority of "have-nots" is elite wishful thinking. It underestimates how far up the pyramid of privilege the floodwaters of America's competitive crisis are going to reach. But Brooks et al. are beginning to understand that the distribution of income and opportunity is likely to dominate the next stage of American politics. Just as NAFTA reflected the political realignment among the classes at the end of the cold war, so the effort to take the integration of the North American economy to the next stage is likely to reflect the shifting politics associated with America's diminishing economic power. The fault lines between the interests of mobile Wall Street and locally rooted Main Street that are hidden by debt-driven prosperity will become more visible. As they widen, we might see growing dissent from neoliberalism on the part of those whose business interests are anchored in the faltering U.S. economy. The globe-trotting pundits of the *New York Times*, CNN, and *Business Week* will deride the retreat from free-market fundamentalism as "protectionism," but their glib mantra of "free trade" will sound increasingly hollow in the hinterland as the cumulative bills for the romance of America's elites with naïve globalization come due.

Simple protectionism—in the sense of isolating the United States from the world—will not pay the bills. Unless the American people are prepared to default on their loans, they will have to sell more to the world and buy less. They will have to spend less and save more. They will have to focus less on how other countries can achieve democracy and prosperity and more on keeping the two together at home.

And unless they are prepared to risk the consequences of ripping apart the economic and financial arteries that now flow into Canada and Mexico, any strategy will have to include their neighbors, who by the accident of geography and the fecklessness of their own elites have irrevocably tied their economic fates to that of the United States.

Under these circumstances, war on terror or no, the majority of American voters are not likely to fight against letting go of the role of global policeman.

In fact, history suggests that ordinary people do not have great attachment to the imperial ambitions of their rulers. Few in America, for example, mourn for the Panama Canal or the loss of the Philippines.

Benedict Anderson notes that the ordinary people of the European imperialist powers "eventually shrugged off the 'losses' of the colonies. . . . In the end, it is always the ruling classes . . . that long mourn the empires, and their grief always has a stagy quality to it."[10] We can expect a certain stagy grief from the Republican right, the American Enterprise Institute, and the Council on Foreign Relations.

But what of the rest of the world? Wouldn't an America that looked inward to its own continent be abandoning others to poverty and lawlessness? Who will be concerned with inequality in Africa and South America? With political instability in Asia and the Middle East?

Substitute "American governing class" for the word "America" and the question turns ironic. By now it is obvious that their own power and the wealth of their transnational investor clients have had the highest priority in the global mission of America's bipartisan elites. This is not to say that the American government is always wrong or never acts in ways that benefit the world—even its poor. But it is not obvious that its interventions, particularly in the last two decades, have been on the whole beneficial. For starters, a good case certainly can be made that the war in Iraq has destabilized the Middle East; the support for transnational oil, mining, and pharmaceutical companies has added to Africa's woes; and the imposition of free-market fundamentalism has crippled Latin America's priorities and undercut its growth.

The basic problem of the people in most of the world's poor societies is not the absence of aid and good advice from people in rich ones. It is located in the corruption, incompetence, and violent repression of their ruling classes. In more cases than not, these classes—happy members of the Party of Davos—are supported by the United States and other western governments. Of course it is not certain that withdrawal of that support would enable people everywhere—or anywhere—to throw off their yoke. But it is even less likely that the United States government, whether led by Democrats or Republicans, would, could, or should support the revolutions needed in much of the developing world. The political fate of Africa lies with Africans, and they are best left to take care of it themselves. The American governing class will, of course, remain important in the world, just not necessarily "indispensable." Its members could still be good global citizens: pay their dues to the UN, provide humanitarian relief, and perhaps even raise their nation's stingy contributions to development aid. Meanwhile, like it or not, they will have to turn their efforts to the task of rebuilding the domestic economy, dealing with all of the internal disputes of domestic politics, questions of poverty in Mexico and energy policy in Canada, and the bothersome electorate that will demand that the benefits of economic growth be widely shared. The elites of Canada and Mexico, having in NAFTA cast their lot with their American counterparts, could similarly be condemned to taking better care of their own people.

So it may well be that the greatest contribution the people and the leaders of these three nations could make to the world would be to demonstrate in their own continental neighborhood a model of economic integration that resolves the Kantian catch-22, that is, one that provides for both growth and democracy. Such an effort could encourage those in Europe working to solve the same problem, and those in South America, Africa, and Asia with a similar regional vision.

This certainly would be a slower path toward globalization than that currently imagined by those who speak for the Party of Davos. But it may well be a surer one to humankind's ancient dream of one world that works for everyone.

Notes

Introduction

1. Jorge Castañeda, *The Mexican Shock* (New York: New Press, 1995), p. 69.
2. Amy Goodman, "*Breaking the Sound Barrier: A Q&A with Democracy Now! Host Amy Goodman*," interview by Alexander Zaitchik, *New York Press*, April 14, 2004.
3. Robert Kuttner, *Everything for Sale: The Virtues and Limits of Markets* (Chicago: University of Chicago Press, 1996).

1. NAFTA: Class Reunion

The epigraph to this chapter is drawn from The White House, Office of the Press Secretary, *Remarks by President Clinton, President Bush, President Carter, President Ford, and Vice President Gore in Signing of NAFTA Side Agreements*, Washington, D.C., September 14, 1993.

1. In Mexico, NAFTA is called a *tratado*, meaning "treaty," but the American version was labeled an "agreement" in order to avoid the constitutional requirement of a two-thirds majority in the U.S. Senate.
2. Bill Clinton, "Town Hall Meeting With Arkansas Governor Bill Clinton," The White House, June 12, 1992, quoted in John R. MacArthur, *Selling Free Trade: NAFTA, Washington, and the Subversion of American Democracy* (New York: Hill and Wang, 2000), p. 158.
3. Bill Clinton, "Expanding Trade and Creating American Jobs," campaign speech in Raleigh, North Carolina, October 4, 1992.
4. Ingrid Negrete, "Mexico Official Defends NAFTA Dispute Process," *Journal of Commerce*, August 20, 1993, p. 3A.
5. Henry Clay, "The American System," Washington, D.C., U.S. Senate, February 2, 3, and 6, 1832, http://www.senate.gov/artandhistory/history/resources/pdf/AmericanSystem.pdf
6. In 1860, tariffs averaged 20 percent of the value of imported goods. In 1865, they averaged 47 percent.
7. Jeffrey Garten, "Business and Foreign Policy," *Foreign Affairs*, May/June 1997, pp. 70–71.
8. The White House, Office of the Press Secretary, *Remarks*.
9. David E. Rosenbaum, "The Nation; They Support Free Trade, Except in the Case of . . ." *New York Times*, November 16, 2003, p. 3.

10. *National Journal,* "Opinion Outlook: Views on National Security," July 31, 1993, p. 1943.

11. Davis S. Broder, "Panetta: President in Trouble on Hill: Agenda at Risk, Trade Pact 'Dead,'" *Washington Post,* April 27, 1993, p. A1.

12. George Stephanopoulos, *All Too Human: A Political Education* (New York: Little, Brown, 1999), p. 220.

13. Hillary Clinton, *Living History* (New York: Simon & Schuster, 2003), p. 182.

14. Peter H. Stone, "Friends, After All," *National Journal* 26, no. 43 (1994): 2440.

15. Maude Barlow and Bruce Campbell, *Straight Through the Heart* (New York: HarperCollins, 1995), p. 105.

16. MacArthur, *Selling Free Trade,* p. 228.

17. The White House, Office of the Press Secretary, *Remarks.*

18. Thea M. Lee and Mark Weisbrot, "The Political Economy of NAFTA: Economics, Ideology and the Media," paper presented at the Union for Radical Political Economy meetings at Allied Social Sciences Association, Boston, January 4, 1994.

19. Howard Kurtz, "The NAFTA Pundit Pack: Sure, They Backed It; How Could They Lose?" *Washington Post,* November 19, 1993, p. D1.

20. *National Journal,* "Opinion Outlook: Views on National Security," July 31, 1993, p. 1943.

21. MacArthur, *Selling Free Trade,* p. 274.

22. Eric Alterman, "Who Speaks for Me?" *Mother Jones,* January/February 1994, http://www.motherjones.com/commentary/columns/1994/01/alterman.html

23. Jorge Castañeda, *The Mexican Shock: Its Meaning for the United States* (New York: New Press, 1995), p. 68.

24. MacArthur, *Selling Free Trade,* p. 275.

25. Theda Skocpol, *Boomerang: Clinton's Health Security Effort and the Turn Against Government in U.S. Politics* (New York: Norton, 1996), p. 79. See also: In a review of nine scholarly studies of NAFTA, University of California Professor Jonathan Fox concludes, "Clinton's investment in NAFTA led him both to miss the window of opportunity for health care reform and contributed to the Republican Congressional win in 1994": *Latin American Research Review* 29, no. 1 (February 2004).

26. Exit polls reported in the *New York Times* (November 13, 1994) showed that registered independents, who had voted 52 percent for House Democrats in 1990, only voted 44 percent for House Democrats in 1994. Self-described conservative independents who voted 43 percent for House Democrats in 1990 only voted 22 percent for House Democrats in 1994.

27. Bill Clinton, *My Life* (New York: Knopf, 2004), p. 557.

28. Antonio Ortiz Mena, personal conversation, February 14, 2003.

29. Alan Sessoms, personal conversation, February 14, 2003.

30. Mark Anderson, personal conversation, October 16, 2003.

31. Robert Kuttner, *Life of the Party* (New York: Elizabeth Silton Books/Viking, 1987), p. 62.

32. Charles Lewis and the Center for Public Integrity, *The Buying of the President* (New York: Avon, 1996), p. 41.

33. G. William Domhoff, *Who Rules America?* 4th ed. (New York: McGraw-Hill, 2002), p. 138.

34. MacArthur, *Selling Free Trade*, p. 150.

35. Ibid.

2. "Good Jobs" and Other Global Deceptions

The epigraph from this chapter is drawn from Jorge Castañeda, *The Mexican Shock* (New York: New Press, 1995), p. 69.

1. The White House, Office of the Press Secretary, *Remarks by President Clinton, President Bush, President Carter, President Ford, and Vice President Gore in Signing of NAFTA Side Agreements*, Washington, D.C., September 14, 1993.

2. H. D. Lasswell, *Politics: Who Gets What and How* (New York: McGraw-Hill, 1936).

3. The White House, Office of the Press Secretary, *Statement by the Press Secretary*, Washington, D.C., September 14, 1993.

4. Jeffrey E. Garten, "The Big Emerging Markets: Changing American Interests in the Global Economy," remarks before the Foreign Policy Association, New York, January 20, 1994.

5. John R. MacArthur, *Selling Free Trade: NAFTA, Washington, and the Subversion of American Democracy* (New York: Hill and Wang, 2000), p. 147.

6. Jonathon D. Salant, "NAFTA Would Put More New Yorkers to Work, White House Argues," *Syracuse Post-Standard*, September 29, 1993, p. 10.

7. Beth Belto, "Pro-NAFTA CEP: More jobs/Gains won't come fast, Bossidy says," *USA Today*, September 13, 1993, p. 7B.

8. Public Citizen, *NAFTA's Broken Promises*, 1997, http://www.citizen.org/trade/nafta/jobs/articles.cfm?ID=1767

9. Ibid.

10. National Association of Manufacturers, *NAFTA: We Need It: How U.S. Companies View Their Business Prospects Under NAFTA*, Washington, D.C., 1993.

11. Public Citizen, *NAFTA's Broken Promises*.

12. Thea M. Lee, "False Prophets: The Selling of NAFTA," briefing paper, Economic Policy Institute, Washington, D.C., 1995.

13. Charles A. Cerami, "Economic Disaster," *Insight*, November 13, 1995, p. 14.

14. Gary Clyde Hufbauer and Jeffrey T. Schott, *North American Free Trade: Issues and Recommendation* (Washington, D.C.: Institute for International Economics, 1992), chapter 3.

15. Dani Rodrik, "Democracies Pay Higher Wages," *Quarterly Journal of Economics*, August 1999, p. 707.

16. Jeff Faux, "The Failed Case for NAFTA," briefing paper, Economic Policy Institute, Washington, D.C., June 1993.

17. Conversation with the author, May 1993.

18. Elizabeth Drew, *On the Edge: The Clinton Presidency* (New York: Simon & Schuster, 1994), p. 299.

19. The White House, Office of the Press Secretary, *Remarks*.

20. Ibid.

21. Frederick W. Mayer, *Interpreting NAFTA: The Science and Art of Political Analysis* (New York: Columbia University Press, 1998), p. 45.

22. Conversation with the author, November 7, 2004.

23. The White House, Office of the Press Secretary, 1993.

24. Andres Oppenheimer, *Bordering on Chaos: Mexico's Roller-Coaster Journey Toward Prosperity* (New York: Back Bay Books, 1998), p. 9.

25. MacArthur, *Selling Free Trade*, pp. 78–79.

26. Oppenheimer, *Bordering on Chaos*, p. 8.

27. Enrique Krauze, *Mexico: Biography of Power* (New York: HarperCollins, 1997), p. 774.

28. "Los Tiempos Peligrosos de Miguel de la Madrid," *La Jornada*, March 24, 2004, p. 1.

29. Krauze, *Mexico: Biography of Power*, p. 770.

30. Conversation with the author, May 14, 2004.

31. White House Office of National Drug Control Policy, *Fact Sheet: Drug Data Summary*, Drug Policy Information Clearinghouse, February 1998, http://www.csdp.org/research/ondcp1.pdf

32. Charles Bowden, *Down by the River: Drugs, Money, Murder, and Family* (New York: Simon & Schuster, 2002), p. 3.

33. Ted Galen Carpenter, *Bad Neighbor Policy: Washington's Futile War on Drugs in Latin America* (New York: Palgrave Macmillan, 2003), p. 176.

34. Carpenter, *Bad Neighbor Policy*, p. 175.

35. Castañeda, *The Mexican Shock*, pp. 167–169.

36. *Dallas Morning News*, "Secretary Expected to Testify About Officials' Drug Links; Witness Worked for Ex-Mexico President's Father," February 26, 1997, p. 12A.

37. Ibid.

38. Jorge G. Castañeda, "Ferocious Differences," *Harper's*, July 1995, p. 70.

39. The White House, Office of the Press Secretary, 1993.

40. Ernest Hollings, "Reform Mexico First," *Foreign Policy*, Winter 1993, p. 8.

3. The Governing Class: America's Worst-Kept Secret

1. Michael Burton, Richard Gunther, and John Higley, "Introduction: Elite Transformations and Democratic Regimes," quoted in John Higley and Richard Gunther, eds., *Elites and Democratic Consolidation in Latin America and Southern Europe* (Cambridge, UK: Cambridge University Press, 1992), p. 8.

2. Eric Alterman, *Who Speaks for America?* (Ithaca, N.Y.: Cornell University Press, 1998), p. 67.

3. Author's analysis tabulating results using LexisNexis. Search terms "American interests or US interests or national interests or America's interests."

4. Joseph Nye, *The Paradox of American Power: Why the World's Only Superpower Can't Go it Alone* (New York: Oxford University Press, 2002), p. 139.

5. This includes Jimmy Carter. Despite the U.S. hostages being held in Tehran, exit polls in 1980 showed that voters regarded unemployment and inflation the first and second most important issues that decided their vote.

6. G. William Domhoff, *Who Rules America?* (Berkeley: University of California Press, 2002), p. 151.

7. Jeffrey H. Birnbaum, "The Road to Riches Is Called K Street," *Washington Post*, June 22, 2005, p. 1A.

8. Center for Public Integrity, "Industry of Influence Nets Almost $13 Billion," special report, April 7, 2003, www.publicintegrity.org

9. Martin Schram, *Speaking Freely: Former Members of Congress Talk about Money in Politics* (Washington, D.C.: Center for Responsive Politics, 1995), http://www.opensecrets.org/pubs/speaking/speakingindex.html

10. Joel Bakan, *The Corporation: The Pathological Pursuit of Profit and Power* (New York: Free Press, 2004), pp. 106–107.

11. Christopher Lee, "Daschle Moving to K Street," *Washington Post*, March 4, 2005, p. 17A.

12. Mike Allen, "Partisans Bury Old Hatchets in Launching a New Business," *Washington Post*, March 3, 2005, p. 4A.

13. Frank Rich, "Will We Need a New 'All the President's Men'?" *New York Times*, October 17, 2004.

14. Angela Partington, ed., *The Oxford Dictionary of Quotations* (New York: Oxford University Press, 1996), p. 650.

15. Thomas Frank, *What's the Matter with Kansas?: How Conservatives Won the Heart of America* (New York, Henry Holt, 2004), p. 249.

16. Elaine Bernard, "Notes on the Prospect of Labor Law Reform in the U.S. and What Failure to Reform Means for Workplace Organizational Change," International Conference on Europe and the United States, Rome, Italy, December 12, 13, 1994.

17. Robert Reich, *Locked in the Cabinet* (New York: Knopf, 1997), p. 176.

18. G. William Domhoff, *Who Rules America?*, p. 27.

19. Ibid., p. 58.

20. Garry Wills, "The Tragedy of Bill Clinton, *New York Review of Books* 51, no. 13 (August 12, 2004).

21. Jack Metzgar, "Politics and the American Class Vernacular," *Working USA*, Summer 2003, p. 49.

22. Robert Perrucci and Earl Wysong, *The New Class Society* (Lanham, Md.: Rowman and Littlefield, 2003), pp. 28–29.

23. Michael Zweig, *The Working Class Majority* (Ithaca, N.Y.: ILR Press, 2000), chapter 1.

24. Domhoff, *Who Rules America?*, p. 67.

25. Actually, the hero of the typical Horatio Alger stories did not succeed through hard work, but through a combination of luck and personal courage, for instance, rescuing a young lady who turns out to be the bank president's daughter.

26. Aaron Bernstein, "Waking Up from the American Dream," *Business Week*, December 1, 2003.

27. Ibid.

28. Samuel Bowles and Herbert Gintis, "The Inheritance of Inequality," *Journal of Economic Perspectives* 16, no. 3 (Summer 2002): 3.

29. United Nations Development Program, *Human Development Report 2003: Millennium Development Goals: A Pact Among Nations to End Poverty* (New York: Oxford University Press, 2003), p. 282, table 13.

30. David Wessel, "Moving Up: Challenges to the American Dream," *Wall Street Journal*, May 13, 2005.

31. See Miles Corak, ed., *Generational Income Mobility in North America and Europe* (New York: Cambridge University Press, 2004), and Anders Björklund and Marcus Jäntti, "Intergenerational income mobility in Sweden compared to the United States," *American Economic Review* 87, no. 5 (December 1997): 1017.

32. Jeffrey I. Bernstein, Richard G. Harris, and Andrew Sharpe, "The Widening Canada-US Manufacturing Productivity Gap," *International Productivity Monitor*, Fall 2002, www.csls.ca/ipm.asp

33. "Mirror, Mirror, on the Wall—Europe vs. America," *Economist*, June 19, 2004. European shortfalls often reported on the U.S. side of the Atlantic are mostly differences in statistical method. For example, Americans count spending on computer software as investment; Europeans count it as a current expense.

34. NCES/Digest of Education Statistics Tables and Figures 2002, http://nces.ed.gov/programs/digest/ (Student Charges and Student Financial Assistance Table 312; accessed September 2, 2004).

35. "Meritocracy in America: Ever higher society, ever harder to ascend," *Economist*, December 29, 2004, p. 15.

36. Jennifer 8. Lee, "Crucial Unpaid Internships Increasingly Separate the Haves from the Have-Nots," *New York Times*, August 10, 2004, sec. A.

37. David Cay Johnston, "Richest Are Leaving Even the Rich Far Behind," *New York Times*, June 5, 2005, p. 1.

38. Lawrence Mishel, Jared Bernstein, and Sylvia Allegretto, *The State of Working America* (Ithaca, N.Y.: ILR Press, 2005), p. 279.

39. "An Immodest Proposal," CNN news report, June 13, 2005.

40. Gretchen Morgenson, "Who Loses the Most at Marsh? Its Workers," *New York Times*, October 24, 2004.

41. Lawrence Mishel, Jared Bernstein, and Sylvia Allegretto, *The State of Working America*, p. 112.

42. Sam Pizzagati, *Greed and Good: Understanding and Overcoming the Inequality That Limits Our Lives* (New York: Apex Press, 2004), p. 27.

43. Ibid., p. 73.

44. Mishel, Bernstein, and Allegretto, *The State of Working America*, pp. 151–156.

45. Barry C. Lynn, *The End of the Line* (New York: Doubleday, 2005), p. 203.

4. How Reagan and Thatcher Stole Globalization

1. John Judis and Michael Lind, "For a New Nationalism," *New Republic*, March 27, 1995, p. 26.

2. Lewis A. Lapham, "Tentacles of Rage," *Harper's*, September 2004, p. 34.

3. *Commanding Heights: The Battle for the World Economy* (Boston: WGBH, 2002), DVD.

4. Ibid.

5. Jeff Faux, *The Party's Not Over* (New York: HarperCollins, 1996), p. 27.

6. Jeff Faux, "Robert Rubin's Contested Legacy," *American Prospect*, February 1, 2004.

7. Vincente Navarro, "La Paz y El Derecho Internacional," panel discussion, University of Salamanca, Spain, June 24, 2004.

8. Judith A. Teichman, *The Politics of Freeing Markets in Latin America: Chile, Argentina, and Mexico* (Chapel Hill: University of North Carolina Press, 2001), chapters 6 and 7; and Sarah Babb, *Managing Mexico: Economists from Nationalism to Neoliberalism* (Princeton, N.J.: Princeton University Press, 2001).

9. Maude Barlow and Bruce Campbell, *Straight Through the Heart: How the Liberals Abandoned the Just Society and What Canadians Can Do About It* (Toronto: HarperCollins Canada, 1995), p. 54.

10. Ibid.

11. William Greider, "Pro Patria, Pro Mundo," *Nation*, October 25, 2001, p. 22, http://www.thenation.com/doc.mhtml%3Fi=20011112&s=greider

12. Ibid.

5. A Bipartisan Empire

1. Bill Clinton, "A New Covenant for American Security," speech at Georgetown University, December 12, 1991.

2. Howard Zinn, *A People's History of the United States: 1492–Present* (New York: HarperCollins, 1995), p. 353.

3. Sherry Jones, "The Crash," *Frontline* (1999), http://www.pbs.org/wgbh/pages/frontline/shows/crash

4. Ibid.

5. John Williamson, "What Washington Means by the Policy Reform," in John Williamson, ed. *Latin American Adjustment: How Much Has Happened?*, Institute for International Economics, 1990, pp. 251–265, http://www.iie.com/publications/papers/williamson1102-2.htm

6. John Gray, *False Dawn* (London: Granta Books, 1998), p. 132.

7. Walter Isaacson and Evan Thomas, *The Wise Men: Six Friends and the World They Made* (New York: Simon & Schuster, 1986), p. 407.

8. Chalmers Johnson, *The Sorrows of Empire: Militarism, Secrecy, and the End of the Republic* (New York: Henry Holt, 2004), p. 255.

9. Lawrence Freedman, "War Is a Force That Gives Us Meaning," *Washington Post Book World*, May 8, 2005, p. 3.

10. Johnson, *The Sorrows of Empire*, p. 56.

11. "The Arithmetic of War," *New York Times*, editorial, September 13, 2004, p. A22.

12. Stanley Hoffman, "TRB from Washington: Too Proud," *New Republic*, January 17, 2000.

13. David Rieff, "Goodbye New World Order," *Mother Jones*, July/August 2003, p. 39.

14. David Remnick, "The Masochism Campaign," *New Yorker*, May 2, 2005, p. 81.

15. *Press Conference with US Trade Representative Robert Zoellick*, September 28, 2001. Copyright 2001 Federal News Service, Inc. Official Kremlin Int'l. News Broadcast.

16. Quoted in Arthur MacEwan, "Is It Oil?," *Dollars and Sense* 247 (May/June 2003): 21.

17. David Bacon, "US Arrests Iraq's Union Leaders," People's NonViolent Response Coalition, December 10, 2003, http://www.pnvrc.net/news/dbDec10.htm

18. Naomi Klein, "Baghdad Year Zero," *Harper's*, September 2004, p. 43.

19. Ariana Eunjung Cha, "$1.9 Billion of Iraq's Money Goes to US contractors," *Washington Post*, August 4, 2004, sec. A.

20. Naomi Klein, "The Double Life of James Baker," *Nation*, November 1, 2004, p. 13.

21. "Let's All Go to the Yard Sale," *Economist*, September 27, 2003.

22. Robert Dreyfuss, "Just the Beginning," *American Prospect*, April 2003, p. 26.

6. Alan, Larry, and Bob Save the Privileged

The epigraph to this chapter is drawn from Thomas Zengotita, "The Romance of Empire and the Politics of Self Love," essay, *Harper's*, July 1, 2003.

1. Nicholas D. Kristof and David E. Sanger, "How U.S. Wooed Asia to Let Cash Flow In," *New York Times*, February 16, 1999, sec. A.

2. Sherry Jones, "The Crash," *Frontline*, June 29, 1999, http://www.pbs.org/wgbh/pages/frontline/shows/crash/etc/script.html

3. Robert E. Rubin and Jacob Weisberg, *In an Uncertain World: Tough Choices from Wall Street to Washington* (New York: Random House, 2004), p. 5.

4. Ibid., p. 23.

5. Ibid., p. 29.

6. Jorge G. Castañeda, *The Mexican Shock: Its Meaning for the United States* (New York: New Press, 1995), p. 202.

7. Rubin and Weisberg, *In an Uncertain World*, p. 5.

8. Tim Carrington, "Rubin's Link to Goldman Is Scrutinized as He Defends Rescue Plan for Mexico," *Wall Street Journal*, February 27, 1995.

9. Rubin and Weisberg, *In an Uncertain World*, p. 282.

10. Paul Blustein, *The Chastening: Inside the Crisis That Rocked the Global Financial System and Humbled the IMF* (New York: Public Affairs Press, 2003), p. 203.

11. Rubin and Weisberg, *In an Uncertain World*, p. 339.

12. Carlos Salinas de Gortari, *Mexico: The Policy and Politics of Modernization* (Barcelona: Plaza and Janés Editores, 2002), p. 412.

13. Phillip L. Zweig, "Goldman Sachs' Spectacular Road Trip," *Business Week*, November 1, 1993, p. 110.

14. Andrew Wheat, "Rubin's Moral Hazard," *Multinationalmonitor.org*, April 1994, http://www.multinationalmonitor.org/hyper/issues/1995/04/

15. Ibid.

16. Ibid.

17. Nora Lustig, *Mexico: The Remaking of an Economy* (Washington, D.C.: Brookings Institution, 1998), pp. 163–164.

18. Julia Preston and Samuel Dillon, *Opening Mexico: The Making of a Democracy* (New York: Farrar, Straus and Giroux, 2004), p. 366.

19. Roberto Gonzales Amador, "Al Rescate de Bancos, 3 Veces Más Recursos que a Infraestructura," *La Jornada*, January 21, 2004.

20. Vanessa Prieto, Instituto Para la Protección del Ahorro Bancario, e-mail message to author, January 13, 2005.

21. Paul Beckett and David Luhnow, "Citigroup Agrees to Buy Mexico's Banacci—Banamex's Parent to Be Sold in Record Deal Totaling $12.5 Billion Cash, Stock," *Wall Street Journal*, May 18, 2001, p. 3A.

22. Patrick McGeehan, "The Paycheck for the Ex-Chief at Citigroup: $111,000 a Day," *New York Times*, March 17, 2004, sec. C.

23. Andres Oppenheimer, *Bordering on Chaos* (New York: Little, Brown, 1996), p. 92.

24. Ibid., p. 89.

25. Ibid., p. 93.

7. NAFTA: Who Got What?

The epigraphs to this chapter are drawn from a joint statement given on July 16, 2004, by U.S. Trade Representative Robert B. Zoellick, Mexico's Secretary of Economy Fernando Canales, and the Honorable James Peterson, Canada's Minister of International Trade; Mary Jordan and Kevin Sullivan, "Migrants' Deaths Reverberate at Home; Friends, Relatives in Mexico Know Risks of Border Crossing," *Washington Post*, May 16, 2003, p. 1A; and John R. MacArthur, *Selling Free Trade: NAFTA, Washington, and the Subversion of American Democracy*, p. 51.

1. *Remarks by Former President George H.W. Bush*, NAFTA at Ten conference, Woodrow Wilson International Center for Scholars, Washington, D.C., December 9, 2002.

2. *Remarks by Prime Minister Brain Mulroney*, NAFTA at Ten conference, Washington, D.C., December 9, 2002.

3. *Remarks by Carlos Salinas*, NAFTA at Ten conference, Washington, D.C., December 9, 2002.

4. "On the Tenth Anniversary of NAFTA," Ipsos-Reid Corporation, December 8, 2002, http://www.ipsos-na.com/news/pdf/media/mr021208-1tb.pdf

5. Robert E. Scott, "The high price of 'free' trade: NAFTA's failure has cost the United States jobs across the nation," Economic Policy Institute, Washington, D.C., November 17, 2003, http://www.epinet.org/content.cfm/briefingpapers _bp147

6. Margo Athans, "U.S. Town Pays Steep Price for Free Trade—Tennessee jobs go to Mexico," *Baltimore Sun*, May 22, 2000.

7. Kate Brofenbrenner, "The Effects of Plant Closings and the Threat of Plant Closings on Worker Rights to Organize," supplement to *Plant Closings and Worker Rights: A Report to the Council of Ministers by the Secretariat of the Commission for Labor Cooperation* (Berman Press, 1993), p. 17, http://www.ilr.cornell.edu/library/downloads/keyWorkplaceDocuments/ReportonPlantClosing.pdf

8. As Andrew Jackson, chief economist of the Canadian Labor Congress, points out, manufacturing productivity growth in Canada fell substantially after 1995, while it accelerated in the United States. Since the trade between the two nations rose, and since trade with the United States loomed much larger in the Canadian economy, one would have expected the labor costs of Canadian producers to rise relative to U.S. competitors. Instead, unit labor costs in U.S. dollars fell faster in Canada, indicating that it was the fall in the Canadian dollar, rather than efficiencies resulting from trade, that increased Canada's surplus with the United States. Andrew Jackson, "From Leaps of Faith to Hard Landings: Fifteen Years of Free Press," Canadian Centre for Policy Alternatives, December 2003, p. 5, http://www.policyalternatives.ca/documents/National_Office_Pubs/leaps_of_faith.pdf

9. Murray Dobbin, "CEO's Sell Out the Nation," *Georgia Vancouver Straight*, British Columbia, April 7, 2005, http://www.straight.com/content.cfm?id=9320

10. Mark Ritchie, Sophia Murphy, and Mary Beth Lake, *United States Dumping on World Agricultural Markets*, Institute for Agriculture and Trade Policy, Minneapolis, Minnesota, 2003, http://www.tradeobservatory.org/library/uploadedfiles/United_States_Dumping_on_World_Agricultural_Ma.pdf; see also Sergio Sarmiento, "Mexico Alert: NAFTA and Mexico's Agriculture," *CSIS Hemisphere Focus* XI, no. 7 (March 4, 2003), http://csis.org/americas.pubs/hf_v11_07.pdf

11. Carlos Salinas Gortari, "NAFTA at Ten: Yesterday, Today and Tomorrow," speech at the NAFTA at Ten conference, Woodrow Wilson International Center for Scholars, Washington, D.C., December 9, 2002.

12. David Luhnow, "US Farm Bill Is Behind Mexican Domino Chain," *Wall Street Journal*, March 5, 2003.

13. UN Food and Agriculture Organization, *FAOSTAT Database*, 2004, http://foastat.fao.org/faostat/collections?version-ext&hasbulk=0&subset=agriculture; USDA Economic Research Service, *Net Value Added (With Net Farm Income)*, 2004, http://www.ers.usda.gov/Data/FarmIncome/FinFidMu.htm

14. Ginger Thompson, "Made in Squalor," *New York Times*, May 6, 2001, p. 1.

15. Tina Rosenberg, "Why Mexico's Small Corn Farmers Go Hungry," *New York Times*, March 3, 2003, p. 22A.

16. John Audley et al., *NAFTA's Promise and Reality: Lessons from Mexico for the Hemisphere* (Washington, D.C.: Carnegie Endowment for International Peace, 2003), p. 15.

17. Enrique de la Garza and Carlos Salas, *La Situación del Trabajo en México, 2003* (México: Plaza y Valdes, 2003), Cuadro III.10, p. 65.

18. León Bendesky, Enrique da la Garza, Javier Melgoza, and Carlos Salas, *La Industria Maquiladora de Exportación en México: Mitos y Realidades* (México, D.F.: Instituto de Estudios Laborales), July 2003.

19. Audley et al., *NAFTA's Promise and Reality*, p. 17.

20. George M. von Furstenberg, "Mexico in NAFTA: Welfare-Benefit Dissipation Due to Lack of a Common Currency," paper presented at the annual meeting of the Allied Social Sciences Associations, Philadelphia, Pa., January 7, 2005, p. 2.

21. Enrique de la Garza and Carlos Salas, *La Situación del Trabajo en México, 2003*, Cuadro III.10, p. 65. The authors report that maquiladoras paid 35 percent of the average Mexican manufacturing wage, which was 14 percent of U.S. wages.

22. Author's calculation using ILO, *LABORSTA Online Database*, 2004, http://laborsta.ilo.org/; IMF, *International Financial Statistics* (CD-ROM), April 2004; and Bureau of Labor Statistics, *Current Employment Statistics Survey*, http://www.bls.gov/data (Object name CEU3000000004).

23. Sabrina Eaton, "Lost Jobs a Bitter Brew: Mr. Coffee story illustrates how and why jobs here often end up overseas," *Cleveland Plain Dealer*, November 14, 2004, p. 1A.

24. José Antonio Gonzales-Anaya, "Why Have Banks Stopped Lending in Mexico Since the Peso Crisis in 1995," Center for Research on Economic Development and Policy Reform, Stanford University, 2003, p. 14.

25. Peter Dorman, "The Free Trade Magic Act: In dubious study, first you see the benefits of globalization, then you don't," Economic Policy Institute, Washington, D.C., September 2001, http://www.epinet.org/content.cfm/briefingpapers_dorman-bp2

26. Mark Weisbrot, David Rosnick, and Dean Baker, "Getting Mexico to Grow with NAFTA," Center for Economic and Political Research, Washington, D.C., September 20, 2004.

27. National Autonomous University of Mexico, Center for Multidisciplinary Analyses, quoted in Susan Ferriss, "Broken Promises: How Economic Reforms Have Failed Mexico," *Austin American-Statesman*, August 10, 2003.

28. Ibid.

29. Enrique de la Garza and Carlos Salas, *La Situacion del Trabajo en Mexico, 2003*, Cuadro III.10, p. 104.

30. U.S. Census Bureau, "Profile of the Foreign-Born Population in the United States: 2000," *Current Population Reports*, December 2001, p. 22, http://www.census.gov/prod/2002pubs/p23-206.pdf

31. Kevin Sullivan, "An Often-Crossed Line in the Sand; Upgraded Security at U.S. Border Hasn't Deterred Illegal Immigration From Mexico," *Washington Post*, March 7, 2005, p. 1A.

32. Mary Jordan and Kevin Sullivan, "Migrants' Deaths Reverberate at Home; Friends, Relatives in Mexico Know Risks of Border Crossing," *Washington Post*, May 16, 2003, p. 1A.

33. Andrés Rozental and Mack McLarty, "Mexico-U.S. Migration: A Shared Responsibility," U.S.-Mexico Migration Panel, 2001, http://www.ceip.org/files/pdf/m%exicoReport2001.pdf

34. There is a growing dispute over these numbers resulting from the wide disparity between the estimates of the remittances made by the Bank of Mexico and much lower estimates drawn from tax records and other surveys of consumer income. One suspicion is that a share of what goes through the banking system as remittances is really illegal money laundering.

35. Karen Brandon, "A Vision Unfulfilled; A Pair of Important Side Deals to the Trade Agreement Gave Labor and Environmental Issues a New, Formal Significance. But Early Tests Have Led to Few Concrete Changes; Workers Say Enforcement is Lacking in Mexico," *Chicago Tribune*, November 29, 1998, p. 1Z.

36. The description of the Han Young case is taken from David Beacon, *Children of NAFTA* (Berkeley: University of California Press, 2004), chapter 4.

37. U.S. Department of Labor, Bureau of International Labor Affairs, U.S. National Administrative Office, *Public Report of Review of NAO Submission No. 2003-01*, August 3, 2004, http://www.dol.gov/ilab/media/reports/nao/pubrep2003-1.htm

38. Keith Gallagher, "Free Trade and the Environment; Mexico, NAFTA and Beyond," Americas Program, Interhemispheric Resource Center, September 17, 2004.

39. Leslie Rockenbach, *The Mexican-American Border: NAFTA and Global Linkages* (*Transnational Business and Corporate Culture: Problems and Opportunities* series) (New York: Routledge, 2001), p. 35.

40. Kevin Gallagher, *Economic Integration, Environment, and Development: Assessing the Mexican Experience*, forthcoming, quoted in John Audley et al., *NAFTA's Promise and Reality: Lessons from Mexico for the Hemisphere* (Washington, D.C.: Carnegie Endowment for International Peace, 2003), p. 18.

41. *Remarks by President Clinton at a Dinner Honoring South Korean President Kim Young Sam and Senate Majority Leader George Mitchell*, November 22, 1993.

42. U.S. State Department, "Deepening US Trade Ties in the Americas: Toward the FTAA," *Remarks by U.S. Trade Representative Robert Zoellick at the Council of the Americas Washington Conference*, Washington, D.C., May 7, 2001.

43. Catherin E. Dalpino, "Does Globalization Promote Democracy?" *Brookings Review*, 19, no. 4 (Fall 2001): 45–48.

44. Roderic Ai Camp, *Mexico's Mandarins: Crafting a Power Elite for the 21st Century* (Berkeley: University of California Press, 2002), p. 204.

45. Still, Mexican intellectuals were generally very much part of the ruling class. Both Paz and, later, Fuentes served as ambassadors for the PRI regime and supported a gradual reform of the PRI from within.

46. Samuel Dillon and Julia Preston, *Opening Mexico: The Making of a Democracy* (New York: Farrar, Straus and Giroux, 2004), p. 434.

47. Jorge Luis Sierra Guzman, *Mexico's Military in the War on Drugs*, Washington Office on Latin America Briefing Paper, April 30, 2003, p. 1.

48. Ibid., p. 6.

49. Dillon and Preston, *Opening Mexico*, p. 343.

50. Ibid., p. 344.

51. John Burnett, "Analysis: Arms Smuggling from the United States to Mexico," *Day to Day*, National Public Radio, May 26, 2005.

52. Roberto Gonzalez Amador, "EU, Renuente a Revisar el Apartado Agrícola del TLC," *La Jornada*, November 22, 2002.

53. Matilde U. Perez, "El TLCAN 'está por encima de la Constitución,' dice Miguel Alemán," *La Jornada*, January 8, 2003.

8. The Constitution According to Davos

The epigraph to this chapter is drawn from Renato Ruggiero, *Remarks at the United Nations Conference on Trade and Development*, October 8, 1996.

1. Bernie Sanders, "The Big Lie about Free Trade; Turns Out It's American Workers Who Are Waving Goodbye to Their Jobs," *Chicago Tribune*, December 31, 2002, p. 25C; Tim Golden, "North of the Border," *New York Times*, Book Review, March 10, 2002, p. 23.

2. David Sanger, "The New Congress: Trade; Clinton Pledges to Push for vote on Trade Accord," *New York Times*, November 17, 1994, p. 1A.

3. Ibid.

4. Ibid.

5. Mike Mills, "Post Criticized on GATT Editorial; 2 Firms Say Newspaper Failed to Disclose Monetary Interest in Bill," *Washington Post*, October 4, 1994, p. 3C.

6. Michael Kranish, "Kantor Sees a Comfortable Win for GATT," *Boston Globe*, December 1, 1994, p. 47.

7. Lori Wallach and Michelle Sforza, *Whose Trade Organization?: A Comprehensive Guide to the World Trade Organization*, 2nd ed. (Washington, D.C.: Public Citizen Inc., 1999), p. x.

8. Ibid., p. 205.

9. Ibid.

10. Ibid., p. 174.

11. Ibid., p. 215.

12. Nancy Dunne, "WTO Hosts Are 'Selling Access,'" *Financial Times*, April 7, 1999, p. 8.

13. Laurie Garrett, e-mail message, "A Candid 'State of the Ruling Class,'" March 28, 2003.

14. Leslie Sklair, *The Transnational Capitalist Class* (Malden, Mass.: Blackwell, 2000), p. 99.

15. Jonathan Duffy, "Bilderberg: The ultimate conspiracy theory," *BBC News Online Magazine*, June 3, 2004, http://news.bbc.co.uk/1/hi/magazine/3773019.stm

16. "Fortune Global 5 Hundred Index," *Fortune*, July 26, 2004.

17. T. R. Reid, *The United States of Europe: The New Superpower and the End of American Supremacy* (New York: Penguin, 2004), p. 115.

18. Joan Lebow, "Japanese to Buy a Rockefeller Group Stake—Mitsubishi Estate Is Offering $846 Million to Get 51% of New Concern," *Wall Street Journal*, October 31, 1989.

19. Sklair, *The Transnational Capitalist Class*, p. 73.

20. Robert B. Reich, *Locked in the Cabinet* (New York: Alfred A. Knopf, 1997), p. 275.

21. Ian Rowley, "So Much for Hallowing Out," *Business Week*, October 11, 2004, p. 64.

22. Jonathan Duffy, "Bilderberg: The ultimate conspiracy theory," *BBC News Online Magazine*, June 3, 2004, http://news.bbc.co.uk/1/hi/magazine/3773019 .stm

23. Judith A. Teichman, *The Politics of Freeing Markets in Latin America: Chile, Argentina, and Mexico* (Chapel Hill: University of North Carolina Press, 2001), p. 60.

24. Anne-Marie Slaughter, *A New World Order* (Princeton, N.J.: Princeton University Press, 2004), p. 4.

25. Ibid., p. 179.

26. Sklair, Leslie, "Democracy and the Transnational Capitalist Class," *Annals of the American Academy of Political and Social Science*, May 2002, http://www .lexisnexis.com/

27. Ibid.

28. See for example, John Cavanagh and Jerry Mander, eds., *Alternatives to Economic Globalization: A Better World Is Possible*, report of the International Forum of Globalization, Benett-Koehler, 2002, also Lori Wallach and Michelle Sforza, *Whose Trade Organization?: A Comprehensive Guide to the World Trade Organization* (New York: New Press, 2004).

29. "Davos Bite (The Davos Report)," *Foreign Policy*, March–April 2004, p. 20.

30. See www.laborrightsnow.org

31. International Confederation of Free Trade Unions, *Annual Survey of Violations of Trade Union Rights*, http://www.icftu.org/displaydocument.asp?Index =991219347&Language=EN

9. America Abandoned

1. Michael J. Mandel, "Does It Matter If China Catches Up to the U.S.? History says it won't—if political stability allows trade to flow freely," *Business Week*, December 6, 2004, p. 122.

2. Pete Engardio and Dexter Roberts, "The China Price," *Business Week*, December 6, 2004, p. 102.

3. TradeStats Express, Office of Trade Analysis, http://tse.export.gov/, National Trade Data, Global Patterns of U.S. Merchandise Trade (accessed March 29, 2005).

4. Engardio and Roberts, "The China Price," p. 102.

5. David Barboza and Elizabeth Becker, "Free of Quotas, China Textiles Flood the U.S. Market," *New York Times*, March 10, 2005, p. 1A.

6. Jeffrey Garten, "The High-Tech Threat from China; America Inc. is rushing Beijing ahead by sharing R&D treasures," *Business Week*, January 31, 2005, p. 22.

7. *President Clinton's New Beginning: The Complete Text, with Illustrations, of the Historic Clinton-Gore Economic Conference* (Little Rock, Ark.: Economic Conference, 1992), pp. 4–5.

8. Dan Morse, "Kentucky Answered Call of the Future—But Got Bad News—Outsourcer Set Up in Hazard, Then Headed Overseas; 'We Were Blindsided,'" *Wall Street Journal*, March 9, 2004.

9. Robert Reich and Sona Shah, "Unemployment Cop-Out? Blaming Lack of Skilled Workers," *"The Flipside,"* CNNfn, February 24, 2004.

10. Jared Bernstein, "The Changing Nature of the Economy, The Critical Roles of Education and Innovation in Creating," testimony before the Committee on Education and the Workforce of the U.S. House of Representatives, March 11, 2004, http://www.epinet.org/content.cfm/webfeatures_viewpoints_changing_economy_testimony

11. Pete Engardio and Bruce Einhorn, "Outsourcing," *Business Week*, March 21, 2005, p. 87.

12. Warren Vieth and Edwin Chen, "The Nation: Bush Supports Shift of Jobs Overseas," *Los Angeles Times*, February 10, 2004, p. 14A.

13. Jeffrey Garten, "Offshoring: You Ain't Seen Nothin' Yet," *Business Week*, June 21, 2004.

14. Anthony Faiola, "Humanoids with Attitude," *Washington Post*, March 11, 2005, p. 5A.

15. Catherine Yang, "Behind in Broadband," *Business Week*, September 6, 2004, p. 88.

16. National Center on Education Statistics, *Digest of Education Statistics*, http://nces.ed.gov/programs/digest/d02/dt057.asp (Table 57, 2002, accessed March 10, 2005).

17. Thomas Friedman, "C.E.O.'s, M.I.A." *New York Times*, May 25, 2005, p. 25.

18. In 2004 the $618 billion trade deficit made up roughly 90 percent of the current account deficit. The rest consisted of net remittances abroad and foreign aid minus a small surplus of investment income in excess of payouts to foreign holders of U.S. assets.

19. Tamara Draut and Adria Scharf, "House of Cards," *Dollars and Sense*, January–February 2005, p. 9.

20. James Burke, "U.S. Investment in China Worsens Trade Deficit: U.S. firms build export-oriented production base in China's low-wage, low labor-protection economy," Economic Policy Institute, Briefing Paper No. 93, May 2000, http://www.epinet.org/content.cfm/briefingpapers_fdi_fdi

21. Actually, countries use U.S. Treasury bills, denominated in dollars, which pay the country interest.

22. "The Passing of the Buck?" *Economist*, December 2, 2004, p. 71.

23. "The disappearing dollar; World economy," *Economist*, sec. leader, December 3, 2004.

24. Studies from economists of different opinions on trade have concluded that the "income elasticities" of U.S. consumers for foreign goods is greater than the elasticities of foreign economies for U.S. goods. See U.S. Trade Deficit Commission, *The US Trade Deficit, Causes, Consequences and Recommendations for Action: Hearing before the US Trade Deficit Review Commission*, Washington, D.C., February 18, 2000, p. 48.

25. Brett Arends, "Economic 'Armageddon' predicted," *BostonHerald.com*, November 24, 2004.

26. *U.S. Senator Kent Conrad (D-ND) Holds a News Conference on the Growth in Foreign-Held U.S. Debt*, Washington, D.C., October 20, 2004. FDCH Political Transcripts.

27. Exchange with the author, panel chaired by Senator Robert Kerrey, Omaha, Nebraska, December 4, 1998.

28. Jeff Faux, "Falling Dollar, Rising Debt; The market is crumbling, accounting's a mess—and we owe the rest of the world about a quarter of our GDP," *American Prospect*, August 12, 2002.

29. Quoted in Jonathan Fuerbringer, "The Dollar? China Gets a Big Vote," *New York Times*, December 19, 2004, p. 9C.

30. Michael Wines, "Dollar's Fall Silences Africa's Garment Factories," *New York Times*, March 12, 2005, p. 1A.

31. Wynne Godley, Alex Izurieta, and Gennaro Zezza, *Prospects and Policies for the U.S. Economy: Why Net Exports Must Now Be the Motor for U.S. Growth* (Hudson, N.Y.: Levy Economics Institute, August 2004).

32. See Dean Baker and Mark Weisbrot, "Fool's Gold: Projections of the US Import Market," Center for Economic and Policy Research, January 8, 2004.

10. After the Fall

1. The World Bank, World Development Indicators, 2004 (series code NY.GDP .MKTP.PP.CD).

2. Stephen Blank, Stephanie R. Golob, and Guy Stanley, *Mapping the New North American Reality*, Institute for Research on Public Policy, September 2004.

3. Victor Cardoso, "Crean gigante ferroviario que unirá México, EU y Canadá," *La Jornada*, April 22, 2003, http://www.jornada.unam.mx/2003/abr03/030422/020n1eco.php?origen=index.html; and NAFTA Railway Web page, http://www.kcsi.com/

4. Earl Fry, "North American Economist Integration; Policy Options," *Policy Papers on the Americas* XIV, Study 8, Center for Strategic and International Studies, July 2003, p. 9. Of the three, Canada is the more decentralized. In Mexico, the formal federal system is somewhat misleading given the historic control of the country's politics by the PRI. Nevertheless, the process of economic integration has itself given more independence to the various Mexican states, particularly those along the northern border.

5. Ibid., pp. 11–12.

6. Aguilar Zinser, personal conversation, Salamanca, Spain, June 25, 2004.

7. Gary Martin, "Stronger North America Links Set," *San Antonio Express-News*, March 4, 2005, p. 1A.

8. John P. Manley et al., "Creating a North American Community: Chairmen's Statement Independent Task Force on the Future of North America," Council on Foreign Relations, March 14, 2005, http://www.cfr.org/pdf/NorthAmerica_TF_eng.pdf

9. Ibid., p. 10. This appears to be modeled after a suggestion of Robert Pastor, director of the Center for North American Studies at American University, for a "quasi-independent" body of "distinguished individuals" to plan the continent's future.

11. Imagining North America

The epigraph to this chapter is drawn from Jean-Marie Guéhenno, *End of the Nation State*, trans. Victoria Elliott (Minneapolis: University of Minnesota Press, 2000), p. 139.

1. Alan Tonelson, "Fight the Outsourcing Focus," *Apparel*, February 2, 2005, http://www.apparelmag.com/bobbin/headlines/viewpoints_display.jsp?vnu _content_id=1000787473

2. Benedict Anderson, *Imagined Communities: Reflections on the Origin and Spread of Nationalism* (New York: Verso, 1991).

3. Ernest Gellner, *Nations and Nationalism (New Perspectives on the Past)* (Ithaca, N.Y.: Cornell University Press, 1983), p. 43.

4. Ross J. S. Hoffman, *Great Britain and the German Trade Rivalry* (New York: Russell & Russell, 1964), pp. 278–279.

5. Suzanne Daley, "Despite European Unity Efforts, to Most Workers There's No Country Like Home," *New York Times*, May 12, 2001, p. 6A.

6. T. R. Reid, *The United States of Europe: The New Superpower and the End of American Supremacy* (New York: Penguin 2004), p. 200.

7. Anthony F. DePalma, *Here: A Biography of the New American Continent* (New York: Public Affairs, 2004), p. 353.

8. Mexico ceded land to the United States that is now Arizona, California, Colorado, Nevada, New Mexico, Utah, and Wyoming with the Treaty of Guadalupe Hidalgo in 1848.

9. "Views of a Changing World 2003; War With Iraq Further Divides," The Pew Research Center for the People and the Press, June 3, 2003, http://people-press .org/reports/display.php3?ReportID=185

10. Michael Adams, Amy Langstaff, and David Jamieson, *Fire and Ice* (New York: Penguin, 2004), p. 52.

11. John Judis and Ruy Teixeira, *The Emerging Democratic Majority* (New York: Scribner, 2002).

12. "Americans and Canadians; The North American Not-so-odd couple," Pew Research Center, January 14, 2004, http://people-press.org/commentary/display .php3?AnalyisID=80

13. "Support for U.S. at new low because of Iraq war: survey," *Toronto Star*, June 4, 2003, p. 11A.

14. "Public Opinion on International Affairs," Program on International and Public Attitudes, February 15, 2002, http://www.americans-world.org/digest/ global_issues/intertrade/data_nafta.cfm

15. Ekos Research/*Toronto Star* Poll, "Political Landscape, Economic Outlook and Globalization," June 1, 2001, Ekos Research, Toronto, www.ekos.com

12. Toward a Continental Democracy

1. Amitai Etzioni, *From Empire to Community* (New York: Palgrave MacMillan, 2004), pp. 192–193.

2. Patricia Muñoz Rios, "En México No se Cumple ni se Respeta la Ley Laboral, Afirma Funcionario de STPS," *La Jornada*, February 21, 2005.

3. Human Rights Watch, *Unfair Advantage: Workers' Freedom of Association in the United States under International Human Rights Standards* (Washington, D.C.:

Human Rights Watch, 2000), p. 8, http://hrw.org/reports/pdfs/u/us/uslbr008 .pdf

4. "What the World Thinks in 2002, How Global Publics View: Their Lives, Their Countries, The World, America," The Pew Research Center for the People and the Press, December 4, 2002, http://people-press.org/reports/display.php3 ?ReportID=165

5. Walter Russell Mead, Jeff Faux, and Angelo Falcon, "NAFTA: A Forum," *Nation*, May 28, 2001, p. 19.

6. Raul Hinojosa Ojeda et al., "Comprehensive Migration Policy Reform in North America: The Key to Sustainable and Equitable Economic Integration," North American Integration and Development Center, November 5–6, 2001, p. 13, http://www.iadb.org/INT/Trade/1_english/4_SpecialInfo/Conference/2002/ a_Nov601-ImpactsTradeLiberalization/IDBFINAL.pdf

7. One early effort to reconfigure the continental map was a 1981 book by journalist Joel Garreau, *The Nine Nations of North America* (New York: Houghton Mifflin, 1981).

8. David Brooks, "The Do-Nothing Conspiracy," *New York Times*, March 19, 2005, p. 27A.

9. Thomas Friedman, *The World is Flat* (New York: Farrar, Straus and Giroux, 2005), p. 221.

10. Benedict Anderson, *Imagined Communities: Reflections on the Origin and Spread of Nationalism* (New York: Verso, 1991), p. 111.

Index

Johnson, Chalmers, 102, 103
Johnson, Lyndon B., 83
Johnson & Johnson, 34, 130
Jordan, 47
Jordan, Phil, 43
Jubilee 2000, 174
Judis, John, 232

Kansas City Southern, 209
Kant, Immauel, 169
Kantor, Mickey, 12, 13, 20, 24, 27, 35, 41
Katrina, Hurricane, 51, 198, 199
Katz, Julius, 35
Kellogg Brown & Root, 106
Kemp, Aaron, 156
Kennedy, John F., 54, 56
Kerry, John, 55, 57, 102, 249
Keynes, John Maynard, and Keynesian economics, 78–79, 80, 83, 84, 85, 87, 230
  foreign trade and, 88
  Mexico and, 89, 90, 136–37
Khrushchev, Nikita, 82
Kimberly-Clark, 130
Kim Dae Jung, 31
King, Martin Luther, Jr., 80
Kinsley, Michael, 23
Kirkpatrick, Jeane, 107
Kissinger, Henry, 21, 25, 38, 58, 120, 165, 170
Kissinger Associates, 105
Klein, Joe, 250
Koch, Bobby, 58
Kosovo, 103
KPMG, 106
Krauze, Enrique, 40, 41
Kristof, Nicholas, 109
Kristol, Irving, 81
Kristol, William, 107
Kucinich, Dennis, 102
Kurtz, Howard, 23
Kuttner, Robert, 5
Kuwait, 106, 107

labor unions, 18, 54, 55, 61, 65, 80, 94, 106, 250
  Clinton's health care plan and, 25
  Continental Bill of Rights and, 240–41
  diminished power of, 62, 70
  in global economy, 89, 175–78
  international, 175–78, 240–41
  lobbyists, 56
  NAFTA and, 62
    the negotiations, 16
    opposition, 10, 16–17, 25, 27
    side agreements, 10, 12, 13, 19, 20, 27, 142–45
  outsourcing and, 18–19
  Reagan and, 5, 85, 87
  state-sponsored violence against, 177
  teachers' unions, 188
  Thatcher and, 86
  WTO and, 161–62
laissez-faire economics, 203
  classical theory, 72, 79
  neoconservatives and, 81, 82, 83–84, 85, 86
  neoliberalism. See neoliberalism
language, integration of nation-states and, 127, 222, 225, 227
Latin America, 252
  extension of NAFTA to, 220, 221
  leftist governments in, 216
Lay, Ken, 21, 55, 70
Leach, Jim, 118
Lee, Thea, 37
leisure time, work vs., 247–48
Lesotho, 196
Lesson from NAFTA for Latin American and Caribbean Countries, 138–39
Levy Institute, Bard College, 197
Lewis, Anthony, 23
Lewis, Charles, 29
Libby, Lewis, 58
Limbaugh, Rush, 23, 112, 120
Lincoln, Abraham, 14

Lippmann, Walter, 49
lobbyists, 55, 56–58
  former congressmen as, 54, 57
  global, 170
  NAFTA and, 9–10
Long Term Capital Management, 118
López Obrador, André Manuel,
    153–54
Lula da Silva, Luiz, 177
Lynn, Barry, 74

MacArthur, John, 24
Magaziner, Ira, 18, 21
Major, John, 107
Malthus, Thomas, 78
Mankiw, N. Gregory, 185
Manley, John, 217
manufacturing industries, 169
  decline of U.S., 18, 197
  in Mexico, 135
  worker productivity and wages,
    131, 132
Marshall Plan, 14–15, 100, 101
Martin, Paul, 214
Maseca, 16
Maximilian, archduke, 229
Mazzoli, Romano, 56
McCaffery, Barry, 152
McGraw-Hill, 159
MCI, 187
McKinnell, Hank, 56
McLarty, Mack, 141, 159
  NAFTA and, 20, 21, 128
McVeigh, Timothy, 165
Means, Gardiner, 72
media, 90–91
  free trade, portrayal of, 2, 251
  government pressure on, 2
  NAFTA's portrayal in the, 23–24,
    32–33, 129–30
  neoconservatives and, 82
  WTO and, 159
Medicare, 198
Menem, Carlos, 31
Merck, 175

Meriwether, John, 118
Metalclad Corporation, 148
Methanex, 148
Mexican Council on Foreign Affairs,
    217
Mexican National Police, 152
Mexican peso, 35
  collapse of, in 1980s, 39
  crisis of 1994–95, 44, 109–16,
    121–23, 124, 127, 128, 150
Mexico. *See also names of individual
    presidents*
  banking system, 123–24
    foreign investment in, 112, 121,
      123, 124, 137–38
  "cohesion" funds for, 242–43
  Constitution of, 240
  continental integration. *See*
      economic integration of
      North America; North
      America, integration of
  corruption and crony capitalism in,
      42–44, 151–52, 239, 240,
      242
  cultural distinctiveness of, 211–12,
      228
  debt crisis of 1982, 90, 123
  drug trafficking and, 37, 41–44,
      151–53, 239, 248
  economic integration with the
      United States and Canada.
      See economic integration of
      North America
  education of leaders of, 39
  farmers in, small, 16, 129,
      133–35, 153
  foreign reserves, 44, 111
  gap between rich and poor in, 6
  imprisoned workers in, 177
  Keynesian economics in, 89
  labor unions in, 240
  leftist government in, fears in the
      United States of, 216
  maquiladoras in, 36, 135–36, 137,
      144, 145, 146–47